GEORGE WHITEFIELD
—THE AWAKENER

" If ever philanthropy burned in the human heart with a pure and intense flame, embracing the whole family of man in the spirit of universal charity, it was in the heart of George Whitefield. He loved the world that hated him, he had no preferences but in favour of the ignorant, the miserable, and the poor."

SIR JAMES STEPHENS.

GEORGE WHITEFIELD
—THE AWAKENER

A MODERN STUDY
OF THE EVANGELICAL REVIVAL

BY

Rev. ALBERT D. BELDEN, B.D.
Superintendent, "Whitefield's," London

WITH AN INTRODUCTION BY
THE RIGHT HONOURABLE
J. RAMSAY MacDONALD, P.C., M.P.

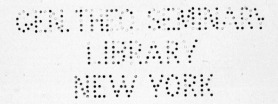
LONDON
SAMPSON LOW, MARSTON & CO., LTD.

MADE AND PRINTED IN GREAT BRITAIN BY PURNELL AND SONS
PAULTON (SOMERSET) AND LONDON

ACKNOWLEDGEMENT

The Publishers acknowledge the kindness of the Rev. George H. McNeal, M.A., for permission to reproduce several of the illustrations appearing in this book from the unique collection of reliquiæ of John and Charles Wesley, at Wesley's Chapel, City Road, London, E.C.1.

AUTHOR'S PREFACE

"GEORGE WHITEFIELD was the first man who treated Great Britain and America as if they belonged to him. He passed from the one to the other as though they were a pair of rural villages and he was the minister in charge of the parish. George Whitefield took a couple of continents under his wing, and the wing proved capacious enough for the task." So writes F. W. Boreham, the Australian essayist, about the subject of this work. The description stresses Whitefield's pioneer character—his sublime audacity in the cause of the Gospel. That is the note the author has tried to honour in this book. Whitefield has a challenge for the youth of the modern world and for the youth of our Evangelical Churches especially. His relentless insistence upon "new birth" for human nature is likely to find a fresh vogue in the hitherto least likely quarters to-day, since by the whirligig of time and thought it is science that just now is preaching a doctrine curiously like the total depravity of human nature, even of the average respectable kind! If our modern world is to be saved, and saved within the terribly narrow time-limit that social evolution seems to be setting, the dynamic of a supernatural power and wisdom must be rediscovered, and harnessed anew to our attempt at realising the ideal social order.

Upon the romantic and thrilling story of Whitefield, therefore, I have dared to impose an outline of thought and policy for the Church of to-day. The attempt has been made in the midst of one of the heaviest tasks that British Congregationalism imposes, and the writer is left wondering how his brilliant predecessor, Charles Silvester Horne, ever found time and energy to spare from this task to write *several* books. But the work, good or ill, is offered now to the world at large, and its chief justification is the motive that lies behind it—the intense desire to quicken the forces of religious revival in modern society.

Naturally I am deeply indebted to all the biographers of Whitefield—to Gillies, and Andrews and Phillips, and especially

AUTHOR'S PREFACE

Tyerman, with his two exhaustive volumes, and to Gledstone and Ninde. I have drawn upon them freely, but always, I hope, with acknowledgement. The amount of new information is scanty, but for certain fresh details I am grateful to Mr. Roland Austin, Librarian of Gloucester, Rev. G. H. Wicks, the Congregational historian of Bristol, and the Rev. C. E. Watson, of Rodborough. For help in obtaining data and in the preparation of the manuscript there are many I should thank, including my friend, Mr. Donald Blackeby, and my son, Kenneth D. Belden, and my little army of ever-faithful and overworked typists. Especially must I thank in this regard Mr. O. W. Burroughs, the Secretary of the Bethesda Orphanage, Savannah, " America's oldest charity ", for most valuable and fresh information supplied by him.

To the Rev. G. H. McNeal, of Wesley Chapel, I am indebted greatly for the gracious way in which he placed at my disposal and that of my publishers the freedom of the Wesley Museum, and the invaluable collection of engravings and portraits at the shrine of Methodism. My thanks also should be offered very fully to the Organising Secretary of Whitefield's, Mr. Harry E. Gaze, for valuable help in regard to the illustrations of this volume, and for the reading of certain chapters in the MS. Finally, my particular thanks are due to my friends, the Rev. R. S. Birch, Ph.D., of West Kensington, for his reading of the book in manuscript, and for valuable criticism on its theological and psychological sections, and to Dr. Sidney M. Berry, Secretary of the Congregational Mission of England and Wales, for his kind encouragement after perusal of the more constructive chapters.

If this volume should inspire any youth to enter upon the great task of the new evangelism, or should induce my fellow ministers to reconsider the relation of the Free Churches to Politics, or if it should cause some of that eager throng of social idealists, who are working for the New Order with such fine devotion, to reconsider the claim of Christ, the author will be more than repaid for his effort, but if this book should start such a quest that fire should fall from Heaven again upon the Churches, then indeed would he be filled with unutterable thanksgiving and praise.

Whitefield's,
Tottenham Court Road, London, W. 1.

FOREWORD

BY

Rt. Hon. J. RAMSAY MacDONALD, P.C., M.P.

THE relation of the Free Churches in this country to the rise and progress of Democracy has always been of the most intimate kind. Whether it was Independency in Cromwell's time, or Methodism in the reigns of the earlier Georges, or both, more or less combined, in the closing years of the last century and the opening years of the present one, we may well regard the Free Churches as one of the pure sources from which Free Democracy came. If, regretfully, we must acknowledge that it was by religious people that many of the harshest oppressions of the Industrial Revolution were perpetrated, blindly and unconsciously perhaps rather than wilfully, yet, as this book shows so effectively, it was by the dynamic of free religion that the masses were inspired to escape from the quagmire of misery and injustice. The faith of the Christian may not have protected the individual from using his economic power oppressively, but it was that faith which preserved the masses from becoming soulless things, obedient to the convenience and advantage of economic forces.

Can those earlier eras of dynamic faith associated with such names as St. Francis and his friars, John Wycliffe and his Lollards, Robert Browne and the Independents, George Whitefield and the Methodists, George Fox and the Quakers, be repeated in our own day on a scale commensurate with this modern world, and with an application of creative value for the future? Such is the inquiry which lies behind the pages of this biography, and modern Democracy, as well as the modern Church, cannot but be vitally interested in such a possibility. The final peak is always the hardest to climb,

xi

and makes the supreme demand on one's powers. Democracy in this country and in America has conquered the foot-hills, it has braved heroically and with bitter sacrifice many a seemingly impossible crag, its eyes are now set upon the bafflingly hard summit. Can it afford now to dispense with that ardour and devotion which only profound religious belief and stern ethical principle can provide? I think not, and therefore recommend this presentation of the challenge of the eighteenth century revival to the Churches and the Masses of our own age. History never repeats itself: it fulfils itself, bringing forth new variations of old causes and new applications of old truths.

This is a peculiarly appropriate moment to go back for refreshment and enlightenment to such times as those of Whitefield, when the permanent things of the spirit were brought into challenging conflict with the rusting and corrupting things of material power. We have reached the end of a phase of Capitalism which I define as the state of society in which the ownership and interests of economic power control the life of society. Some people say that Capitalism is decaying: it is only transforming itself, and is bringing society more and more under its control. In the reconstruction which is inevitable, it is not only sacrificing wealth but humanity, as was the case in the days of the Industrial Revolution. To make the economics of the reconstruction socially advantageous requires not only political power (which is so often inadequate to control economic evolution) but spiritual power. Social policy should not aim at subsidising humanity but at preserving its spirit. Whitefield's work gave men self-respect and pride, and did not merely arm them with claims for sharing in this world's goods. The problem is still unsolved how to make man his own master. It never will be solved by rectifying differences in status, or in material possessions. Class conflicts will only mislead us, and give victories which will be barren of results. "God give us men." He will not. We have to make them. Whitefield and Wesley, John Knox and George Fox—each in his own way and in spite of apparent differences, helped to make them in the only way they can be made. They awakened manhood. Bolingbroke said that, regarding the downfall of Rome, "losing the spirit of Liberty was the cause, and losing Liberty was the effect." The generation which loses the spirit of life loses everything worth having. Let us not pride ourselves that we are progressing if we let go the interests and inspirations which brought the Free Churches into being.

It is particularly happy that this story of the greatest evangelist of the English-speaking race—George Whitefield—should be a heritage held in common by our American cousins and ourselves. Both nations are equally and permanently indebted to this intrepid apostle of faith. It is well to be reminded of our common baptism in one free faith at a time like the present, when we are trying to unite in the essentially religious task of establishing, if possible on a permanent basis, the Peace of Mankind throughout the world.

CONTENTS

PART I—EARLY DAYS

PART II—THE APOSTLE OF TWO WORLDS

PART III—THE REVIVAL IN FLOOD

xv

CONTENTS

PART IV—THE AWAKENER'S CHALLENGE

ILLUSTRATIONS

xvii

GEORGE WHITEFIELD
—THE AWAKENER

INTRODUCTORY CHAPTER

CAN THE EVANGELICAL REVIVAL BE REPEATED?

"I love those that thunder out the Word. The Christian World is in a dead sleep. Nothing but a loud voice can awaken them out of it."—GEORGE WHITEFIELD.

THE time is ripe for the greatest religious revival of history. The people are ready. The terrible tragedy of the Great War has ploughed deep into the human heart of our time, bringing to light great evil and great good. Despair and fear and bitter agony have plunged a host of lives into reckless sinning, whilst hard social conditions have broken the spirit of many. Repeated disappointment and breakdown in the struggle for an ideal social order have produced on every hand a new unbelief in human nostrums and panaceas—an unbelief which covers a great secret yearning for Divine resource. This explains why there is a widespread popular interest in religion, side by side with a general forsaking of organised Christianity. The people have lost faith in the Church, but they have also lost faith in themselves, and they are looking round wistfully for God "if haply they may find Him."

The Church is ready. Its congregations, if smaller, are more genuine. It is no longer fashionable to attend Church; neither is it any longer particularly good business to do so. Those who attend regularly can safely be presumed to care. Great popular auxiliary movements like the Y.M.C.A., the Student Christian Movement, the Brotherhood Movement,

Adult School Movement, Toc H, and many smaller organisations are helping to conserve and develop much of the man-power otherwise lost to the Church. The Church's indifference to the material well-being of the common people and to social justice which, as we shall see, seriously retarded and greatly minimised the full effects of the Evangelical Revival of the eighteenth century, is now, in the main, ended for ever, and under the stress of the urgency of modern-world-problems, such as those of War and Industry, the Church is steadily proceeding to clarify her Gospel and to determine true Christian method.[1] She has a new and deep concern for the success of the Gospel with the mass of mankind in every land, and is facing missionary problems in a broader spirit. Her unity is still unachieved, but never was the Church more stricken in conscience concerning her disunity than to-day. "Judgment," as the apostle claims, "must begin at the house of God," but it is beginning.

In this connection we may note the formation of the United Church of Canada, the recent stirring achievement of unity in the Scottish Presbyterian Church, the approaching union of the Methodist Churches, and the rise of a great united Church movement in South India. The Lausanne Conference on Faith and Order, and the Jerusalem Missionary Conference of Easter, 1928, were pointers towards the same ultimate goal.[2]

The world is ready.

> " There is a tide in the affairs of men
> Which, taken at the flood, leads on to fortune.
>
>   .   .   .   .   .
>
> On such a full sea are we now afloat."

Such a tide is flowing to-day. Never was there an age so eminently suited for propaganda of all kinds, religious included. There is the enormous power of the Press. Men, the world over, are ceasing to be illiterate. They are increasingly sensitive to the printed page. Newspaper, magazine and book are magic vehicles to-day for truth as much as for error. For a Church that knows its own mind here is an instrument of

---

[1] *Cf.* the findings of the Lambeth Conference and the Archbishops' Report upon Industry—also the great effort known as C O P E C, namely, the Christian Conference on Politics, Economics and Citizenship—the " blue-books " of which are very valuable, and published by Longman's.

[2] Also we should recall the Life and Work Œcumenical Conference at Stockholm, 1925, held exactly sixteen hundred years from the last one.

information and instruction mightier than anything of its kind in other days.

There is the still novel, but even vaster, appeal of the radio. The broadcasting of religion to audiences of millions is the greatest aeration of religion that has ever taken place. A Church that was sure of its Gospel would scarcely need to worry over empty pews whilst it could fling its challenge adequately over the ether into millions of family circles. Moreover, the radio is more than a means of appeal. The World-voice that God, through Science, has given us, is but the prelude, surely, to an ultimate World-mind, a new common World-culture and World-will to Truth and thus to Righteousness.

Again, the increasing stability of Peace throughout the world enlarges the opportunity of World-evangelisation. At the time this was written, a joint message from Britain and the United States, the result of personal conversations between Mr. Macdonald and Mr. Hoover, declared:

"In signing the Paris Peace Pact, fifty-six nations have declared that war shall not be used as an instrument of national policy. . . . Our conversations have been largely confined to the mutual relations of the two countries in the light of the situation created by the signing of the Peace Pact.

"Therefore, in a new and reinforced sense, the two Governments not only declare that war between them is unthinkable, but that distrust and suspicions arising from doubts and fears, which may have been justified before the Peace Pact, must now cease to influence our national policy.

"We approach the old historical problems from a new angle and in a new atmosphere."

This momentous declaration, from so responsible a source, is the high-water mark of Peace hopes in the modern world since the Great War. Should these hopes be realised, if only in part, and over a considerable period of time merely, such a Peace would, at the worst, provide a breathing-space between cataclysmic wars, which, if well-used by a strong evangelism, might usher in the final peace of a redeemed humanity. Owing to factors such as these and to the amazing development of transport facilities in our age, humanity is flowing together to-day into one vast pool of common life.

GEORGE WHITEFIELD—THE AWAKENER

The great slogan used by both Whitefield and Wesley, "The world is my parish,"[1] would seem, therefore, to be still more justified on the lips of the modern Church. It would seem incredible that the increasing unity of the world should not react with final effect upon the disunity of the Church, bringing steadily into being the One Church of the One Saviour for the One World, and leading on to final victory for Christianity. Whilst, moreover, for such a stupendous achievement great Christian personalities will be required, it is difficult to believe that in such an unusual situation such personalities will not be forthcoming. They will arise, however, the more readily, out of a new atmosphere of passion, out of a revival of "enthusiasm" among Christian people.

It is here we touch the unique splendour of George Whitefield, the greatest evangelist of the British race. Whilst Wesley was the steady light of revival, Whitefield was the raging flame, the kindling torch whose fiery zeal caused him to run ahead of others in his time and blaze a new trail of more daring endeavour for Christ. Without that pioneer achievement there might well have been no Evangelical Revival, no Methodist Church, no mighty social emancipation such as resulted therefrom. Indeed there is much to be said in favour of Southey's verdict : "If the Wesleys had never existed Whitefield would have given birth to Methodism." It is this burning passion which it is so urgent for us to share anew to-day. Hence this book. To wave aloft this brilliant torch over the youth of our time may be to kindle other torches, possibly no less brilliant.

From the time he began as a lad to preach, to the very hour and article of death, through thirty-four years of ceaseless labour, George Whitefield knew no abatement of evangelistic passion. From end to end of that remarkable career his soul was a furnace of burning zeal for the salvation of men. In some features he was less than other men, but in this he has no equal, and to this he sacrificed everything, even, we may well assume, some of those other powers. "God forbid that I should travel with anybody a quarter of an hour without speaking of Christ to them," he cried. "Believe me, I am willing to go to prison and to death for you. But I am not willing to go to heaven

---

[1] This seems to have been a general slogan of the members of " The Holy Club." —Tyerman. Vol. I. p. 316.

without you," he declared. "Day after day, from early morning, the house where the preacher was entertained was besieged with weeping men and women, begging for a word of prayer and counsel, that they might find God." Such was his life. No preacher of the Gospel before or since has gathered such audiences, no evangelist has achieved such magnitude in results, no single life has had a wider impact upon our English-speaking race.[1]

The power that attended this man's preaching was little short of miraculous. It is doubtful whether a more powerful vocal instrument has been known to the pulpit before or since—a voice capable of addressing crowds of ten, twenty and even thirty thousand people in the open air! Nor did this man catch the popular ear with clap-trap and cheap-jack wiles. Intensely human and dramatic as he was, the testimony of sceptics like Lord Chesterfield and Lord Bolingbroke argues a quality of piercing conviction in his preaching that even their habitual cynicism could not withstand. Said Bolingbroke of Whitefield, "He is the most extraordinary man in our times; he has the most commanding eloquence I ever heard in any person." Hume, the historian—who could hardly be expected to endorse anything shallow—declared "it was worth going twenty miles to hear him." We shall have occasion later to record the friendship of that cool-headed American philosopher, Benjamin Franklin, of Philadelphia, for Whitefield, but here let us recall that he was astounded at the revolution in the manners of his fellow townsmen as the result of Whitefield's preaching. Benjamin Franklin says, "From being thoughtless and indifferent about religion, it seemed as if all the world were growing religious." That last sentence sums up George

[1] Yet neither in Great Britain nor America has due honour on a national scale been paid to this man. His bones lie in the old South Presbyterian Church at Newburyport, near Boston, U.S.A., under conditions of insufficient dignity. No adequate memorial of him exists in this country save in the Churches he himself founded. The Smithsonian Institute of Washington possesses no Whitefield relic, and the portrait in our own National Portrait Gallery is, to quote a verdict the writer heard expressed not long ago, " a poor one, with a woman in rhapsody gazing up at him, almost a caricature." Save for the Orphan House of Bethesda, which still exists, and the fine statue by Tait Mackenzie, which stands in the campus of Pennsylvania University, and a stone at Exeter (U.S.A.), which marks the scene of his last open air sermon, the American continent holds no fitting public memorial of him, and Great Britain is in similar case. One underlying cause doubtless of this neglect lies in the great honour deservedly paid to John Wesley, but paid somewhat unconsciously to the under-estimation of Whitefield and to the ignoring of Wesley's debt to the great pioneer.

Whitefield's work. He recalled the English-speaking world of his time back to religion. He stemmed and turned the tide of indifference, scepticism and immorality that threatened to engulf and destroy the Church and the Nation in the eighteenth century. His life and work should appeal to all Protestant Christendom, for there is scarcely a Church in Protestantism that his labours did not refresh. Whitefield rejoiced whole-heartedly in his standing as an ordained Church of England priest, and the challenge of his teaching and his passion for the people stung the conscience of that community at last into a new sensitiveness. Yet Whitefield seized every opening for preaching afforded him by Dissenting Communities, whilst refusing to distinguish finally between any form of Church government and polity. His work stands to-day, therefore, as a kind of watershed of Divine grace behind the total Church life of England, Scotland and Wales. It nourished into stronger life in Great Britain the then existing Churches of Presby-terianism and Congregationalism, whilst it helped to bring into being the new Communions of Methodism in their various forms, Wesleyan, Calvinistic, Primitive, and still further, the Countess of Huntingdon's Connexion! Similarly, Whitefield's work stands with equal benefit behind every form of Church life in the United States. All Churches to-day, therefore, might well combine to do him honour in that way which best would reach his great heart wheresoever it is beating now in God's universe—by a new and really passionate concern for the winning of the people to Christ. The finest memorial of George Whitefield would be another Evangelical Revival on a world-scale. As we turn to look at his life again, with such an end in view, we may fittingly allow the eloquence of John Whittier to focus our attention on the manly figure of this prince of evangelists.

> " Lo! by the Merrimac WHITEFIELD stands
> In the temple that never was made by hands,
> Curtains of azure, and crystal wall,
> And dome of the sunshine over all!
> A homeless pilgrim, with dubious name
> Blown about on the winds of fame;
> Now as an angel of blessing classed,
> And now as a mad enthusiast.

CAN THE EVANGELICAL REVIVAL BE REPEATED?

> Called in his youth to sound and gauge
> The moral lapse of his race and age,
> And, sharp as truth, the contrast draw
> Of human frailty and human law;
> Possessed by the one dread thought that lent
> Its goad to his fiery Temperament,
> Up and down the world he went
> A John the Baptist crying, 'Repent'."
>
> WHITTIER: The Preacher.

PART I

EARLY DAYS

CHAPTER I

BOYHOOD AND EDUCATION

"The only way to be a true scholar is to be striving to be a true saint."—GEORGE WHITEFIELD.

THE interior of a tavern in a provincial city of the eighteenth century must have been a squalid affair, even under respectable management. The gross poverty, both physical and mental, that affected the period, together with its moral depravity, would ensure a sufficiently poisonous atmosphere. Yet out of such unpromising ground there sprang a life that was to become a flaming torch of moral grandeur and of spiritual challenge to its age. It was at the Bell Inn, Gloucester,[1] that George Whitefield[2] was born on December 16th (old style)[3] 1714. The inn still stands under the name of the Bell Hotel, although it has been drastically renovated and brought up to date during the intervening years. There is still to be seen, however, "the Oak room", dating from 1650, indicative, possibly, of the fact that the inn was of the higher rather than the lower type. The fact that George Whitefield sprang of clerical stock, his great-grandfather, Samuel, being rector first of North Ledyard,[4] in Wiltshire, and then of Rockhampton, near Thornbury, in Gloucestershire, may have helped the boy

[1] In 1872 this inn was in the possession of John and Sybella Philpotts, whose family contained some brilliant and fortunate children. One, John, became a barrister, another was a general in the regular Army, a son, Thomas, became a West Indian planter, and the youngest, Henry, became Bishop Philpotts of Exeter.
[2] Spelt in both ways—Whitfield and Whitefield, and pronounced Whit-field. At Tottenham Court Road Chapel there are MSS. bearing Whitefield's own signature in both styles.
[3] December 27th new style.
[4] Tyerman says there is no such place in Wiltshire. The name probably should be Liddiard Melicent, three miles from Wootton Bassett, Wilts, a parish curiously enough, in the gift of Pembroke College, Oxford. This traditional association of the family with Pembroke may have been useful in getting George to Oxford.

in such an environment. The rector had two sons, one of whom succeeded him in the living of Rockhampton, the other, Andrew, living as a private gentleman of means. It was the latter's son, Thomas, a wine-merchant of Bristol, and afterwards owner of the Bell Inn, Gloucester, who was the father of the great evangelist. He died when George, the youngst of seven children, was but two years old. The inn did not prosper—perhaps because it was too respectable—and to remedy matters, Mrs. Thomas Whitefield married again, this time an ironmonger of the city, named Capel Longden, when George was ten years of age. The evangelist left on record in later life a caustic comment upon this marriage, declaring that it was "not attended with very happy results, especially as regards 'temporals'."

Whitefield's mother, who was related to the Blackwells and Dimours, of Bristol, seems to have discharged her educational duty to her youngest son with fine conscientiousness. At twelve years of age we find him accepted by the Gloucester Free Grammar School at St. Mary's de Crypt. More recent research, however, has discovered his name enrolled earlier than this as a scholar at the King's School connected with the Cathedral.[1] At St. Mary de Crypt, Whitefield made good progress in classical studies, but he seems to have leapt to the fore particularly through a natural gift of elocution. So marked was this that on the occasion of the annual visit to the school of the Mayor and Corporation it became customary for George Whitefield to "make the speech." He also frequently played truant from school for days at a time preparing himself for parts in various dramatic plays, the reading of which was a great delight to him.[2] In this way he gained, very early in life, a power of public address.

At fifteen, the business still failing, Whitefield was taken from school and "putting on the blue apron" he was soon "washing the mops, cleaning the rooms, and becoming common drawer to his mother's customers."[3] The mischief that is part of the normal boy's constitution was happily not missing from George Whitefield, and possibly life at the inn gave him

[1] This fact was ascertained by Mr. Roland Austin, chief librarian of Gloucester to whom the author is indebted for the information.
[2] Whitefield's *Journal.*
[3] ibid.

The Bell at
Gloucester in
Whitefield's day. Ed. Burrow. 1900.

[Face page 12

a double share. We are told that although he often slipped into the Southgate Independent Chapel to hear its minister, Mr. Cole, preach, he did so chiefly that he might return home to mimic the preacher for the benefit of boon companions at the Bell Inn. He is reputed to have broken in, with some of his cronies, upon a service conducted at the Cordwainers' Hall by Cole, with cries of "Old Cole, Old Cole!" Mr. Cole was more alive than most ministers of his time, and seems to have had a real affection for his unruly young hearer. Learning that one of young Whitefield's points of mimicry and ridicule was his minister's habit of telling anecdotes, and that Whitefield used to declare that if he were a minister he would never behave in that way, Mr. Cole stored the report in memory. Years afterwards, when Whitefield actually preached from the pulpit of the Independent Chapel, the old minister remarked to him afterwards, "I find young Whitefield can tell stories as well as old Cole!" It looks as though "old Cole" had already, in those early days, perceived the boy's promise. Certain it is that later we find Mr. Cole serving humbly as one of Whitefield's itinerating preachers.[1]

At the end of a year the business was taken over by George's eldest brother, Richard, and, finding himself at variance with his sister-in-law, George removed to Bristol on a visit to another brother. Although before this he had been much impressed by Bishop Ken's *Manual for Winchester Scholars*, it was here that he received his first marked impetus to a change of heart and life through a sermon preached at St. John's Church. The difference was noticed by all on his return to Gloucester. Residing now, not at the inn, but with his mother, whose circumstances were greatly reduced, he plunged into devotional reading, setting aside his schoolbred fondness for plays. It is more than probable that, but for this simple choice of reading matter, an actor greater than David Garrick might have taken the place of the greatest of Christian Revivalists.

George Whitefield published, in 1740, the only account of his boyhood that is in existence, in the form of an octavo pamphlet of seventy-six pages, written during his first voyage

---

[1] *Whitefield's Legacy to Bristol and the Cotswolds*, by Rev. George Hoskin Wicks.

to America. It was not republished in its entirety until his biographer, the Rev. L. Tyerman, reproduced it in the first volume of his *Life of Whitefield*. We shall have occasion to refer to this pamphlet more than once, as a guide to White-field's character and temperament. It is particularly notable at this juncture for the confession of boyish sinfulness that it contains. Tyerman, with other biographers, deprecates Whitefield's low opinion of himself as a boy, and doubtless there is some truth in the charge of exaggeration. But modern judgment would view the situation differently. It would agree that the "guilt" was exaggerated, but scarcely the condition or the facts, particularly in such a period. Whitefield writes:

"I can date some very early acts of uncleanness. I soon gave frequent proofs of an impudent temper. Lying, filthy talking, foolish jesting I was much addicted to even when very young. Sometimes I used to curse, if not swear. Stealing from my mother I thought no theft at all, and used to make no scruple of taking money out of her pocket before she was up."

That is the worst he has to tell of himself, but although it is not a pleasant picture, modern psychology sees in it simply the natural reaction of an immature and emotional mind to early environment. These things probably were so, but their meaning was not nearly so depraved as the religious teaching of that period would have declared. We must insist upon the reality of boyish spiritual experience, and the relative importance of current verdicts even for the child of tender years, but the true interpretation of them may be other than Whitefield gives. This matter, which has considerable bearing upon the psychology of the great evangelist, will be dealt with more fully in the last section of this book. It is noted here as a vital remembrance of Whitefield in regard to his early years. This aspect of his boyhood was important to him because moral values had come to be supreme in his estima-tion, and this confession does credit therefore both to his candour and his earnestness. It is curious that Tyerman, whilst disputing the wisdom and propriety and truthfulness of Whitefield's account of himself as a boyish sinner, should nevertheless make the following admission, which accords so well with the more modern judgment of the matter.

GRAMMAR SCHOOL OF ST. MARY DE CRYPT, GLOUCESTER, WHERE WHITEFIELD WAS EDUCATED

BOYHOOD AND EDUCATION

"As in the case of so many others, Whitefield's boyhood was a strange admixture of sin and penitence. At intervals we find the boy a liar, a petty thief, a potential rake, a dandy, almost an infidel; and then we find him spending his scantily collected pence in buying the Manual of Bishop Ken; composing sermons; delighting in Thomas à Kempis . . . religiously watching over his own thoughts, words and actions, praying in private, worshipping in public, receiving the Sacrament once a month, and during Lent and at other times frequently fasting for eighteen hours."[1]

George Whitefield is certainly not the only city lad in whom saint and sinner have badly jostled each other. This early setting, however, of the lists of moral battle may help greatly to account for the amazing maturity of Whitefield's moral passion and spiritual power, at so young an age.

[1] Tyerman. Vol. I. p. 11.

CHAPTER II

OXFORD AND THE HOLY CLUB

"Whenever I go to Oxford I cannot help running to the spot where Jesus Christ first revealed Himself to me, and gave me the new birth."—GEORGE WHITEFIELD.

WHITEFIELD'S life on his return to Gloucester from Bristol was too uncertain in its prospect and occupation to be a happy one. He confesses frankly in his *Journal* that he fell into a godless way of life, and hints darkly at secret and besetting sin. There is no reason to doubt the substantial accuracy of such a report, or to minimise its moral seriousness for him at such a time. He tells us that, led away by a crew of "atheistical" acquaintances, he went to public service only to make a sport of it. But the work of grace had begun in his soul, and was already too deep to be easily obliterated. Coming downstairs one day he overheard friends speaking well of him, and the knowledge of his hypocrisy struck shame into his soul. There and then he experienced an accession of moral power whereby he overcame his secret sin. "I had then power given me over my secret and darling sin," he says. Is the true evangelist, I wonder, ever made excepting by that definite experience of deliverance from the power of sin? One remembers how vividly St. Paul and St. Augustine and St. Francis all experienced it. However that may be, it is a fact that shortly afterwards Whitefield felt himself in the grip of that sense of destiny which so often seems to be the "shadow cast before" by coming greatness. "One morning as I was reading a play to my sister, said I, 'God intends something for me which I know not of. As I have been diligent in business, I believe many would gladly have me for an apprentice, but every way seems to be barred up, so that I think God will provide for me some way or other that

16

JOHN WESLEY GREETING GEORGE WHITEFIELD OUTSIDE THE HOLY CLUB, OXFORD

[*Face page* 16

we cannot comprehend'." [1] Not long after his prophecy an old schoolfellow, a servitor of Pembroke College, Oxford, paid a visit to Whitefield's home. It was this youth's proud boast that by his diligent service he had been able to discharge all his college expenses and have something over. Mrs. Whitefield was quick to see the possibility of an Oxford education in such an achievement, not only for this servitor, but also for her own boy. "This will do for my son," she cried, then almost in the next breath, "Will you go to Oxford, George?" The lad replied sensibly enough, "With all my heart!" Thereupon, with commendable energy, mother and son set to work, the one to secure the patronage that would obtain for her son a servitor's position at Pembroke, the other to polish up his scholarship again with his old schoolmaster and his old books. Very proudly does Whitefield tell us that in the Latin test he made only one inconsiderable mistake, much to his master's surprise.

The way to the new opportunity was soon opened up. A friend was kind enough to lend him ten pounds with which to pay his entrance fee, and George entered upon University life. This was in 1732, and Whitefield was eighteen years of age. It was an eventful change, for there was awaiting Whitefield at Oxford just that human environment which, out of all his generation, could best minister to the peculiar genius slumbering within him. John and Charles Wesley were there, and the Holy Club! [2]

There are few instances in history of personal influence so perfectly mutual, so profound and far-reaching in their effects on the world at large as the shuttle-like impacts of these three men on one another. They form a triangle of constantly-interchanging forces. John captures Charles, Charles lays hold of Whitefield, Whitefield bursts into flame, and in turn, pioneers John and Charles into the greatest religious achievement of the century, and John, through a long and laborious life, carries on and consolidates the pioneer's work. If ever

---

[1] *Whitefield's Journal.*
[2] This met generally in John Wesley's rooms in Lincoln College, "the first-floor rooms on the south or right-hand side of the first quadrangle, shaded by the famous Lincoln line and opposite the clock-tower."—Overton's *John Wesley.*

It is an interesting coincidence that at the time of going to press a new Oxford Movement is springing into being called "The Oxford Group Movement" based upon the Buchman Group Movement of America.

three men were brought together by God for His purpose it was these three. Charles Wesley, forty years afterwards, wrote thus of his meeting with Whitefield:

> " Can I the memorable day forget
> When first we by Divine appointment met?
> Where undisturbed the thoughtful student roves
> In search of truth, through academic groves;
> A most modest youth, who mused alone,
> Industrious the frequented path to shun
> An Israelite, without disguise or art
> I saw, I loved, and clasped him to my heart,
> A stranger as my bosom friend caressed
> And unawares received an angel-guest."

It is good to have that glowing picture of Whitefield, the student, from a pen sobered by forty years of further experience of life, and, be it noted, further knowledge of the evangelist.

There is little need, doubtless, to enlarge very much upon the Holy Club. Suffice it to say that the description was one of several, such as the Godly Club, the Bible Moths, Bible Bigots, Sacramentarians and especially Method-ists, applied derisively by their fellow-students to the group which gathered about the Wesleys at Oxford. It was their novel earnestness in religious exercises, and more especially their living by rule or method which earned them the interest, scorn and fierce opposition of those about them, and led to their being dubbed Method-ists. The term " Methodists " was first applied, by a fellow-graduate of Wesley versed in Classic lore, directly from a School of Medicine that flourished in Rome in the days of Nero, and which was renowned for the strict regimen and rule of life it recommended to its patients—they were called Method-ists.[1] When Whitefield arrived at the University their numbers were about fifteen, and though at a subsequent period, through John Wesley's influence, the number rose to twenty-seven, before Whitefield had actually joined them the number had dwindled to seven, largely because of the stern discipline involved in the policy of the Club.[2] These were John Wesley, Charles Wesley, James Hervey, author of *Meditations* and *Theron and Aspasia*, Mr. Morgan, of Christ Church, Mr. Ingham,

[1] See John Wesley's address on laying the foundation "of the new Chapel, near the City Road, London, April 21, 1777." Quoted also by Overton, *John Wesley, p. 28.*

[2] Andrew's *Life of Whitefield.*

18

PEMBROKE COLLEGE, OXFORD (1835)

[*Face page* 18

of King's College, Mr. Broughton, of Exeter, and Mr. Clayton, of Brasenose.

The steps by which George Whitefield came into this circle are worthy of notice. It could not have been easy for him to endure the hard life of a servitor in the College, adding to his innumerable menial tasks a round of constant strenuous study. Moreover, Whitefield was not the sort to fail of putting his utmost energy into his duties. His lot was, therefore, both so lowly and so busy that it was some time before any opportunity arose of fellowship with the Methodists. It was not till the end of his first year that an occasion arose which brought him into acquaintance with Charles Wesley, but the contact at once bore vital fruit. Charles Wesley lent to Whitefield certain books, among them being the book that was the means of Whitefield's conversion. This was Henry Scougal's *Life of God in the Soul of Man*, and its teaching broke upon Whitefield's groping soul like a great blaze of light. "At my first reading," he says in his *Journal*, "I wondered what the author meant by saying that 'some falsely placed religion in going to church, doing hurt to no one, being constant in the duties of the closet, and now and then reaching out their hands to give alms to their poor neighbours'. Alas, thought I, if this be not true religion, what is? God soon showed me, for in reading a few lines further, that 'true religion was union of the soul with God, and Christ proved within us,' a ray of Divine light was instantaneously darted in upon my soul, and from that moment, but not till then, did I know that I must be a new creature." So George Whitefield took the first steps towards that experience of "new birth" which he afterwards made the test and standard of all genuine conversion. There now began, for Whitefield, a process of rapid but most profound spiritual education. It is no small tribute to his spiritual genius that within a few months he had struggled to the fiery heart of the Gospel of Christ, whilst the Wesleys were still stumbling in the mazes of salvation by conduct. It took John Wesley, older than Whitefield by eleven years, three more years to reach that profound change of heart which eventually transformed him as amazingly as it transformed Whitefield. This is not necessarily to Wesley's detriment, for perceptions and temperaments differ greatly, but it does stress effectively Whitefield's claim to be regarded as essentially the pioneer spirit of the great revival. That able biographer of Whitefield, the Rev. James Paterson Gledstone, points out that after this experience Whitefield "never becomes entangled in doubts concerning the Divine method of saving sinners, and never hesitates between rival plans of practical living. He tried all three great plans of being a Christian, and of serving God which have gained favour with large sections of mankind";[1] and finding satisfaction in the one which he ultimately adopted he "felt no temptation ever afterward to leave it." "The pupil was the first to become a safe teacher; he knew the 'liberty of the sons of God' while the Wesleys were struggling in chains he had broken."

Indeed, as far as one can be sure of facts gathered from slightly conflicting evidence, it would seem that the Wesleys at this juncture came near to quenching the flame that had been kindled in the soul of Whitefield. Introduced by Charles to the Holy Club, Whitefield, after his first faint glimpse of the true light, began to live by rule with a fanaticism that could not be excelled. He has told the story with moving eloquence in his *Journal*. To live by rule was the glory of the Holy Club, and Whitefield set out bravely and stubbornly to live the narrowest and hardest life conceivable. "The redemption of time became a primary virtue, and he hoarded the moments as if they were years." Sacrament every Sunday, fasting every Wednesday and Friday, sick persons and prisoners visited and poor people read to, and one hour every day given to acts of charity! No books to be read "but such as entered into the heart of religion and led him directly into an experimental knowledge of Jesus Christ and Him crucified!" Added to this, was the petty persecution that fell to the lot of every Methodist, but perhaps even more so to a poor servitor whose position in the University was less dignified. Some withdrew their pay from him, others were actively brutal to him, pelting him with dirt, friends fell away from him, masters and tutors rebuked him. He had a full baptism of that contempt which was to harass him still more later on in his strenuous life. But, saddest result of all, the light he had seen for one glorious moment in Scougal's teaching was, for the time being, quenched,

[1] Namely, Good works, Asceticism and Quietism.

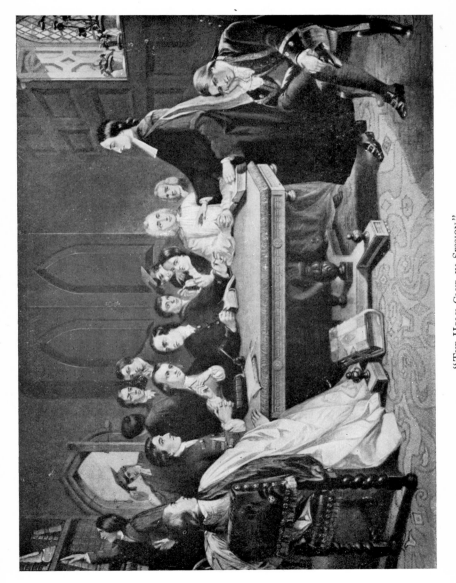

"The Holy Club in Session"

From Marshall Claxton's picture. The scene is the actual room, and the faces were painted from authoritative portraits of the time.

and with it all inward joy. Fear and horror of the devil took possession of his soul, "and unusual weight and impression, attended with inward darkness."

"My memory," he says, "quite failed me. My whole soul was barren and dry, and I could fancy myself to be like nothing so much as a man locked up in armour. Whenever I kneeled down I felt great heavings in my body, and have often prayed under the weight of them till the sweat came through me. At this time Satan used to terrify me much, and threatened to punish me if I forgot his wiles. . . . And he so troubled me when I lay down to rest, that, for some weeks I scarce slept above three hours at a time. God only knows how many nights I have lain upon my bed groaning under the weight I felt, and bidding Satan depart from me in the name of Jesus. Whole days and weeks have I spent lying prostrate on the ground and begging freedom from those proud hellish thoughts that used to crowd in upon and distract my soul. . . . Having no one to show me a better way, I thought to get peace and purity by outward austerities. Accordingly, by degrees, I began to leave off eating fruits and such like, and gave the money I usually spent in that way to the poor. Afterwards I always chose the worst sort of food, though my place furnished me with variety. I fasted twice a week. My apparel was mean. I thought it unbecoming for a penitent to have his hair powdered. I wore woollen gloves, a patched gown and dirty shoes, and therefore looked upon myself as very humble."[1]

Reading in Castaniza's *Spiritual Combat* that "he that is employed in mortifying his will is as well employed as if he were converting Indians," he set himself the task of mortifying his will. He gave himself up to incessant prayer, but was as far from finding peace as ever. Denying himself every pleasure, he at last began to feel that even the pleasure of meeting his fellow Methodists was an indulgence he must surrender. This brought Charles Wesley to him in a hurry, and after some inquiry he counselled Whitefield to consult John. But John's advice was too much after the manner of that which George had already been doing to be of any real help. It is a dramatic picture, this, of Wesley, as the father of the Holy Club, counselling its latest and most raw recruit, with Whitefield as humble inquirer, receiving not so much bread as a stone—"advice," as Gledstone says, "which might have driven him mad, not a ray of comfort in it, not a drop of the love of God." Did the memory of that interview ever recur to John Wesley's mind in later years, when he as Arminian,

[1] *Whitefield's Journal.*

was crossing dialectical swords with Whitefield, the Calvinist? In qualification of this reference to Wesley it is only fair to recall that in the original edition of his *Journal*, Whitefield pens the following words about John Wesley's influence at this time:—

"And at length, by his excellent advice and management of me, under God, I was delivered from these wiles of Satan."

From his 1756 edition, however, Whitefield omitted this paragraph. Did he feel that his previous remark might be misunderstood as meaning that Wesley led him all the way into the new great experience? Of that experience as being something distinct from the self-righteous strivings of a soul that would justify itself, Whitefield was, we know, always very jealous. In any case, it would seem clear that Wesley could hardly have carried Whitefield to a point he himself had not reached as yet.

Whitefield's violent asceticism, in his search for salvation, brought him at last to a sick bed. But the enforced cessation of his own feverish endeavours gave that light which once had visited his soul and was now all but quenched by neglect, a new opportunity of shining.

"About the end of the seventh week, after having undergone innumerable buffetings of Satan and many months' inexpressible trials by night and day under the spirit of bondage, God was pleased at length to remove the heavy load, to enable me to lay hold on His dear Son by a living faith, and by giving me the spirit of adoption, to seal me, as I humbly hope, even to the day of everlasting redemption."

Then he bursts out in triumph:

"But oh, with what joy, joy unspeakable, even joy that was full of and big with glory, was my soul filled when this weight of sin went off, and an abiding sense of the pardoning love of God and a full assurance of faith broke in upon my disconsolate soul! Surely it was the day of my espousal—a day to be had in everlasting remembrance. At first my joys were like a spring tide and, as it were, overflowed the banks. Go where I would, I could not avoid singing of Psalms almost aloud; afterwards it became more settled, and blessed be God! saving a few casual intervals, has abode and increased in my soul ever since. Thus were the days of my mourning ended. *After a long night of desertion and temptation*

KEY TO CLAXTON'S PICTURE OF THE HOLY CLUB

1. John Wesley, A.M.
2. George Whitefield
3. James Hervey, Author of "Meditations"
4. William Morgan, Visitor of the Prisons

5. Rev. Charles Wesley, A.M.
6. Benjamin Ingham, Founder of the Inghamite Sect
7. John Clayton
8. Thomas Broughton
9 to 16. Students mentioned in Wesley's Life

[Face page 22

the Star which I had seen at a distance before, began to appear again and the Day Star arose in my heart." [1,2]

Yet the pitiful struggle he had been through was not by any means wasted. Whitefield repeatedly claims in his *Journal* that seasons and experiences of solace and power punctuated his travail. Something of the Methodist discipline of those early days remained with both Whitefield and Wesley all through their careers and was one of the secrets of their remarkable achievements. Undoubtedly, too, in the Methodist programme of charity Whitefield found the kindling of that philanthropic passion to which he was to give expression later in such a singularly selfless manner. Meanwhile, one might well ask, what was happening to Whitefield's academic studies all this time? It is hardly to be supposed that he could be the friend and intimate of John Wesley, a Fellow of Lincoln, of Charles, a College tutor, without being conscientious in the general work of the University. It is generally assumed that he had no great distinction in learning, but we must remember that preaching of the type favoured by the Methodists was not likely ever to lend itself to a display of learning. What we do find in Whitefield is a faultlessly easy English style, a deep understanding of human nature, and a keen business aptitude, especially in other people's and his own philanthropic interests. It is a profound mistake, therefore, to imagine that because Whitefield was exceptionally emotional, and because the very nature of his call from God compelled him to concentrate upon evangelism and not upon such constructive work as fell to Wesley's lot and talent, he was therefore of inferior intellectual power. The work that Whitefield did and the way in which he did it were possible only to an exceptionally able and robust mind, and he doubtless accepted the inevitable limitations of expression forced upon him by the peculiar nature of his task, with a noble cheerfulness and self-denial.

[1] *Whitefield's Journal* (Edit. 1756).

[2] I notice that Mr. Edward S. Ninde, in his otherwise excellent account *George Whitefield—Prophet-Preacher*, makes the error of assuming that the reading of Scougal's book *followed* the struggles of Whitefield to find peace through ascetic practices and quietism, whereas the *Journal* makes it quite clear that these were rather an interlude between the first ray of vision occasioned by Scougal's teaching, and the ultimate clear shining of truth revealed in the time of sickness. Hence my italics for the closing sentence of the extract. This order of events is confirmed also by Andrews, Tyerman and Gledstone in their respective volumes.

CHAPTER III

"I would not but be a poor despised minister of Jesus Christ for ten thousand worlds."—GEORGE WHITEFIELD.

THE illness that had been so signally blessed to Whitefield necessitated his taking a real holiday from his studies and duties at Oxford. He had kept no less than nine terms without a break—terms not merely of hard work, but of cruel asceticism, and his body urgently required rest and recuperation.

He, therefore, returned to Gloucester and did so with his heart aglow over the new discovery he had made of the grace of God in Christ. He found, however, that the spiritual atmosphere of Gloucester was not that of the Methodist group at Oxford, and felt his spirit checked and chilled.

"Being unaccustomed for some time to live without spiritual companions, and finding none that would join heartily with me—no, not one—I watched unto prayer all the day long, beseeching God to raise me some religious associates in His own way and time." So he launched out into his first achievements at evangelism on the new basis, and sought out a lady, an old friend of his childhood, and endeavoured to secure her conversion. "God was pleased to bless the visit with the desired effect. Not long after, God made me instrumental to several young persons, *who soon formed themselves into a little Society*."

We see from this how inevitably the policy of forming Societies arose for the Methodists, and later Wesley developed it in a most thorough-going fashion. The very deadness and dullness of the religious world around them compelled these initiated and illuminated souls to gather to each other in their own very simple form of organisation.[1]

Whitefield was extremely poor at this time, his sickness having swallowed up any little resources he had gathered at Oxford. He had already formed the simple habit of relying upon God for temporal supplies, living frugally, giving freely, and praying for his own relief when in need. "This is still my practice," he writes in his *Journal*, "and I never yet failed of success." There were to come in his life much fiercer financial crises than those of his simple personal expenses, and in this way he was well prepared.

There is a vital note in his *Journal* at this point. After a glowing account of rich and refreshing experiences of communion with God at Gloucester, he sets down the considered verdict: "I always observed, as my inward strength increased, so my outward sphere of action increased proportionately." We shall see that all through his great ministry Whitefield was careful to honour that principle. He made sure of the inward depths that he might secure the utmost reaches. He also tells us at this juncture of fresh enlightenment on the matter of justification by faith only, and expresses wonder that his friends at Oxford did not rejoice more fully in it. It seems, however, that it was long before he ventured to include the idea in his preaching.[2]

Here at Gloucester, too, he first appears in print with certain articles upon Laws' "Absolute Unlawfulness of State Entertainments," which appeared in six successive issues of the local "News." "And God," says Whitefield, "was pleased to give it His blessing!"

In a letter to Wesley explaining why his return to Oxford was delayed, appears the paragraph.

"My friends here are for drawing me into orders, but I trust God will still provide for me without it. I know I am not qualified, and therefore, by the help of the Lord Jesus, I will not comply."

[1] Whitefield and Wesley in this matter were following a precedent, dating from 1675, which had brought into being various "Religious Societies." They were concerned mainly with the application of Christian principles to social life, closing houses of ill-fame, relieving the sick, burying the poor, encouraging charity schools for the education of the children, etc. At this time, moreover, they were in a depressed and moribund condition. *Cf.* Gledstone, p. 69.

[2] Tyerman. Vol. I. p. 37.

Whitefield continued in Gloucester for another three months, strengthening and adding to his little Society. Then, fresh financial supplies being forthcoming, he returned to Oxford. His mind at this time was full of the question of taking orders, but his modesty caused him to wrestle with a most painful sense of unworthiness and unfitness.

"I was not solicitous," he says, "what place should be prepared for me, but how I should be prepared for a place. Oftentimes I have been in an agony of prayer when under convictions of my insufficiency for so great a work."

In one of the last sermons of his life Whitefield made a most interesting reference to this struggle.

"I never prayed against any corruption, I think, in my life so much as I did against going into Holy Orders. I have prayed a thousand times until the sweat dropped from my face like rain, that God in His infinite mercy would not let me enter the Church *before He called me*. I remember once at Gloucester—I know the room, I look up at the window when I am there and walk along the street —I know the bedside and the floor where I prostrated myself and cried, 'Lord, I cannot go! I shall be puffed up with pride. I am unfit to preach in Thy great Name. Send me not, Lord; send me not yet'."

Nevertheless, long before this Whitefield, in a dream, had seen himself in the palace of the Bishop of Gloucester, good Dr. Benson, receiving at his hand some gold. The dream now literally became true. Lady Selwyn, who had already helped Whitefield financially, mentioned the possibility of his ordination to Bishop Benson, who presently sent for Whitefield. After some conversation and inquiry about Whitefield's age, which was then twenty-one, the Bishop said: "Notwithstanding I have declared I would not ordain anyone under three-and-twenty, yet I shall think it my duty to ordain you whenever you come for Holy Orders," and he gave Whitefield a present of five guineas. The pressure of his friends increased with this news, and Whitefield began to feel that if he held out longer, he would be fighting against God.

Meanwhile, Sir John Philips, Bart., of Picton Castle, Pembrokeshire, a good "encourager of the Methodists," had prevailed on Whitefield to continue at Oxford at the head of the Methodists, John and Charles Wesley having left for Georgia, and had promised him an allowance of £30 a year. So, his sphere of labour being determined, Whitefield applied for Holy Orders.

It was characteristic of Whitefield that after spending the whole day before the memorable Sunday of the ceremony in abstinence and prayer, at night he climbed a hill near Gloucester and remained there in fervent prayer for two more hours, interceding, not only for himself, but also for those who should be ordained with him.

Sunday, June 20th, 1736, was the great day—a day that carried momentous issues in itself, not only for George White-field, but for his age and for succeeding generations in two continents. Only five years had elapsed since this youth of twenty-one was a common tapster in a local public-house. Now he was on the verge of acquiring his Bachelor of Arts degree from his University, and was about to preach his first sermon as a deacon in Holy Orders. Two or three years before he had told his mother that he meant to be a clergyman, and she had rebuked him for presumption. Here we find him with his ambition fulfilled, and his mother a wondering listener to his first eloquence. How one would like a glimpse of that first audience! Was Robert Raikes there, the printer and editor of the *Gloucester Journal*, a firm friend of Whitefield's, and himself a benefactor of the world? Good "old Cole" was undoubtedly there, and Gabriel Harris, an early friend of the young ordinand—doubtless, too, some of those mayors and aldermen and councillors who had listened admiringly to the orations of the young scholar of St. Mary de Crypt! A letter of Whitefield's, referring to the solemn occasion, is worth quoting for the glimpse it gives of his mind:

"Gloucester,
"June 20, 1736.

"This is a day much to be remembered; for about noon I was solemnly admitted by good Bishop Benson before many witnesses, into Holy Orders. I endeavoured to behave with unaffected devotion. I trust I answered every question from the bottom of my heart. I hope the good of souls will be my only principle of action. Let come what will, life or death, I shall henceforward live like one who this day, in the presence of men and angels, took the holy sacrament upon the profession of being inwardly moved by the

27

Holy Ghost to take upon him the ministration in the Church. This I began with reading prayers to the prisoners in the County gaol. Whether I myself shall ever have the honour of styling myself a prisoner of the Lord, I know not; but, indeed, my dear friend, I can call heaven and earth to witness that when the Bishop laid his hand upon me, I gave myself up to be a martyr for Him who hung upon the Cross for me. Known unto Him are all future events and contingencies. I have thrown myself blindfold, and I trust without reserve, into His almighty hands."

A week later, on Sunday, June 27th, Whitefield preached his first sermon, entitled "The Necessity and Benefit of Religious Society," in the church of St. Mary de Crypt, where he had been baptized, and where he had taken his first Communion. Here is an interesting extract from a letter that he wrote to a friend a few days later:

"Curiosity, as you may easily guess, drew a large congregation together. The sight at first a little awed me; but I was comforted with a heartfelt sense of the Divine Presence, and soon found the unspeakable advantage of having been accustomed to public speaking when a boy at school, and of exhorting and teaching the prisoners, and poor people at their private houses, whilst at the University. By these means I was kept from being daunted overmuch. As I progressed, I perceived a fire kindled, till at last, though so young, and amidst a crowd who knew me in my childish days, I trust I was enabled to speak with some degree of Gospel authority. A few mocked, but most for the present seemed struck; and I have since heard that a complaint had been made to the bishop that I drove fifteen mad. The worthy prelate, as I am informed, wished that the madness might not be forgotten before next Sunday."

His first sermon, and fifteen people already "drunk with the Spirit!" Not a bad beginning, George Whitefield!

It may be well to look at this boy-preacher as he stands before us here in the pulpit of St. Mary de Crypt, before that congregation composed so largely of his own people. He is just turned twenty-one years in age, above the middle height in stature, slender but well-proportioned, in manner graceful, regular in features, with a fair complexion. His eyes, however, are remarkable. They are small and dark-blue, but lively and piercing to a degree, and in the left eye there is a distinct cast, evident in his portraits. This squint was the result of a nurse's neglect during his childhood's bout of measles, and in later

28

years it gained for him the unenviable sobriquet of " Dr. Squintum." It is declared by some that this cast in the eye was by no means a disadvantage to Whitefield as a preacher. Rather, it had the curious effect of making everyone of his hearers feel that the eye was upon him, and could not be escaped. To compensate for this marred feature, however, and to compensate amply, Whitefield's voice was a gift of God. Used with perfect though natural art, its modulations were of an extraordinary variety, running the whole gamut of feeling, and in strength it was as clear as a bell and capable of amazing expansion when necessary.

One of his less-educated hearers of this first sermon could find no better way of describing the event than to say, "He preached like a lion." It was an apt reference to one aspect of the achievement, but we are assured that it quite misses "the melting charity, the earnestness of persuasion, the outpouring of redundant love which characterised the preaching of this youthful evangelist for the next four and thirty years."[1]

It looked at first as though Oxford would claim the services of Whitefield for some years after his ordination, but he returned there only for a few weeks. He took his degree of Bachelor of Arts, administered the funds (about £40 per annum) raised by the Methodists and their friends for the "poor prisoners" of Oxford gaol, inspected three small charity schools that the Methodists had started, and generally, in the absence of the Wesleys, acted as the central figure of the now sadly-diminished group. But a greater destiny was already drawing George Whitefield towards itself. A friend of his Holy Club days, Mr. Broughton, Curate at the Tower of London, having to be away in Hampshire for some time, invited Whitefield to officiate there. Accordingly Whitefield went to London on Wednesday, August 4th, and stayed there two months. He was very elated at the idea of preaching in London, Whitefield tells us, but "God sent something to ballast it, for as I passed along the streets, many came out of their shops to see so young a person in a gown and cassock, and one cried out, 'There's a boy parson,' which served to mortify my pride and put me also upon turning the apostolical exhortation into prayer, 'Let no man despise your youth.'"

[1] Tyerman. Vol. I. p. 51.

Whitefield's first preaching in London was at Bishopsgate Church on Sunday, August 8th, and as he went up the pulpit stairs Whitefield felt the revulsion in the congregation caused by his extreme youth, but when the service was over there was great inquiry as to who this youth was. "And," says Whitefield, surely with a chuckle, "nobody could tell them." His work at the Tower was mainly visitation of sick soldiers and the reading of prayers twice a week, but he preached in Ludgate Prison every Tuesday, and to his preaching services every Sunday in the Chapel of the Tower a crowd was very quickly drawn. From the very first moment of contact with London audiences Whitefield had the ear of the London crowd. The Tower Chapel was packed Sunday after Sunday by people drawn from every part of London to hear him "discourse about the new birth and the necessity of renouncing all in affection in order to follow Jesus Christ." From the very beginning to the very end of this man's ministry, with very few exceptions,[1] he preached only to crowded congregations. There was no slow winning of fame in Whitefield's case. As though the very finger of God had pointed him out, the common people flocked to him wherever he went.

During this first brief London ministry, foretaste of greater things to come, Whitefield heard from the Wesleys in Georgia. Their news fired his quick and eager spirit with the hope of joining them, but he set the hope resolutely on one side and returned to Oxford to gather about him more youths ready to be Methodists.[2] Many of these youths were desperately poor, but help was secured for them from Lady Betty Hastings, sister-in-law of Selina, Countess of Huntingdon, who afterwards became Whitefield's chief benefactor and friend.

But again, and very soon, his work was broken by the summons to preach. This time it was an invitation to Dummer, a small village of Hampshire, to take the place of its Vicar, Mr. Kinchin. Of this visit, it is enough to record that Whitefield promptly applied to his work the "method" and discipline that his life at Oxford had made habitual. He writes:

[1] As for example just after his return from America the second time. *Cf.* p. 121.
[2] " Several dear youths were quickened greatly, and met daily at my rooms to build up each other in their most holy faith." (*Further account of God's dealings with George Whitefield*, 1747.)

"I generally divided the day into three parts—eight hours for study and retirement, eight hours for sleep and meals, and eight hours for reading prayers, catechising, and visiting the parish. The profit I reaped by these exercises, and conversing with the poor country people, was unspeakable. I frequently learned as much by an afternoon's visit as in a week's study."

Whilst at Dummer, where his preaching was no less effective than in London, Whitefield had the offer of a lucrative curacy in London. The invitation came to him at a time when he was desperately poor, and his recent success in London might easily have inclined him towards acceptance. It is interesting to reflect that had he done so his great work in and for America might never have been done. He might have become the greatest Anglican preacher of his age, and nothing more! But it was not to be. Doubtless the very improvement in worldly fortune which it would confer warned the ascetic young Methodist against such a policy, and hard upon the heels of this temptation came a new and fascinating opportunity from America. Charles Wesley arrived home, and in a letter to George Whitefield explained that he had returned to find fresh workers for Georgia. This appeal coincided with a letter from John Wesley containing the following words:

"Only Mr. Delamotte is with me, till God shall stir up the hearts of some of His servants, who, putting their lives in His hands, shall come over and help us, where the harvest is so great and the labourers so few. What if thou art the man, Mr. Whitefield?"

In another letter appeared this sentence:

"Do you ask me what you shall have? Food to eat, and raiment to put on; a house to lay your head in, such as your Lord had not and a crown of glory that fadeth not away."

"Upon reading this," says Whitefield, "my heart leaped within me, and, as it were, echoed to the call!"

Simultaneously the way was cleared at Oxford for Whitefield's release from his responsibilities there. Mr. Kinchin, late of Dummer, now Dean of Corpus Christi, was willing to take over the work among the prisoners, and James Hervey, Methodist, and member of the Holy Club, was ready to step into the pulpit at Dummer. With characteristic humility, Whitefield also adds, "Mr. Wesley was my dear friend, and I thought it would be a great advantage to be under his tuition." We catch a glimpse in that remark, and also in the following, of that inner diffidence that always afflicted the soul of Whitefield, and which indicates the existence of a perpetual inward struggle. He writes:

"I at length resolved to embark for Georgia and knowing that I should never put my resolution into practice if I conferred with flesh and blood, I wrote to my relations to inform them of my design, and withal told them, if they would promise not to dissuade me from my intended voyage, I would come and take a personal leave of them; if otherwise, knowing my own weakness, I was determined to embark without visiting them at all."

So Whitefield, at the age of twenty-one, decided, under a sense of Divine Call, to become a missionary. But before his resolution could be put into effect there occurred the first rumblings and stirrings of that mighty storm of religious revival which was approaching.

The quiet retirement of life at Dummer, though for some two months only, November and December, 1736, was undoubtedly a great blessing to Whitefield. He seems then to have thought long and deeply. Eight hours every day in study and retirement! There is a rule of life to challenge the modern ministry! Is it any wonder that when such a disciplined spirit essayed to speak the world stood still to listen?

Whitefield found that by a series of unavoidable delays he could not embark for Georgia inside twelve months. An unexpected and cruel check it must have seemed to his eager spirit—a rich blessing in disguise it turned out to be. The year was spent in preaching—preaching that startled the nation.

Circumstances conspired to set Whitefield peculiarly free, just at this time, for preaching whenever and wherever opportunity offered. The taste of freedom that he enjoyed in this position intoxicated him for life. Never again could he be content to be bound down for long to one sphere, or one Church even. He became, to use his own description, a "Gospel rover." Every congregation before which he appeared in this "year of wonder" was literally taken by storm. He became at once both the sensation and the embarrassment of the Church of England, whilst the attention of every part of the country was riveted upon him by the reports that were spread abroad of his marvellous preaching. Within a year of his ordination as a deacon, before he had yet taken priestly orders, his name was a household word throughout the land. The fact, of course, that he was a Methodist was of additional and even vital interest. Whilst Wesley was far across the ocean, this young stripling with the golden voice was laying the foundation of that Methodist popularity and preaching repute which was to become the outstanding religious feature of the century, and without which Wesley's work could hardly have been done. Tyerman's comment is undoubtedly justified:

"It may be fairly doubted whether Wesley's preaching in 1739 would have attracted the attention which it did if Whitefield had not preceded him in 1737."

When the Wesleys set out at last upon their own great and memorable itinerary they found and followed a trail already blazed by their young comrade Whitefield. Their one-time humble follower was already showing them the way. Here is a snapshot of that wonderful year of preaching taken from an account given by Whitefield of a visit to Bristol at this juncture. After visiting Gloucester to inform his relatives of his decision about Georgia, he went on to Bristol on the same errand, and, moved doubtless by memories of those first stirrings of his soul occasioned by a sermon at St. John's Church, he attended there the Thursday after his arrival:

"Whilst the psalm was singing after the prayers, the Minister came to my seat and asked me to give the congregation a sermon. Having my notes about me, I complied. The hearers seemed startled, and, after sermon, inquiry was made who I was. The next day there was another lecture at St. Stephen's. Many crowded there in expectation of hearing me again. The lecturer asked me to preach. I again complied, and the alarm given here was so general that on the following Lord's Day many of all denominations were obliged to return from the Churches where I preached, for want of room. Afterwards I was called by the Mayor to preach before him and the corporation. For some time following, I preached all the lectures on week-days and twice on Sundays, besides visiting the Religious Societies. The word, through the mighty power of God, was sharper than any two-edged sword. The doctrine of the new birth and justification by faith in Jesus Christ (though I was not so clear in it as afterwards) made its way like lightning into the hearers' consciences . . . and my whole time between one lecture and another . . . was wholly occupied in talking with people under religious concern."

During this work Whitefield found time to slip away from Bristol to Bath—England's fashion resort, the home of "Beau" Nash and the fast set of that day, where he preached twice in the Abbey Church.

This popularity was heady wine for such a youth, but Methodist discipline had done its work, and Whitefield was alive to the danger.

"Oh, pray, dear Mr. Harris," he wrote to a friend, "that God would always keep me humble, and fully convinced that I am nothing without Him, and that all the good which is done upon earth, God doeth it Himself."

Moreover, in a letter written to John Wesley at this time, Whitefield makes only the slightest allusion to the immense fame that had descended upon his preaching. He reveals, however, the interesting fact that he commenced that collecting for the needs of the poor folk of Georgia which was afterwards to become such a beacon light of philanthropy in an age of cruelty, and that he had raised already a sum of £200.[1]

After visits back to Gloucester and Oxford, and thence to London to meet James Oglethorpe and the trustees of the Georgian Colony—during which visit he met Dr. Potter, the Archbishop of Canterbury, Mr. Bedford, Chaplain to the Prince of Wales, and Dr. Edmund Gibson, the saintly Bishop of London—Whitefield paid a flying visit to Stonehouse, in Gloucestershire, which is particularly memorable as being the occasion when the idea of open-air preaching may first seriously have entered his mind:

"Neither church nor house could contain the people that came. . . . One night, when I had been expounding to many people,

[1] Tyerman. Vol. I. p. 76.

34

it happened to lighten exceedingly, and some being afraid to go home, I thought it my duty to accompany them, and improve the occasion to stir them up to prepare for the coming of the Son of Man. Every week the congregations increased; and on Ascension day, when I took my leave, their sighs and tears almost broke my heart."

That was a fortunate thunderstorm if it gave Whitefield his first taste of preaching in the open-air.[1]

From Stonehouse, Whitefield went again to Bristol in response to urgent requests. "Multitudes came on foot, and many in coaches, a mile outside the city to meet me, and almost all saluted and blessed me as I went along the street." On this occasion he preached five times a week; "People hung upon the rails of the organ-loft, climbed upon the leads of the church, and made the church itself so hot with their breath that the steam fell from the pillars like drops of rain. . . . It was with great difficulty that I got into the desk to read prayers or preach."

When after a month spent in this way the Bristol audiences were told by Whitefield of his impending departure to Georgia, their grief knew no bounds. "Multitudes, after sermon, followed me home, weeping, and the next day I was employed from seven in the morning till midnight, in talking and giving spiritual advice to awakened souls."

Whitefield came to London in this wonder-year, about the end of August. It was the occasion, too, of his first publication. The following advertisement appeared in the *Weekly Miscellany* of July 22nd, 1737:

[1] There has been quite unnecessary mystery attached to the problem of the date of Whitefield's first open-air preaching. Very commonly the preaching in Islington Churchyard, April 27th, 1739, is referred to as the initial instance. This, however, is to overlook at least two well authenticated previous occasions. One is that recorded by Whitefield as taking place " on a mount " at Kingswood when he preached to the poor colliers on February 17th, 1739, the other was in Stonehouse Churchyard on April 17th, 1739,[2] as reported in the *Gloucester Journal* of April 24th of that year. The idea of preaching in the open-air was strongly in his mind when a thousand people had to be shut out of Bermondsey Church in January, 1739, when he preached there one Sunday afternoon. So impressed was he that, when he went to preach the following Sunday at Ironmonger's Almshouses, he took two sermons with him, one for indoors and one for outside. Unhappily the overflow was not large enough to warrant his taking the step. When he mentioned the project to his friends they told him it was a " mad notion."

[2] *Whitefield's Connection with Stonehouse*, by C. L. S.

"Speedily will be published (price sixpence, or two guineas per hundred, to those who give them away). 'The New Nature, and the Necessity of our New Birth in Christ Jesus in Order to Salvation'—a sermon preached in the Church of St. Mary's, Radcliffe in Bristol, by George Whitefield, B.A., of Pembroke College, Oxford.

"Published at the request of several of the hearers. Printed by C. Rivington, in St. Paul's Churchyard, and sold by Messrs. Harris, Senior and Junior, in Gloucester; Mr. Wilson in Bristol; and Mr. Combe, in Bath."

Before the year was out, this sermon passed through three editions.

Whitefield came to London expecting to sail for Georgia, but General Oglethorpe was not yet ready to embark, and once again the pulpit called for its latest and youngest genius. He was dragged from the retirement and prayer in which he tried to bury himself, to preach in Cripplegate, St. Ann's, and Forster Lane churches at six o'clock on Sunday mornings, and to help administer Holy Communion. Such crowds gathered that it became necessary to consecrate fresh supplies of the elements three times over. Wapping Chapel, the Tower, the Ludgate and Newgate prisons, these also received once more the "boy-preacher," and again the numbers were so great that Whitefield had to preach four times on the Sunday.

The first mention of Whitefield in the Press was made at this time over a charity sermon that he preached, in the course of which was discovered his extraordinary capacity for opening the pockets as well as the hearts of his hearers. The reference would not appear to have been very exciting, judged by press reports and methods of to-day:

"There is a young gentleman going volunteer to Georgia. He has preached at St. Swithin's and collected £8, instead of 10s., £3 of which was in half-pence; he is to preach next Wednesday before the Societies at their general quarterly meeting."

"This advertisement," says Whitefield, "chagrined me. I immediately sent to the printer, desiring he would put me in his paper no more." The result, of course, was still more public curiosity. In three months the crowds of London of all classes were flocking to hear this young herald of a newer and sterner gospel than ever they had heard:

36

"As I was to embark shortly, they procured the liberty of the churches on the week-days—a thing never known before. I sometimes had more than a dozen names of different churches, at which I had promised to preach, upon my slate-book at once, and when I preached, constables were obliged to be placed at the door, to keep the people in order. The sight of the congregations was awful. One might, as it were, walk upon the people's heads, and thousands went away from the largest churches for want of room. They were all attention, and heard like people hearing for eternity. I now preached generally nine times a week. . . . I always preached gratis, and gave myself."

But now, however, signs of trouble began to appear. With the baptism of a miraculous popularity there was soon raised the baleful fires of jealousy and hate. There is no greater curse in the ranks of the Christian ministry than professional jealousy, and the spirit of career-mongering that takes offence at the popularity of others. Soon many of the clergy got angry at the way the crowds were running after this boy and accordingly forsaking themselves.

"Complaints were made that the churches were so crowded that there was no room for parishioners, and that the pews were spoiled. Some called me a spiritual pickpocket, and others thought I made use of a kind of charm to get the people's money."

But another disturbing factor entered in. Whitefield could hardly be preaching so effectively a real gospel without attracting the attention of the best minds in London among the Dissenters. Many of these sought interviews with him, and entertained him for discussion. To Whitefield's credit, he found not the slightest difficulty in such intercourse. "My practice in visiting and associating with them, I thought, was quite agreeable to the word of God." But this free contact with people sharply opposed to the Church of England gave offence to many.

To add further to his difficulties, large offers began to pour in upon him to remain in England. The seed he had sown at Gloucester, Bristol, Bath, was found to have life in itself, and to be springing up and multiplying. Everywhere he had been, he was called for again. He needed all his carefully-guarded inward resource of close dependence upon the Spirit of God to guide him safely through crowds of friends and crowds of foes. Perhaps it was as well that a great interlude was about to come for him.

"At length, on December 28th, I left London and went on board the *Whitaker*, after having preached in a good part of the London churches, collected about £1,000 for the charity schools,[1] and £300 for the poor, among my friends!"

Thus closes the preliminary chapter of the great revival. God's chosen mouthpiece had been shaped, revealed and permitted to speak, and now, with an infinite wisdom, was withdrawn for a time that the all too youthful spirit might mellow to the great task yet to be achieved.

A boy of twenty-two had shaken London. This, mark you, was Charles Wesley's twenty-seventh year, which he began "in a murmuring and discontented spirit, reading over and over the third of Job." Poor, worthy Charles! And God, that very year, flung fire upon the earth!

[1] Schools for the education of the poor, established by the Religious Societies, and by the Society for Promoting Christian Knowledge. In 1747 there were in London 136 of these schools, with 5,069 scholars.

PART II

THE APOSTLE OF TWO WORLDS

CHAPTER I

ACROSS THE ATLANTIC

" My heart leaped within me . . .
and echoed to the call."—
WHITEFIELD (*on receiving invitation to Georgia*).

To people of the twentieth century it seems a very simple matter that Whitefield should set out for Georgia. During his ministry to two nations, Whitefield was to accomplish that journey to and fro across the ocean no fewer than thirteen times. That was an unusual achievement in an age when nobody dreamed of ocean travel for pleasure, and for a person outside the ranks of the sea-faring community. It was anything but a simple enterprise in the eighteenth century. Few ships engaged in such ventures were above fifty tons, and many were much less. In mid-ocean they could have seemed no better than the proverbial cockle-shell. Moreover, they were so small that prolonged calm was almost as fatal as storm —as Whitefield was to discover—through failure of provisions and fresh water.

Nor was it Nature only that was to be feared by these tiny but gallant craft in their long and tedious voyages, but also "man's inhumanity to man," for during most of Whitefield's career England was at war with either France or Spain, and privateers were constantly on the outlook to capture or destroy British shipping, whilst piracy was by no means uncommon.

Yet with that fine heroism that Whitefield shows consistently through life, the young evangelist cheerfully took such risks over and over again. Whitefield was actually at sea no fewer than seven hundred and thirty-two days of his life. With such unwieldy craft, too, the voyages were incredibly slow, and arrival very uncertain as to date. His longest was in

1744, and took eleven weeks; his quickest only twenty-eight days.[1]

On this first voyage Whitefield embarked on the *Whitaker*, and with him went General James Edward Oglethorpe, the philanthropic member of Parliament, gallant colonist and personal friend of Dr. Johnson, together with a regiment of soldiers whose purpose it was to reinforce English Florida against certain threats that had been directed against it by Spain.

On its way down the Channel the ship was detained for three weeks in Deal harbour, and, taking lodgings in the town, Whitefield speedily fell to preaching. "He preached in the house of his landlady on shore, and the people came in such numbers that the poor woman feared the floor would break through."

On the very day of final sailing, there came into the harbour an American vessel with John Wesley on board. Inquiring as to the *Whitaker*, which lay in the offing, Wesley learned that Whitefield was about to sail for the very colony whose dust he had but just shaken from his feet. With that somewhat extravagant sense of personal responsibility with which all these young men were rather heavily laden, John Wesley inquired of the Lord by the casting of lots as to whether Whitefield should continue on his way or return. The lot fell against Whitefield's going, and Wesley, without troubling about a personal interview (confident, apparently, in the infallibility of this guidance from God) sent Whitefield a brief note advising him to return home, and, without waiting for a reply, continued his own Journey to London. Doubtless the bitterness of Wesley's experience in Georgia explains his attitude, but his advice was entirely lost on Whitefield. The latter might be highly emotional, but he had an abundant share of common sense, and although he was moved by Wesley's advice so far as to turn to Scripture for counsel, he did not waver in his belief in God's call to Georgia, and his determination to proceed at all costs.

"When I received this I was somewhat surprised. Here was a good man telling me he had cast a lot and that God would have me

[1] E. Ninde, *Whitefield—Prophet and Preacher.*

return to London. On the other hand, I knew that my call was to Georgia, and that I had taken leave of London, and could not justly go from the soldiers who were committed to my charge."

Such is Whitefield's sensible comment.

All men, however great, make mistakes at times, but if Whitefield had obeyed Wesley at this juncture it would doubtless have been a grave disaster for the world at large. Not only would Whitefield have forfeited the confidence of many of his late hearers in London and elsewhere, but he might never have established that contact with America which was to be of such life-giving value to the cause of religion in that land. There is little doubt that Wesley's superstition in appealing to sortilege in this way shook, rather deeply, Whitefield's confidence in his judgment.

The young evangelist's position on board ship was by no means an easy one for a youth of two-and-twenty. The vessel was crowded beyond its capacity, with one hundred passengers over and above the soldiers. To the latter, both officers and men, their boyish-looking chaplain seemed a good joke. If one wants a ready test of Whitefield's sheer ability, his behaviour and his conquest on this first voyage form a convincing instance. Without a tactless word or gesture, without toadying or coaxing, in perfect dignity and poise, he proceeded to discharge his duties *thoroughly*. He tells us that on the first Sunday, "nothing was to be seen but cards, and little heard but cursing and blasphemy. I could do no more for a season than, whilst I was waiting, now and then turn my head by way of reproof, to a lieutenant who swore as though he was born of a swearing constitution." When he told the captain of the military that he would like to have prayers every day for the officers, he was greeted with, "I think we may, when we have nothing else to do!" So Whitefield simply proceeded to hold voluntary services on deck every morning, seizing every opportunity to preach. He also organised groups of such soldiers and passengers as were willing to accept regular instruction. His attention to the sick was utterly selfless in its constancy and devotion, and this was no mean task, with outbreaks of fever on board. One night a terrific storm burst upon the vessel, and the water broke through the hatches.

43

"I arose," says Whitefield, "and called upon God for myself and those that sailed with me. Then, creeping on my hands and knees, I went between decks, and sang Psalms with and comforted the poor, wet people."

Yet in the midst of that confusion Whitefield finished preparing a sermon before he went to bed, in spite of being "a little sick by the late shaking of the ship, and the heat and smell of the people between decks!"

Gradually he won his way with both officers and men, neglecting no opportunity, even of personal evangelism. He walked the decks discussing with the chief mate and the other officers, both of the ship and the military, about religion.

Soon both captains were offering him better facilities for his services, and at last we find him "pedestalled in triumph," with officers all about him, conducting regular drum-head worship.

A fine tribute, both to his preaching ability and his magnificent voice is to be found in the fact that often the two smaller vessels—the *Amy* and the *Lightfoot*, which attended the *Whitaker* —would draw near to their consort and Whitefield would preach to the total company of his shipboard parish from the larger vessel. Was there ever such a chapter in sea-evangelism as this? Three tiny vessels grouped in mid-Atlantic, their crews and passengers listening hungrily and eagerly to a preacher perched in one of them, whose voice soared easily above the wash and roar of the ocean!

It would be fascinating to detail the extraordinary cargo that Whitefield took aboard with him. It was varied enough to excite a smile. £300 had been given him for the poor of his new parish, Savannah, and, with extraordinary forethought and care in one so young, Whitefield laid out some of the money in purchases likely to be of use to his new parishioners. There is room here to mention only the following, which will suffice to indicate market values in England in the year 1737.

"Stockings for men, women, boys and girls at from 10s. to 15s. per dozen pairs. Shoes at from 6s. 6d. to 3s. 6d. per pair, caps for boys at 6d., three dozen hats, £2 2s. 6d, six dozen women's caps, £2 8s. 6d., twenty-six pairs canvas breeches, 28s., thread, cotton, laces, handkerchiefs, and twelve dozens of shirt buttons."

Whitefield's exhaustive biographer, Tyerman, says very shrewdly:

"They (the purchases) suggest one reason why Whitefield was more successful in Georgia than his friend Wesley. The latter had no funds to purchase gifts for the motley colonists; the former had more than £300 for this important purpose. Wesley's ritualism repelled the people; Whitefield's donations attracted them."

A further instance of Whitefield's amazing adaptability to occasions is found in his work at Gibraltar, at which the *Whitaker* and her attendant ships called. Whitefield was asked by the Governor to preach every Prayer Day whilst in Gibraltar, and, as usual, captured all hearts. He also discovered that a society of devout soldiers had been formed, calling themselves the New Lights, and to these he gave every encouragement, overjoyed to find something of the Methodist idea working spontaneously in hearts so far removed from Oxford. His audience shot up rapidly from three hundred to a thousand and more, whilst unheard-of enthusiasm fell upon his hearers.

Writing of this experience, Whitefield says truly:

"God, I find, has a people everywhere; Christ has a flock, though but a little one, in all places. God be praised that we are of this flock, and that it will be our Father's good pleasure to give us the Kingdom."

During these preachings to the soldiery, both ashore and on board, Whitefield made special attacks, with great effect, upon the swearing and profane speech that was so rife among them, and also upon the drunkenness to which they were prone. One day on board ship after such a sermon, Captain Mackay asked the soldiers to stay behind, and he then humbly confessed that he had been a notorious swearer, but that "he had now left off and he exhorted them, for Christ's sake, to go and do likewise."

At last the little vessels reached Savannah, arriving on May 7th. Whitefield, at the end of the voyage, suffered a sharp attack of fever, but such was his indomitable will that, although very ill, he insisted upon preaching a farewell sermon, in the course of which he spoke very directly, with deep affection and with heart-melting power, to each section of his ship-board congregation—straight words of warning and appeal to the men, of stern rebuke and good, common-sense counsel to the women, and warm appreciation to the officers—altogether a masterly utterance in the homiletic tone of the time. Needless to say, they parted from him with real and deep sorrow.

The colony of Georgia was the latest of England's planting on the Atlantic sea-board of America, its charter dating from 1732. It was undertaken as a measure of precaution against Spanish Florida and against possible inroads of the Indians. Unhappily, its first settlers were of a very mixed description, being composed of released debtors from English prisons, a company of Saltzburghers, who were very poor though high-principled Protestant exiles, from Germany, a number of Scotch Highlanders who founded New Inverness, and two sets of very godly but rather narrow-minded Moravians.[1] Whitefield had been appointed really to Frederica, but as yet there was no church there, so he commenced operations in Savannah, the port and chief town of Georgia.

Although so ill and weak from the fever, the evangelist began his public labours at five o'clock on his first morning in Savannah, his first congregation in America numbering only seventeen adults and twenty-five children. The rest of the day he spent in interviews with leading people of the colony, including Wesley's bitter enemy, Thomas Causton. The magistrates promised him a house and church at Frederica, encouraging him meanwhile to work at Savannah. Whitefield writes:

"I find there are many divisions amongst the inhabitants, but God, I hope, will make me an instrument of composing them."

William Stevens, secretary to the Trustees of Georgia, and a resident at Savannah, has left on record in his first volume of *A Journal of the Proceedings in Georgia*, the following interesting references to Whitefield:

[1] This sect features strongly in the story of the Evangelical Revival. Founded in 1467 by Peter Chilczicky, a contemporary of Huss, they held that all Christians should lay aside distinctiveness of rank, abstain from military service and the use of oaths, and live in literal accordance with the teaching of Jesus. Count Zinzendorf became their bishop in 1737, and was their chief advocate till his death in 1760, and profoundly influenced the movement.

"1738, May 21.—Mr. Whitefield officiated this day at the church, and made a sermon very engaging to the most thronged congregation I had ever seen there."

"May 28.—Mr. Whitefield manifests great ability in the Ministry, and his sermons to-day were very rousing."

"June 4.—Mr. Whitefield's auditors increase daily, and the place of worship is far too small to contain people who seek his doctrine."

"July 2.—Mr. Whitefield gains more and more on the affections of the people by his labour and assiduity in the performance of the Divine offices, to which an open and easy deportment, without show of austerity or singularity of behaviour in conversation, contribute not a little, and open the way for him to inculcate good precepts, with greater success, among his willing hearers."[1]

It had never been Whitefield's intention to stay long upon his first visit to Georgia, because of his desire to add priest's orders to his diaconal standing in the Church of England. Other reasons, however, combined with this to urge him presently to return to the home-country. He arrived in May, and left again in August of the same year. But not before he had surveyed the position in every quarter of the colony, visiting the Saltzburghers and Highlanders and Indians, and moving very freely among the poorer folk in every place. It was the very close knowledge he obtained of the condition of the colonists that produced further urgent reasons for return. There were certain things in the government of the colony he wished to get altered, and especially did he realise the urgent need of an Orphan House to take in the unhappy children who were left without parents, for whom nothing was done, and whose number was increasing. Both intoxicating spirits and slavery were prohibited in Georgia. "Slavery," General Oglethorpe had said, "is against the Gospel as well as against the fundamental law of England. Besides, the colony is an asylum for the distressed, and it is necessary, therefore, not to permit slaves in such a country, for the slaves starve out the poor labourer."

But several of the best citizens in Savannah thought otherwise, and in 1736 they petitioned the Trustees "for the use of negroes."[2]

It is curious to find Whitefield in favour of this petition, and his judgment in this matter is a serious blemish upon his

[1] Tyerman. Vol. I. p. 131.   [2] Bancroft, *History of the United States.*

record, though it is one shared, unhappily, with many of the greatest and best of his time.

Whitefield's own presentation of the matter is at least vivid and practical. He writes:

"The people were denied the use both of rum and slaves. The lands were allotted them according to a particular plan, whether good or bad, and the female heirs were prohibited from inheriting. So that in reality to place people there on such a footing was little better than to tie their legs and bid them walk. The scheme was well-meant at home, but was absolutely impracticable in so hot a country abroad. However, that rendered what I had brought over from my friends more acceptable to the poor inhabitants, and gave me an ocular demonstration of the great necessity of an Orphan House, which I now determined to set about in earnest. The Saltzburghers, at Ebenezer, had one, and having heard and read of what Professor Francke had done in that way in Germany, I confidently hoped that something of a like nature might succeed in Georgia. Many poor orphans were there already, and the number was likely soon to be increased. . . . I was really happy in my little foreign cure, and could have cheerfully remained among them had I not been obliged to return to England to receive priest's orders, and to make a beginning towards laying a foundation to the Orphan Home."

Thus practically and earnestly did Whitefield address himself to the task of promoting the well-being of his parish. We may differ from his judgment on "rum and slaves," though he was not the first superlatively great man to possess a blind spot in his vision. We cannot deny the sincerity of his motives, or his profound and self-sacrificing humanity within the limits of current social custom. Whitefield always generously espoused the right of the slaves to perfectly humane and kindly treatment, and more than once incurred the wrath and hatred of slave-owners by his denunciation of cruelty and wrong done to their charges.

How completely Whitefield had won the hearts of his constituency is seen from the following note, dated August 28th, 1738:

"This being the day of my departure, it was mostly spent in taking leave of my flock, who expressed their affection now more than ever. They came to me from the morning to the time I left them with tears in their eyes, wishing me a prosperous voyage and safe return.

They also brought me wine, ale, cake, coffee, tea and other things proper for my passage, and their love seemed to be without dissimulation. My heart was full, and I took the first opportunity of venting it in prayers and tears. I think I never parted from a place with more regret. I have great hope some good will come out of Savannah, because the longer I continued there the larger the congregations grew. I scarce knew a night, though we had divine service twice a day, when the Church House has not been nearly full."

Whitefield had been as signally successful as the Wesleys had been failures, and the secret lies without doubt in that profound experience of grace and new birth that Whitefield had undergone, and that dwelt as a fountain of fire within him, kindling other hearts. Had the Wesleys obtained their great spiritual baptism before visiting Georgia, probably their story would have been different; yet, in the Providence of God, it may have required the irritation of that failure to level down the spiritual pride which was one of the supreme dangers of the Methodist attitude and discipline, at least in its early years, and with which they were all to a degree afflicted. No more lifelike and humorous picture has been given of the Wesleys in Georgia than the delightful and valuable novel Miss Marie Conway Oemler has written under the title of *The Holy Lover*.[1] It gives in vivid story the facts of John Wesley's love for beautiful Sophia Hopkey, the unhappy ward of Thomas Causton. It shows the hopelessly stiff and pedantic type of lover that Wesley made, and the tangle of events which at last conspired so to alienate Wesley from his parishioners that it was wise for him to retire from the scene and return to England.[2]

The fundamental fact is that Wesley's soul was in chains to the tyranny of Methodist asceticism and good works, until his great enlightenment in 1738. It takes a free soul to be a great lover.

---

[1] *The Holy Lover*, by Marie Conway Oemler. (Heinemann.)
[2] John was so slow in his wooing, so beset with scruples as to whether he should, or should not, that at last Sophia lost her patience and encouraged another lover, Mr. Williamson, and eventually married him. Wesley could not keep himself from interfering as their spiritual superior, and refused to admit Sophia to the Sacrament, whereupon Mr. Williamson sued him for defamation of character. The issue never came to the courts, but it finished Wesley in Georgia.

Whitefield's return voyage illustrates tragically the peril of such adventures in his day. The vessel, driven out of its course by storms, ran short of provisions. On November 4th Whitefield recorded as follows:

"Our allowance of water now is but a pint a day, so that we dare not eat much salt beef. Our sails are exceeding thin; some more of them split last night, and no one knows where we are, but God does and that is sufficient."

A week later:

"Still we are floating about, not knowing where we are, but our people seem yet to have hopes of seeing Ireland. The weather now begins to be cold, so that I can say with the Apostle, 'I am in hungerings and thirstings, cold and fastings often.' My outward man sensibly decayeth, but the spiritual man, I trust, is renewed day by day. Our ship is much out of repair, and our food by no means enough to support nature—an ounce or two of salt beef, a pint of water, and a cake made of flour and skimmings of the pot; but I think of Him Who preserved Moses in the ark of bulrushes, and so long as I look upwards my faith will not fail."

The next day, with only half a pint of water left, land was sighted. It proved to be Ireland: provisions were speedily brought aboard, and an Irish "country gentleman," Mr. McMahon, took charge of Whitefield and sped him on his way. Whitefield's final comment on the voyage is typical of his point of view:

"The voyage has been greatly to my good, for I have had a glorious opportunity of searching the Scriptures, composing discourses, writing letters, and communing with my own heart. We have been on board just nine weeks and three days—a long and perilous but profitable voyage to my soul: for I hope it has taught me in some measure to endure hardships as becometh a Minister of Christ. My clothes have not been off (except to change me) all the passage. Part of the time I lay on open deck, part on a chest, and the remainder of the time on a bedstead covered with my buffalo's skin. These things, though little in themselves, are great in their consequences, and whosoever despiseth the small acts of bodily discipline, it is to be feared, will insensibly lose his spiritual life little by little. As for the success of my ministry on board, I shall only say much sin has been prevented, and one,[1] I hope, effectually converted who is to be my fellow-traveller to England."

[1] This was Captain Gladman.

En route across Ireland Whitefield's progress was punctuated by preachings—his fame having gone before him. The Cathedral pulpit at Limerick was offered to him, and he preached "to a very numerous audience who seemed universally affected." The good Bishop, Dr. Burscough, was so affected that he kissed the young preacher on his departure. In Dublin he preached in the churches of St. Wedburgh and St. Andrew, and met the celebrated Dr. Delany, also Dr. Rundle, Bishop of Londonderry, and Dr. Boulter, Archbishop of Armagh, that extraordinary benefactor of the Protestant Church in Ireland.[1]

So Whitefield came back to England on November 30th, 1738, having established himself firmly as an apostle of note in two continents, and with a future before him of bewildering and dazzling promise.

Before proceeding to London, which he was eager to reach, Whitefield called at Nantwich, and then went to Manchester, to renew acquaintance with John Clayton of the Holy Club. Here he preached to thronged and attentive crowds in his friend's church, and enjoyed "judicious Christian conversation." By December the 8th, however, he was "received with much joy" in London, and a few days later greeted John Wesley, who, hearing of his return, hastened from Oxford to London to meet him.

"On December 12th, God gave us once more to take sweet counsel together."

Whitefield, however, found London very changed in its attitude towards him. The Wesleys had been busy in his absence in close association with the Moravian Society. Charles had found the light of free salvation, and had revelled in preaching it wherever he could, including even Westminster Abbey, and had become a sort of curate to the Rev. George Stonehouse, Vicar of Islington. John had preached his memorable sermon on "Salvation by faith" in St. Mary's, Oxford,

[1] A former chaplain of George I, who expended £30,000 (an enormous sum then) in helping small livings, erecting hospitals, supporting sons of poor clergy at Universities, establishing Protestant schools, and providing food in times of scarcity. He died four years after this meeting with Whitefield. (Tyerman, Vol. I. p. 147.)

had drawn up a set of rules for the Moravian Societies in London, and had published his first "Collection of Psalms and Hymns." This activity, whilst contributing to the cause of Revival, had made them marked men, and subject to much criticism on the part of the clergy. The result was that although Whitefield was favourably received by the Archbishop of Canterbury, he found the churches steadily closing against him as a friend and associate of Methodists. He made, however, good use of such pulpits as would accept him, as in the case of St. Helen's, where one of the Holy Club members, Mr. Broughton, was vicar.

"I heard," Charles Wesley writes, "George Whitefield preach to a vast throng at St. Helen's."

Islington, Christ Church, Spitalfields and Wapping Chapel were the only other churches where he could secure a hearing. Without doubt, a further reason that operated against him, besides his friendship for the Wesleys, was the publication by friends without his knowledge of his two *Journals of a Voyage from London to Gibraltar, and from Gibraltar to Savannah*, with their naïve egotism and unusual "enthusiasm," features which appealed to the clergy as sheer bombast in one so young. A pamphlet of thirty-two pages appeared in condemnation of the *Journals*. There was also reasoned theological opposition to the great doctrines propounded as the essence of the Gospel by Whitefield and Wesley, and sermons were being preached by learned divines deliberately assailing the teaching of "free grace" and "new birth."

This opposition, however, proved to be a profound blessing, as we shall see, for it precipitated that new way of preaching which brought the "breath of God" back to the common people in the common ways of life. The Revival began to take definite form, and gain real momentum. Before, however, plunging into the story of its rise and progress, let us first look at the condition of the nation and the Churches in those memorable days.

CHAPTER II

THE AERATION OF RELIGION

"I should think it was no scandal to hear it affirmed that none but the poor attended my ministry. Their souls are as precious to our Lord Jesus Christ as the souls of the greatest men. . . . The poor are dear to my soul."
—GEORGE WHITEFIELD.

IF we are inclined on occasion to be depressed with the state of the Christian Churches in our own time, it may be of some encouragement to us to reflect that they are not nearly so sunken in depths of apathy and shame as was the Church of the eighteenth century.

That century was in many features both the worst and the best in our history. The industrial revolution brought upon the masses of the people a nightmare of ferocious cruelty and wrong. Great numbers of the population were swept off the countryside to be herded round factory, mill and mine, in working and housing conditions that were as crudely as they were rapidly devised. Not only did men and women find themselves in bondage to masters as relentless and ruthless as their new machinery, but little children, even of the tenderest years, were caught also in the toils of the new money-making, death-dealing Moloch—the factory system.

Meanwhile, in the higher strata of society the pendulum of conduct having swung heavily away from the Puritanism of Commonwealth days to the wide-open license of the Restoration period, was now settling with a grim and cynical determination at a steady but blasé indulgence. As a penetrating modern writer has said:

"The reaction from Puritan rigour to Restoration license is the most familiar of platitudes. The reaction to a mundane materialism was more gradual, more general and ultimately of greater significance.

53

The profligacy of the courtier had its decorous counterpart in the economic orgies of the tradesman and the merchant."[1]

It was no shame for statesmen and society leaders to be publicly drunk. When Robert Walpole and his father sat together for a carouse, it was the father's custom to pour out a double draught for his son saying, "Come, Robert, you shall drink twice to my once, for I will not permit the son in his sober senses to be witness of his father's intoxication." The courtly Lord Chesterfield thought it proper to instruct his son in the "art of seduction as part of a polite education." Swift tells us that "gambling was the bane of English nobility." Among the poor, drinking knew no limit. Every sixth house in London was a saloon for the sale of liquor. Hogarth's famously infamous cartoons and engravings reflect the period without much exaggeration, and in the corner of one of them, "Gin Alley," is to be found the announcement said to be common at the time:

> " Drunk for one penny
> Dead drunk for twopence
> Clean straw for nothing."

That same good Dr. Benson, Bishop of Gloucester, who ordained Whitefield, burst out once in protest in a letter to Bishop Berkeley: "Our people are now become what they never were before, cruel. Those accursed, spirituous liquors which, to the shame of the Government, are so easily to be had, and in such quantities drunk, have changed the very nature of our people." Any visitor to the British Museum to-day may take from the library shelf a huge portfolio of broadsheets and handbills such as were commonly distributed in those not-so-distant days, but so foul and obscene that anyone repeating them to-day would be arrested.

In spite of revolting savagery on the part of the law, crime was rampant among all classes.[2] The death penalty applied to no less than one hundred and sixty offences. Consequently crime was attended by every incentive to violence and murder

---

[1] R. H. Tawney, *Religion and the Rise of Capitalism.*

[2] *Cf. The Town Labourer*, by J. L. and B. Hammond, chapter ' Justice.' As late as 1800 a child of ten was sentenced to death for secreting notes at the Chelmsford Post Office. (Sentence afterwards commuted to transportation.) In 1814 a boy of fourteen was hung at Newport for stealing!

on the grounds that one might as well "be hung for a sheep as a lamb," and that to finish off your victim reduced the risk of conviction. Horace Walpole waxes gently satirical about the state of siege in which society lived. "Is it not delightful," he inquires, "not to dare to stir out of one's own castle but armed for battle?" Residents in London rarely travelled after dusk even to the nearest suburbs, excepting in armed companies and groups. Says one authority, "At no time in our history were morals and religion more deeply submerged."

And in such an England where was the Church and Christianity? Bishop Butler, writing his famous *Analogy* in this period, placed it on record that "it had come to be taken for granted that Christianity is not so much a subject for inquiry, but that it is now discovered to be fictitious." On his return to France in 1731 Montesquieu reported that the English people had no religion, and that not more than four or five members of the House of Commons attended Church. As for the clergy, "a converted minister," we are told, "was as rare as a comet." They spent their time to an alarming and outrageous degree in every form of pleasure—foxhunting, gambling, playhouse-gadding and drinking. The Bishop of Chester one day reproved one of his incumbents for drunkenness. "But, my lord," protested the surprised cleric, "I was never drunk on duty!" "On duty!" thundered the bishop, "pray, sir, when is a clergyman not on duty?" "True, my lord," stammered the culprit, "I—er—never thought of that!"

Even the Palace of the Archbishop of Canterbury (Archbishop Cornwallis) was so notorious a scene of routs and feastings that Lady Huntingdon, Whitefield's generous patron, felt it her duty to make a private protest to the Archbishop and his Lady.[1] Finding that unavailing, she appealed, with much courage, to the King and Queen themselves. The following highly interesting letter from King George II to the Archbishop was the result:

"My good Lord Prelate,
"I would not delay giving you a notification of the great concern with which my breast was affected at receiving authentic information

---

[1] *The Countess of Huntingdon and her Circle*, S. Tytler.

that routs had made their way into your Palace. At the same time I must signify to you my sentiments on the subject, which hold these levities and vain dissipations as utterly inexpedient, if not unlawful, to pass in a residence for many centuries devoted to divine studies, religious retirement, and the extensive use of charity and benevolence; I add, in a place where so many of your predecessors have led their lives in such sanctity as has thrown lustre on the pure religion they professed to adorn.

"From the dissatisfaction with which you must perceive I behold these improprieties—not to speak in harder terms—and on still more pious principles, I trust you will suppress them immediately, so that I may not have occasion to show any further marks of my displeasure, or to interfere in a different manner.

"May God take your Grace into His Almighty protection.

"I remain, my Lord Primate,

"Your gracious friend,

"G.R."

Even gay Lord Bolingbroke, without holding exactly a brief for saints, was moved to protest. "Let me seriously tell you," he cried, pointing the finger of scorn at a group of clergymen, "that the greatest miracle in the world is the subsistence of Christianity and its continued preservation as a religion, when the preaching of it is committed to the care of such un-Christian men as you."

No wonder that the foulest wrongs and most hideous cruelties were perpetrated by a supposedly Christian nation to both its own offspring and to the child-races of Africa in such a period—almost naked English women used as draught-cattle in mines, little English boys sent up filthy chimneys at the risk of burning, thousands of innocent lives destroyed in the occupations of civil society as well as in perpetual wars abroad, and the slave trade running incessantly between Africa and the West Indies!

Where was the remedy for such a hell upon earth? The country was not without noble and high-souled men in every class. Many and bright were the stars that shone in the firmament of letters in that century; brilliant sons of the Church there were, too, in plenty, but these were all too preoccupied with their own way of life, and essentially too academic and dainty in their approach to life to provide a remedy. Not in the polished irony of Addison, nor in the eloquence of Burke, or even the statesmanship of Walpole or the Pitts, nor, indeed, in the satirical gibes of Samuel Johnson or Dean Swift was deliverance to be found.[1]   No, not in these was there any hope, but instead were chosen—a pot-boy out of Gloucester! a son out of the manse! What poetic justice! What romance of reform! The liquor interest and the faithless clergy raided by Providence to provide the twin-flames of a heroic selfless-ness that could purge and cleanse and heal the nation with a Divine efficacy!

Of Whitefield, the tapster, a lad plucked from the heart of that trade which was the ruin of the people, God made a Crusader of torrential eloquence, and of John Wesley, a child of ecclesiastical piety and scholarship, God made a Builder of surpassing wisdom. Thus it was that a century which saw the mighty river of Human Liberty in full spate, and saw it, in France, dyed red with the blood of the slain, saw that same river pouring controlledly and with ever-increasing health and volume through the life of England, of the Empire, and of America, sweetened and guided by the Gospel of Christ.

The first task was to rescue religion from the palsied hands of an institution moribund with respectability and complacency, and cursed with academic irrelevance. A mere boy arrogating to himself the oracles of the Church with an apparent vanity intolerably insulting to the complacent clergy of the time! What neater method could be devised to precipitate expulsion? The Church herself should discharge religion from her own fusty interiors, so that it might again become the treasure of the multitude!

This was Whitefield's particular achievement, the successful aeration of the common ways of our English life with the breezes of true and powerful religion. That religion, released from the dim aisles and naves and crypts where it had been so long imprisoned and befouled, poured like a tonic whirlwind across the fields and hills of the countryside, into the hovels and alleys, the slums and the streets, the factories and mines of the new industrial cities and of the growing metropolis— a rushing, mighty Wind of the Spirit, destined to blow those cities at long last very clean! Not content with that, it began

---

[1] " Where Chatham moved hundreds, Whitefield drove to a very madness of religious fervour many thousands." (Turberville, *English Men and Manners in the XVIIIth Century*.)

to fill the sails of ship after ship laden with treasure of Heaven, bound for the distant shores of the New World. Hard upon the flying heels of the ocean-crossing Whitefield, and the steadier trotting of the ceaselessly-riding Wesley, there came a mighty wave of missionary adventure, the pouring forth of the Gospel into the lands of India, China, Africa and the Islands of the Pacific. Whitefield's aeration of England with simple Christianity blew at last so fierce a gale of the Spirit back upon the Churches as to lift their revived Gospel to the very ends of the earth!

But underlying this gigantic achievement on the part of these two men, aided by their gentler lieutenant, Charles Wesley, there lies a most fundamental fact which it is impossible for us to ignore. *All three men passed through a definite experience of conversion without which it is inconceivable that they should have been either moved to essay their great adventure, or could have been equipped for its achievement.*

John Wesley entered upon his transforming experience just after his return from Georgia, and in this we may recognise the overruling of Providence indeed, for it brought him, all aflame, into the situation which Whitefield's fiery eloquence had created in London in time to prevent the fire from dying down. Immediately upon his return Wesley paid a visit to Herrnhuth, in Germany, in company with Ingham, where he had close intercourse with the Moravians, whose spiritual condition he deeply envied.

"I resolved to seek it unto the end," he says. "I continued to seek it until May 24th, 1738."

That Wednesday morning he opened his Bible, and there leaped up at him the text, "Thou art not far from the Kingdom of God." He felt strangely reassured.

"In the evening," he writes, "I went very unwillingly to a society in Aldersgate Street, where one was reading Luther's preface to the Epistle to the Romans. About a quarter before nine, while he was describing the change which God works in the heart through faith in Christ, I felt my heart strangely warmed. I felt I did trust in Christ, Christ alone, for salvation; and an assurance was given me that He had taken away my sins, even mine, and saved me from the law of sin and death."

That is the classic record, and it is a new John Wesley the world knows after that memorable evening. Mr. Arnold Lunn, in his recent volume, *John Wesley*, attempts, somewhat unfortunately in the present writer's judgment, to minimise the significance of this occasion. He quotes with evident approval Dr. Piette's fatuous remark, "Had he not recorded the incident in his *Journal*, it is probable that Wesley would have entirely forgotten it." Authors may have blundered, as Dr. Piette contends, in painting Wesley as a great sinner before this conversion, but that error on their part does not minimise the rubicon-character of the change that transpired.

Wesley had discovered—as Whitefield and Charles before him—the freedom, the liberating glory, of salvation *by grace through faith*. One has only to study Wesley in Georgia to see that his soul is fretting in bondage, longing to be free, but knowing not the way to "the liberty of the sons of God." The Methodism of the Holy Club, the Methodism of the Wesleys in Georgia, was not its true self. It was only Method-ism, a new and more virile and stringent religious legality. It only became Methodism, a return to the saving spiritual profundity of the Gospel, when law was swallowed up in grace, and fear was transformed into faith. Methodism in this sense really dates from Whitefield's sick-bed in 1735, and from Wesley's illumination in the Aldersgate meeting on May 24th, 1738.[1] Let Wesley's own words corroborate the truth of this verdict and the absolute cruciality of his conversion. Replying to his brother, Samuel, in a letter in this very year, 1738, in reply to the question what he meant by being a Christian, Wesley wrote:

"By being a Christian I mean one who so believes in Christ as that sin hath no more dominion over him, and in this obvious sense of the word I was not a Christian till the 24th of May last past. Till then sin had dominion over me, although I fought with it continually, but from that time to this it hath not. Such is the free grace of God in Christ."

[1] Is it quite fair to overlook the former of these two springs of Methodism? Lecky, for example, writes: " It is, however, scarcely an exaggeration to say that the scene which took place at the humble meeting in Aldersgate Street forms an epoch in English history. The conviction which then flashed upon one of the most powerful and most active intellects in England is the true source of English Methodism." (*History of England in the Eighteenth Century*. Vol. III. p. 48.)

Compare this calm, definite statement with his heart-broken cries before his experience, such as, "I had even then the faith of a servant, though not that of a son," or, "I went to America to convert the Indians, but oh! who shall convert me?"

We need to see this issue very clearly, because it was this very Gospel of Grace presented by the Wesleys as "justification by faith," and by Whitefield mainly as the power of "the new birth," that met the peculiarly desperate and outcast state of the common people with such an exquisite precision that opposition and unbelief melted away before it. Moreover, it is to be doubted whether any other Gospel than this can ever really serve the desperate pass into which sin and sorrow combined bring the souls of ordinary men and women in every generation—our own not excepted.

So Wesley and his brother kept the sacred fire burning until once again the "Awakener" was on the scene. It is from the reunion of the holy three at this time that the Revival may be said to have started seriously and consciously.

For some while these three friends enjoyed a feast of profound devotion, mainly in the Moravian Society that met in Fetter Lane. Here, with others like-minded, they "mused until the fire burned," and burn it did! Here was held what was probably the first watch-night meeting.

"About three in the morning," says Wesley, "as we were continuing instant in prayer the power of God came mightily upon us, inasmuch that many cried out for exceeding joy, and many fell to the ground. As soon as we were recovered a little from that awe and amazement at the presence of His Majesty, we broke out with one voice, 'We praise Thee, O God! We acknowledge Thee to be the Lord!'"

Five nights later, "eight ministers of Jesus Christ, despised Methodists, whom God in His providence had brought together," met at Islington to consider the situation, and, after much prayer and discussion, parted in the small hours of the morning with "the conviction that God was about to do great things." Still another night in that week was given by Whitefield to all-night devotion at the Fetter Lane Society. "There was a great deal of Divine influence among us." So was the Revival born in Pentecostal atmosphere!

With this holy fire in his bosom, and having received formal appointment by the Trustees of Georgia to the incumbency of Savannah, Whitefield went to Oxford to receive at the same hands of good Bishop Benson, of Gloucester, who had ordained him as a deacon, his orders as a priest. This was on January 14th, 1739. Writing on the matter to Lord Huntingdon, the bishop says:

"I hope that will give some satisfaction to my lady, and that she will not have occasion to find fault with your lordship's old tutor. Though mistaken on some points, I think him (Mr. Whitefield) a very pious, well-meaning young man, with good abilities and great zeal. I find His Grace of Canterbury thinks highly of him. I pray God grant him great success in all his undertakings for the good of mankind and a revival of true religion and holiness among us in these degenerate days; in which prayer I am sure your lordship and my kind, good Lady Huntingdon will most heartily join."

There came a time later on when Bishop Benson, sorely tried by the enthusiastic evangelist, told the Countess that he "bitterly lamented" having ordained him. The noble lady's reply reveals the soundness of her judgment, as well as the warmth of her heart. "Mark my words," she said, "when you come upon your dying bed, that will be one of the few ordinations you will reflect upon with complacence." The prophecy was a sound one. From his death-bed the good old man sent Whitefield a kindly message and a gift of ten guineas.

The name of Selina, Countess of Huntingdon, was to become famous in the annals of British religion, largely through her interest in George Whitefield. At this point in the story it is enough to remark that through her patronage others of the high aristocracy also became interested in Whitefield's ministry. The Duchess of Marlborough, of great influence in the Cabinet, in a letter to the Countess concerning Whitefield, let fall the very accurate sentiment:

"My dear Lady Huntingdon is always so very good to me that I must accept your very obliging invitation to accompany you to hear Mr. Whitefield. God knows we all need mending, and none more than myself . . . for good, alas, I do want, but where among the corrupt sons and daughters of Adam am I to find it?"

The quasi-royal Duchess of Buckingham, natural daughter of King James the Second, went to hear the Methodist preachers, but expressed herself in any but complimentary terms. She wrote:

"I thank your ladyship for the information concerning the Methodist preachers. Their doctrines are most repulsive and strongly tinctured with impertinence and disrespect towards their superiors, in perpetually endeavouring to level all ranks and do away with all distinctions. It is monstrous to be told that you have a heart as sinful as the common wretches that crawl on the earth, and I cannot but wonder that your ladyship should relish any sentiments so much at variance with high rank and good breeding. However, I shall be most happy to accept your kind offer to accompany me to hear your favourite preacher, and shall await your arrival. The Duchess of Queensbury . . . will be an addition to our party."

This latter was the celebrated Duchess of Queensbury, whose beauty and talent were extolled by Prior, Pope, Swift and others of the time. She was a constant attendant for some while upon the ministeries of George Whitefield and Charles Wesley.

Another of Whitefield's highly-placed admirers was Lady Anne Frankland, who in turn interested the Princesses Anne, Amelia and Caroline.

Thus Whitefield's teaching found its way into the palaces and mansions of high society, as well as into the hovels and cottages of the poorest in the land.

It was at this time that Whitefield made his first acquaintance with Isaac Watts. The stern old Dissenting hymn-writer was to prove eventually, with Philip Doddridge, a good friend to Whitefield when nearly all Dissenting leaders were against him. Whitefield was too "enthusiastic" for the staid old Puritan philosopher, but the latter was constrained at last to utter the following verdict:

"My opinion is that Whitefield does more good with his wild notes than we do with our set music."

people hung upon those lips that were touched with Divine fire. The famous entry in his *Journal* runs thus:

"Having no righteousness of their own to renounce, they were glad to hear of a Jesus who was a friend to publicans, and came not to call the righteous but sinners to repentance. The first discovery of their being affected was to see the white gutters made by their tears which plentifully fell down their black cheeks as they came out of the coal-pits. Hundreds and hundreds of them were soon brought under deep convictions which (as the event proved) happily ended in a sound and thorough conversion. . . . The open firmament above me, the prospect of the adjacent fields, with the sight of thousands and thousands, some in coaches, some on horseback, and some in the trees, and at times all affected and drenched in tears together, to which sometimes was added the solemnity of the approaching evening, was almost too much for, and quite overcame, me."

From Bristol Whitefield slipped over the border into Wales, upon which country he was destined to have a profound influence. The Welsh valleys and hills had already been sown with the good seed of Methodism by two devoted and able men, Griffith Jones and Howell Harris. The former, rector of Llanddowror in Carmarthenshire, was the most noted preacher of his day in Wales, a man of great force of character. He, too, had been driven to preach in the open air by the closing of the pulpits against him. Howell Harris was a man of much simpler character, but, within his limits, a great spiritual genius. Wherever he preached the crowd gathered and departed, mightily moved to reformation of character and life. Yet he was refused Orders in the Church of England in Wales!

Whitefield's fame had long since endeared him to the hearts of these men. Indeed, Whitefield, hearing of Harris's good work, had written him a glowing letter of congratulation and encouragement.

On this first flying visit, Whitefield preached in the Cardiff Town Hall, and addressed several religious societies before he returned to Bristol, having cemented a fast friendship with Howell Harris.

Hostile indeed was Whitefield's reception in Bristol this time. He was even refused a privilege he deeply prized, that of preaching to the prisoners in the Newgate prison, where the keeper, Mr. Dagge,[1] was a convert of his. But he resumed the Kingswood open-air meetings, and other opportunities were forthcoming. Thus, one gentleman offered him the use of a bowling green, and on this unusual site for a religious service no fewer than five thousand people gathered. This was his first open-air preaching quite early in the morning.

He also preached, in the yards of the glass factories, to thousands of the roughest and most abandoned of the city's population.

Feeling, however, that he must return to London, Whitefield begged Wesley to come to Bristol and carry on the great movement he had begun. Wesley resorted to his lot-finding again to discover whether he should go, but with an amusing result. The first Scripture he obtained in this way was:

"Get thee up into this mountain, and die in the mount whither thou goest up."

Not liking this, he appealed to the Fetter Lane meeting to take up the inquiry. They tried, and turned up:

"Son of man, behold I take from thee the desire of thine eyes at a stroke; yet thou shalt not mourn nor weep, neither shall thy tears run down."

Not satisfied even yet, the brethren tried once more, only to learn:

"And Ahaz slept with his fathers, and they buried him in the city, even in Jerusalem."[2]

In spite of this, to Wesley's credit be it said, he went to Bristol. We notice, too, the struggles of the donnish little Oxonian to reconcile himself to Whitefield's new practice of open-air preaching.

"I could scarce reconcile myself at first to this strange way of preaching in the fields, of which he set me an example on the Sunday, having been all my life (till very lately) so tenacious of every point relating to decency and order, that I should have thought the saving of souls almost a sin if it had not been done in Church."

[1] Immortalised by Samuel Johnson.
[2] Tyerman, *Life of John Wesley*.

Commenting on this attitude of Wesley's, Gledstone pens a shrewd note regarding him.[1]

"True to his cautious, practical mind, Wesley adopted field preaching only when he had seen its worth, just as he took up the class-meeting idea from others, and only consented to lay preaching because it had been started by men more headlong than himself, and these supported by the wisdom and piety of his mother, who warned him not to hinder a work of God. Others moved, he quietly followed, and if it was found practicable, passed on and took the lead."

Whitefield conducted Wesley round his constituency from meeting to meeting, at the bowling green, in the Kingswood fields [2] and elsewhere, introducing him to the great audiences that gathered, and himself taking leave of them. In the evening, going to say "Good-bye" to one of the societies, he found the way so crowded that he could only get to it by using a ladder and climbing over the tiling of the adjoining house!

Before Whitefield had gone from Bristol three hours, Wesley had proved himself a worthy successor by submitting, as he put it, to "make myself more vile," and preaching in the streets to about three thousand people. So the good work of aerating religion went on, whilst Whitefield sped to the metropolis.

---

[1] Gledstone's *George Whitefield*, p. 85.
[2] On this occasion, having been given a piece of land, Whitefield laid the foundation of the Kingswood School—a school which was the direct outcome of his work for the colliers.

CHAPTER III

WITH THE LONDON CROWDS

"Field-preaching is my plan; in this I am carried as on eagles' wings."—GEORGE WHITEFIELD.

ON April 25th, 1739, Whitefield, accompanied by his staunch friends, William Seward and Howell Harris, arrived again in London. From then until the end of June there befell London the first great storm of Revival. Only one church was willing to open its pulpit to Whitefield on this visit, and that was the Islington Parish Church, whose vicar was, as already noted, the Rev. George Stonehouse, who had experienced conversion under the guidance of Charles Wesley. But alas, the vicar had reckoned without his churchwardens, who objected so strenuously to Whitefield's preaching that the latter, out of consideration for his friend, decided to preach in the church-yard instead, "being assured my Master now called me out here, as well as in Bristol."

". . . they have thrust me out," wrote Whitefield, "And since the self-righteous men of this generation count themselves unworthy, I go out to the highways and hedges and compel harlots, publicans, and sinners to come in that the Master's house may be filled. They who are sinners will follow after me to hear the word of God!"

Two days after, Charles Wesley suffered the same fate of exclusion. But how true it is that God can make even "the wrath of men" to praise Him. By human short-sightedness and bigotry Whitefield was being thrust forth to bigger congregations than any building could ever hold and to a prouder pulpit than any church could boast.[1]

[1] Read's *Weekly Journal* of May 5th, 1739, says that Whitefield's exclusion was decided upon by a committee of ten whose verdict was unanimous.

WHITEFIELD PREACHING AT ISLINGTON

This was the first open-air preaching in London by Whitefield

WITH THE LONDON CROWDS

So Whitefield preached in the churchyard of Islington parish, and if tradition speaks truly he had several illustrious personages in his audience.[1] It was the first step towards approaching the London crowds on their own grounds. The idea gained rapidly upon the mind of Whitefield. "To-morrow I am to repeat the mad trick, and, on Sunday, I go out to Moorfields." But he found he could not stop at that—the flood had caught him. Moorfields had been originally a swamp on the edge of the city, and it had passed through a variety of changes, having been successively London's first brickyard, an exercise ground for the City archers, the site of Bedlam, the madhouse, and afterwards the City Mall, where fashion displayed itself. It was at this time "a park laid out in grass plots, intersected by broad gravel walks and shaded by rows of well-grown elms." To this open space the rabble of London in jealousy of the "quality" used to flock on every opportunity. It was a favourite spot for shows, many of them grossly indecent.

"When he spoke," we are told, "and they heard his strong sweet voice exquisitely undulated to express the deepest, strongest passion, or the soberest introduction, or the most indignant remonstrance, they stood charmed and subdued. Then his message was so solemn and gracious, something in which everyone was interested for time and for eternity; and he delivered it as if it were all real to him, as indeed it was; as if he believed it and loved it and wanted them also to accept it, as indeed he did. No scoffer durst raise a shout, no disturber durst meddle with his neighbour as the thrilling text flew all round, everyone hearing it."[2]

We know what Whitefield said on that memorable occasion. His text was "Watch, therefore, for ye know neither the day nor the hour in which the Son of Man cometh." Here are some moving sentences of appeal from that sermon:

"Oh do not turn a deaf ear to me, do not reject the message on account of the meanness of the messenger! I am a child, a youth

[1] There is a fine picture of this scene, painted by Sintzenich, temporarily in possession of Whitefield's Central Mission, Tottenham Court Road, in the foreground of which are figures apparently representing Samuel Johnson, Lord Chesterfield, the Countess of Huntingdon and other celebrities of the time.

[2] Gledstone, p. 91.

69

of uncircumcised lips, but the Lord has chosen me that the glory might be all His own. Had He sent to invite you by a learned Rabbi you might have been tempted to think the man had done something. But now God has sent a child that cannot speak, that the power may be seen to be not of men but of God . . . and I am persuaded if any of you should be set upon your watch by this preaching, you will have no reason to repent that God sent a child to cry 'Behold the Bridegroom cometh' . . . let that cry . . . be continually sounding in your ears; and begin now to live as though you were assured this was the night in which you were to be summoned to go forth to Him.''

So encouraged was Whitefield by this experience at Moorfields, that he promptly arranged to do the same thing in another of London's famous out-of-door resorts—Kennington Common. This was at that time "two miles from London, and a mile beyond the hamlet of Newington." It had been the scene of hundreds of ghastly hangings and gibbetings, and was a notorious *rendez-vous* of the worst characters of the city. Upon this spot the intrepid herald of a new life took his stand not once but many times. On this first occasion "no less than thirty thousand"[1] people were supposed to be present. "The wind being for me, carried the voice to the extremest part of the audience. All stood attentive and joined in the Psalm and Lord's Prayer most regularly. I scarce ever preached more quietly in any church. All agreed it was never seen in this wise before."[2] Whitefield preached regularly in these two open-air cathedrals of his every Sunday whilst in London. Enterprising business men were quick to seize the opportunity of providing the great crowds with

---

[1] These numbers have been thought to be exaggerated but the records of similar gatherings contained in John Wesley's Journal is sufficient confirmation. Curnock in his edition of *Wesley's Journals*, disputes even Wesley's figures. But the *Gentleman's Magazine*, reporting independently on Whitefield's service at the Three Mounts, Bristol, on February 15th, 1739, numbered the crowd at 20,000. In both cases, of course, there may at times have been miscalculations. A writer, "Thoninonca," in the *Gentleman's Magazine*, August, 1739, who was present at one of Whitefield's sermons at Moorfields, reckoned, by several marks that he erected on the edge of the crowd, that 25,443 persons were present. This was allowing 9 persons to a square yard. The Editor however pointed out that soldiers in close order only stood 4 to the square yard and on that basis the numbers would be only 11,338. Such phenomenal figures, however, if halved are remarkable enough.

[2] *Whitefield's Journal.*

scaffolds, wagons, seats, stands, from which they could see better or hear better and the people gladly paid the dues exacted.

The singing of these vast audiences could be heard two miles off, and Whitefield's voice is said to have had a range of one mile. The quality of London attended as well as the common people, there being at the second Moorfields preaching no less than eighty coaches!

It was not long, of course, before the general population of London, realising the new thing that was happening, began to make opportunities for themselves of hearing the marvellous young orator even if religion was his theme. Thus on Tuesday, May 1st, having addressed another vast throng in Islington Churchyard, he made his way to the house of a Mr. C......l on Dowgate Hill. When he arrived there a crowd of some two or three thousand people filled the vicinity, and would not disperse till he had preached to them from the upstairs window!

"Now I know," writes Whitefield, "that the Lord calls me to the fields, for no house or street is large enough to contain the people who come to hear the Word."

In between these colossal and exhausting preachings at Moorfields, Islington and Kennington, Whitefield was interviewing hundreds of souls, directing them to religious societies and groups for their further development, and expounding Scripture at innumerable smaller gatherings, yet in between he had wisdom sometimes to refuse to preach for a whole day in order to pay attention to the affairs of Georgia and his great project for an Orphan House.

When Whitefield returned from the provinces just before leaving again for Georgia, he seems to have sought out still other open spaces for preaching-ground. Hackney Marsh was one so chosen—the more so because it was a frequent scene of horse-racing. Here on Thursday, July 26th, 1739, Whitefield preached to a concourse of ten thousand people who had gathered for the races. "Very few left the sermon to see the race and some of these soon returned. By the help of God," says Whitefield, "I will go on to attack the devil in his strongest holds. The common people go to these diversions for want of knowing better."

Marylebone Fields were also used for the great work, and on Wednesday, August 1st, of the same year Whitefield might have been found there preaching to a crowd of no less than thirty thousand.

One of the most remarkable features of these great open-air services conducted by Whitefield was his genial audacity in taking collections for his Orphanage scheme. The problem is, how were those collections taken, and how was it that the disreputable elements in these crowds respected these large sums of money? Whitefield tells us that he himself did some of the collecting, but he must also have had very trustworthy stewards, and obviously even then, judging by the amounts, many must have failed to contribute. In any case, it is another tribute to his organising and business capacity, whilst doubtless the awe inspired in the multitude by his preaching kept the offertories sacred from profane and thieving hands. Here are a few specimens of such collections [1] taken from *Whitefield's Journal* :

From twenty thousand at Kennington, £47. (£16 in halfpence, equals 7,680 coins!)

From a crowd at Moorfields, £52 17s. 6d. (£20 in halfpence) "they were more than one man could carry home."

"Preached in evening to near sixty thousand people—after sermon I made *another* collection of £29 17s. 8d. Preached at Moorfields and Kennington Common and at both places collected near £50 for the Orphan House. A visible alteration is made in the behaviour of the people, for though there were near fifteen thousand in the morning, and double the number in the afternoon they were as quiet as though there had not been above fifty persons present."

This record is typical of Whitefield's work with the London crowds repeated over and over and over again in the course of his ministry. It would be hopelessly monotonous to the reader to repeat the detail of such proceedings, but it is necessary to understand that Whitefield was constantly alternating such attacks upon the London multitudes with his extensive provincial tours.

Such events, of course, did not occur without exciting the

[1] The amounts should be trebled to yield modern values.

contempt and ridicule of many. The London *Daily Post* published the following:

"On Mr. Whitefield's preaching in Moorfields, near Bedlam:

> " *Map*, *Ward* and *Taylor*, did our wonder raise
> Now *Whitefield* has the giddy rabble's praise;
> Infatuated crowds to hear him flock,
> As once to *France* for Mississippi stock
> A proof more madmen out of Bedlam dwell
> Than are confined within that spacious cell."

Still more dangerous was the often uncertain temper of the crowd, filled as it was with large numbers of disreputable and very unhappy people. Thus at Moorfields on the first occasion:

"Whitefield went in between two friends who in the pressure of the crowd were soon parted from him, and were obliged to leave him at the mercy of the rabble; but these, instead of hurting him, found a lane for him along which he was carried to the middle of the fields where a table had been placed, which was broken in pieces by the crowd, and afterwards back again to the wall that parted the upper and lower Moorfields, from whence he preached without molestation, although many had previously told him that he would never come out of the place alive."

The clerical attack was led by Dr. Trapp, who in 1733 had been made rector of Harlington, in Sussex, by Lord Bolingbroke, and was also, at this time, joint-lecturer at St. Martin-in-the-Fields. He, like Whitefield, was Gloucestershire born, and an Oxonian. George Whitefield, with that touch of simple and courageous frankness that makes him so lovable, actually sat in the audience of Christ Church, Newgate Street, to hear the first of a series of sermons by Dr. Trapp against himself and the Methodists. The text was appropriate enough to the issue between the opposing parties: "Be not righteous overmuch, for why shouldest thou destroy thyself," from Ecclesiastes. Whitefield writes:

"God gave me great serenity of mind; but alas the preacher was not so calm as I wished him. His sermon was founded upon wrong suppositions, not to say that there were many direct untruths in it. And he argued so strenuously against the *inward feelings* that he plainly proved that with all his learning, he knew nothing as yet he ought to know."

These sermons against Whitefield and his companions were published in a pamphlet of sixty-five pages, called " *The Nature, Folly, Sin and Danger of being Righteous Overmuch*, with a particular view to the Doctrines and Practices of certain Modern Enthusiasts. Being the substance of four discourses lately preached at the Parish Church of Christ Church and St. Lawrence, Jewry, London, and St. Martin-in-the-Fields, Westminster, by Joseph Trapp, D.D."

The following extract shows the temper of the dispute, and the real point of issue between Whitefield and his fellow-clergymen :

"Suppose another, though in holy orders, yet a raw novice very lately initiated into them, shall take upon him, at his first setting out, to execute as it were, the office of an apostle—to be a teacher, not only of all the laity in all parts of the Kingdom, but of the teachers themselves, the learned clergy, many of them learned before he was born—to reflect upon and censure them as if they did not know their duty, or would not do it without being instructed and reproved by him—what is this but an outrage upon common decency and common sense? the height of presumption, confidence, and self-sufficiency, so ridiculous as to create the greatest laughter, were it not so deplorable and detestable as to create the greatest grief and abhorrence; especially if vast multitudes are so sottish and wicked too, as in a tumultuous manner, to run madding after him? Surely it is shocking and prodigious for *so young a son of Levi to take so much upon him.*"

So young, and so successful—there was the rub for the older clergy! One's thoughts go naturally to the lonely figure of Another! That young Rabbi of an earlier time after whom the multitudes flocked, and with whom also the priests were furiously angry! So young! So successful!

As a further instance of the fury aroused in ecclesiastical quarters by the conduct of Whitefield, we may cite the out-pourings of the *Weekly Miscellany*, the principal organ of the Church of England at that time, and edited by Dr. Hooker. In its issue of May 5th, 1739, a whole column was filled with "Queries to Mr. Whitefield" concerning "Principles, Doctrines, Articles of Faith, Motives and Extraordinary Light" in a tone of ridicule. Of Whitefield the following complaint appears in the issue of May 12th, which gave up no less than two pages to denunciation (some indication of the magnitude of the commotion created by Whitefield!)

" Immediately after his ordination to the *priesthood*, without a licence from any bishop; contrary to the rules of the Christian Church, contrary to the canons and constitutions of our own Church, which so lately gave him orders, contrary to the laws of the land—he goes strolling about the Kingdom, showing the greatest contempt for our excellent liturgy,[1] and all forms of prayer, and using extemporary effusions; preaching doctrines different from those which he subscribed before the bishop, with an unparalleled degree of vanity and vainglory; extolling himself and with the most unchristian spirit of censoriousness, undervaluing and blaming the established clergy.

"If Whitefield and the Wesleys are permitted to hold their conventicles at pleasure, and to ramble up and down, singing psalms, and preaching in the open streets, or in the more open fields, wanton curiosity will carry thousands to hear them; hundreds of the ignorant multitude will innocently be corrupted and the preacher's vanity and enthusiasm, if possible, will be still more inflamed by a foul imagination that their hearers are all *admirers*, whereas most of them would as eagerly attend any other monster equally as strange as that of a clergyman preaching in a gown and cassock on a common."

Whitefield's most careful biographer, Tyerman, comments upon this:

"It must be allowed that one of Whitefield's besetting sins, or rather one of his infirmities, was an unconsciously indulged inflatedness of mind which led him to the employment of bombastic expressions and to the utterance of sentiments often silly, sometimes fanatical, and generally such as a more prudent and worldly wise man would not have used."

The fairness of this comment may be admitted, but Whitefield's extreme youth must be taken into account, and also his overwhelming concern for the winning of souls, which made him impatient of petty restrictions and minor ecclesiastical conventions.

A very effective and temperate reply to Dr. Trapp's pamphlet was made voluntarily on behalf of Whitefield by a Rev. Robert

---

[1] This, of course, was quite untrue. Whitefield loved and used the liturgy.

Seagrave, M.A., under the title "An Answer to the Rev. Dr. Trapp's four sermons against Mr. Whitefield showing the Sin and Folly of being Angry overmuch," the last sentence being a good play on the words of Dr. Trapp's first text. Mr. Seagrave was the author of a volume of hymns, and became minister of a company that gathered at the Leather-Cutters' Hall in Basinghall Street. The following extract from his defence is valuable for the further light it throws on this historic quarrel between the Church and the Methodists:

"Little or nothing was objected to the Methodists by the clergy, while they continued in our churches, excepting some disorders and inconvenience arising by their means to our places of worship; but from the time they unexpectedly undertook to preach in fields, and in a manner not altogether favourable to *ecclesiastical maxims* and *church authority* they have commenced impostors, enthusiasts and novelists. They have likewise acquired additional blame for asserting that they discern several valuable and worthy Christians amongst Dissenters of every branch." "To which I reply (1) Does preaching in a field annul that character or *commission* of a minister, in all respects ordained like the rest, which divines themselves call an *indelible* character? A discovery seems to be made, that the exercise of a minister's function subsists no longer than he shall *absolutely* coincide with the majority of his, or shall think as his, diocesan. (2) The Dissenters have morally *kept* the old truths which now begin to be discovered. Why should we confine *all* religion, *all* learning, and *all* knowledge to our own Church? The Methodists think they see *more* religion and real knowledge at present amongst Dissenters than (I am sorry to say it) is commonly seen in our own Church; and they have the impartiality not to deny it. . . . Nothing but obstinacy and envy can deny that a *great* reformation has arisen upon the manners of the age by the *itinerants* preaching. If the Gospel be preached in the Church, it is well and desirable; but when the clergy leave the old truths, and are fallen into the scheme of Deism, though they may not discern it, men have a right to hear the truth *in the field* or in a *meeting-house*, supposing they can find it nowhere else."

Whilst Whitefield was charming the London crowds into the hearing of the Gospel, Wesley, as his successor in field-preaching at Bristol, was equally busy in the same kind of work, and reports arrived that "numbers were falling on the ground as if thunderstruck." It is a curious fact that whilst Whitefield led the way for an all too reluctant Wesley in open-air preaching, yet once Wesley was convinced and gave himself to the task with his customary wholeheartedness, more signs and disturbances, greater emotional upheavals, attended his preaching than that of Whitefield.[1] There is a psychological reason, doubtless, for this difference to be found in the fact that Whitefield's more dramatic and warmer emotional style in preaching expressed a degree of the audience's emotion for them, and so served as a safety valve, whereas Wesley's colder type of utterance, his more statuesque delivery,[2] left his hearers pent up emotionally, and liable, therefore, to sudden convulsive and even physical outbreaks.

But what was that power running through the strikingly different styles of these preachers and smiting the people like lightning from heaven? Undoubtedly there was a curious coincidence between Methodist doctrine and popular moral and spiritual need. The state of the people was so intrinsically miserable and hopeless that they could not do other than fling themselves upon Divine grace when they received such bold and eloquent assurance of its reality and welcome. But when this coincidence has been explored to the full, some tribute still needs to be paid to *the state of exquisite purity* into which these two living vehicles of Divine truth had been brought by much discipline of body and travail of soul, and by virtue of which they were such favoured and effective instruments of the Divine Spirit.

[1] See p. 269.
[2] Stoughton, *History of Religion in England*, Vol. VI.

CHAPTER IV

TO AMERICA AGAIN

" As there is here the same sun so there is here the same God
—in America as in England.   I bless God all places are equal
to me."—GEORGE WHITEFIELD.

AFTER sundry visits in the provinces, including Cirencester,
Tewkesbury, Bristol, Basingstoke, Rodborough, Stroud, and
Hampton Common,[1] during which he preached several times
at Gloucester to a great concourse of people in a field adjoining
the Bell Inn (his brother's property and his own birth-place),
Whitefield found himself due at last to return to his task in
Georgia. Doubtless he little dreamed that the storm of
revival would blow across the Atlantic in his person to engulf
also the cities of the New World.

Accompanying him was a group of men worthy of our
notice. There was John Periam, who had been thrown by
Whitefield's preaching into such emotional stress and strain
that his relatives imprisoned him in a mad-house, from which
Whitefield had only been able to free him with great difficulty.
There was Captain Gladman, whom Whitefield had befriended
on his first visit to Savannah, and converted during that terrible
voyage home together, and who now, in gratitude, attached
himself to Whitefield to serve in whatever way might open
up. The third was William Seward, a gentleman of Evesham,
whose heart had been changed and captured by Methodism,
and who volunteered to accompany Whitefield as a kind of
business friend and counsellor. But for his untimely death
a little later at the hands of a West of England mob, he would
probably have proved, as Gledstone hints, Whitefield's Boswell.

[1] " Hasted to Hampton Common and found no less than 20,000 on horseback and foot to hear me."—*Journal*, 1739. Whitefield's favourite pulpit
here was a long-barrow mound, just above Amberley, still known as " Whitefield's Tump."

His friendship for Whitefield, however, was embarrassing at times in its lack of discretion. He allowed his enthusiasm to run away with his imagination, and even to distort facts.[1] With that touch of spiritual genius which never failed him, Whitefield made the eleven weeks' voyage an occasion of great self-examination, passionate prayer and earnest study of the Scriptures and doctrine. "The Searcher of hearts," he wrote, "alone knows what agonies of soul I have undergone since my retirement from the world."

In those days of still crude navigation, it was not always easy to arrive precisely at the port one wanted, and Whitefield's party was eventually landed at Lewis Town, one hundred and fifty miles from Philadelphia on October 30th, 1739. The ship had run out of provisions, and had it not been for Whitefield's private stock, actual starvation would have faced them all.

Travelling overland, the Awakener came to Philadelphia, where another vital contact in this human epic was awaiting him. Philadelphia was at this time the largest city in America,[2] and it contained that remarkable man, Benjamin Franklin, who became successively, printer, philosopher, scientist and ambassador, and was at this time editor of the *Pennsylvania Gazette* and compiler of "Poor Richard's Almanack." This celebrated man was then thirty-three years of age. Nineteen years before he had entered the city ragged and poverty-stricken, his only possession one Dutch dollar. Now he was a printer, publisher, alderman and magistrate, and a leading publicist, destined to be one of America's most distinguished and attractive sons. Alert for fresh business, Franklin was interested in the new arrival, and arranged to print his sermons and *Journals*. Thus began a warm friendship, that remained through life, and is an abiding tribute to the mental quality of Whitefield. The pulpits of Philadelphia were opened immediately to the famous young preacher from England, but the congregations were speedily too great for any building to

[1] "Thus in Philadelphia Seward took steps forcibly to prevent a dance-hall from being opened, and in a press report written by himself attributed the closing of the hall to Whitefield's preaching." *Cf.* Gledstone, p. 139.

[2] At this period the population of America was very small and sparse, there being only three cities of any size—Boston, 16,000; New York, 23,000; Philadelphia, 32,000. *Cf.* Ninde, p. 128.

hold, and Whitefield was offered the steps of the Court House for an open-air rostrum.

The enthusiasm roused by his direct and searching appeals knew no bounds, and a constant and delighted hearer was the none too easily satisfied, sceptically-minded printer, Franklin. Needless to say, Whitefield took collections for his Orphan House, and when he consulted Franklin about his plans, the latter strongly advised him to build the Orphanage at Philadelphia, and bring the children to that city. When Whitefield rejected his idea, Benjamin Franklin calmly buttoned up his pocket and refused the smallest subscription. "Poor Richard," to quote Franklin's pseudonym, had not reckoned, however, with his new friend's oratory.

"I happened," he says, "soon afterwards to attend one of his sermons, in the course of which I perceived he intended to finish with a collection, and I silently resolved he should get nothing from me. I had in my pocket a handful of copper money, three or four silver dollars, and five in gold. As he proceeded I began to soften and concluded to give the copper. Another stroke of his oratory made me ashamed of that and determined me to give the silver, and he finished so admirably that I emptied my pocket into the collection dish, gold and all."

Franklin goes on to tell of a Quaker friend of his who had taken the precaution to attend the sermon with empty pockets. He, too, however, relented, and turned to a neighbour with the request that he should lend him some money. "The request was made, perhaps, to the only man in the company who had the firmness not to be affected by the preacher. His answer was, 'At any other time, Friend Hopkinson, I would lend thee freely, but not now, for thee seems to be out of thy right senses.'"

It was at this time that Whitefield made the acquaintance of the famous Tennent family. The elder Tennent had founded a school at Neshaminy, not far from the city, for ministerial students. This "Log College," as it was called, is now Princeton University, and "became the parent of every Presbyterian College and theological seminary in America."[1] Tennent's son, Gilbert, minister at Brunswick, a man of

[1] Ninde, p. 139.

BENJAMIN FRANKLIN

[*Face page* 80

terrific though sombre oratory, who imitated the scanty, rough
dress of a John the Baptist, was also an apostle of the new
faith. He threw in his lot enthusiastically with the movement
which Whitefield's preaching had launched, and accompanied
the latter on his visit from Philadelphia to New York. Here
Whitefield was not so generously received. Being denied the
use of the churches, he accordingly took to his favourite pulpit,
the fields, again, and the people thronged to hear his message.

It was not long, however, before the usual champion arose
for him. The Rev. Ebenezer Pemberton, who became minister
of the Presbyterian Church in New York in 1727, offered
Whitefield the use of his meeting-house. Here the Awakener
preached for several days to increasing crowds, and an eye-
witness of these services has left the following records:

"I never saw in my life such attentive audiences as Mr. Whitefield's
in New York. All he said was demonstrative life and power. The
people's eyes and ears hung upon his words. . . . He is a man of
middle stature, of a slender body, of a fair complexion and of a
comely appearance. He is of a sprightly, cheerful temper, and acts
and moves with great agility and life. The endowments of his
mind are uncommon, his wit is quick and piercing, his imagination
lively and florid, and, as far as I can discern, both are under the
direction of a solid judgment. He has a most ready memory, and,
I think, speaks entirely without notes. He has a clear and musical
voice, and a wonderful command of it. He uses much gesture but
with great propriety. Every accent of his voice, every motion of
his body *speaks*; and both are natural and unaffected. If his
delivery be the product of art, it is certainly the perfection of it, for
it is entirely concealed. He has a great mastery of words, but
studies much plainness of speech. He spends not his zeal in trifles.
He breathes the most catholic spirit, and professes that his whole
design is to bring men to Christ, and that, if he can obtain this end,
his converts may go to what church, and worship God in what form,
they like best."

From New York, Whitefield had some correspondence with the
Rev. Benjamin Colman, D.D., of Boston, which is a matter of interest chiefly because of Dr. Colman's testimony, in a letter to Dr.
Watts dated Boston, January 16th, 1740, confirming the greatness
of the work Whitefield was doing at this time. He writes:

"Mr. Whitefield arrived some months ago at Philadelphia where,
and through the Jerseys and New York, he preached daily to incredible multitudes with great eloquence and zeal. America is like to

do him much honour. He proposes to see Boston in his return to Europe, about June next; and our town and country stand ready to receive him as an angel of God. Ministers and people, all but his own church, speak of him with great esteem and love. He seems spirited from on high, in an extraordinary manner assisted and prospered."[1]

From New York, too, Whitefield wrote to his mother, and it is perhaps indicative of the almost inevitable tendency of the most sweetly human evangelist to harden into the professional soul-saver that this letter is couched in terms of public exhortation. Queen Victoria is reputed to have complained that Mr. Gladstone would address her as though she were a public meeting, and it is one of the little failings of the overworked preacher that he is apt to treat his friends, even those nearest and dearest, as though they were public meetings!

"Honoured Mother," wrote Whitefield, "new friends are raised up every day, whithersoever we go. The people of Philadelphia have used me most courteously, and many, I believe, have been pricked to the heart. . . . Oh, my honoured mother, my soul is in distress for you. Flee, flee, I beseech you, to Jesus Christ, by faith. Lay hold on Him, and do not let him go. God has given you convictions. Arise, arise, and never rest till they end in sound conversion. Dare to deny yourself. My honoured mother, I beseech you, by the mercies of God in Christ Jesus, dare to take up your cross and follow Christ."

One suspects that the reiterated "honoured mother" hides a scruple in the heart of the evangelist that his doubts about his mother's spiritual security scarcely do sufficient honour to the faithfulness of her motherhood. But considering the stilted style of address, especially religious address, common in the period, this letter might have been much worse.

Whitefield's return to Philadelphia was a triumphal progress through Elizabeth Town, New Brunswick, Maidenhead, Neshaminy, where his audience numbered three thousand people (over a thousand on horseback), and Abingdon.

All the preaching on this remarkable journey was done in Dissenting meeting-houses or in the lovely glades of the Pennsylvanian forests. Whitefield said in a letter to John Wesley:

[1] *Life and Times of Dr. Isaac Watts*, Milner.

TO AMERICA AGAIN

"Do you ask what I am doing? I answer 'ranging and hunting in the American woods after poor sinners'."

It was highly irregular work for a Church of England clergyman, but Whitefield allowed himself no uneasiness. The freedom with which the Word ran through the people and the fire that attended its course were sufficient warrant for his great heart.

The Presbyterian atmosphere, however, of these associations undoubtedly affected Whitefield's spiritual outlook and theological thinking very deeply. It is from this time that Calvinism begins to have a special value for him, and doubtless all through the controversy with Wesley, which was to follow, Whitefield was subtly bound to the Calvinistic position, not only by his conscious conviction, but also by a subconscious realisation that without it his American work would be rendered utterly impossible.

At Philadelphia the storm of revival broke once again. On Saturday, November 24th, he preached to a vast concourse of all denominations in the English Episcopal Church—on Tuesday, the 27th, at German Town seven miles away he preached to six thousand persons from the balcony of a house. On Wednesday, back again in Philadelphia, the crowds were so great that the attempt to preach in church was abandoned and the fields were sought once more. On the day of his departure, November 29th, the people thronged his door from seven o'clock in the morning, in tears, seeking God. A company of over two hundred horsemen escorted him from the city, and on reaching Chester he was met by some three thousand people, many of whom had come out from Philadelphia, clamouring for him to preach. The justices were in session at the time, but sent word to Whitefield that they would defer their business till his meeting was ended!

On through Maryland, Virginia, Carolina, the never-resting Awakener sped. In spite of the sparsely-populated character of the country, such was Whitefield's fame that most remarkable audiences came together from all directions and over long distances. At Newcastle, on December 1st, he preached to two thousand people in the streets and again, later in the day, to a similar crowd at Christian Bridge. The next day, Sunday, December 2nd, saw ten thousand people waiting upon his words at the same place, several hundreds being on horse-back. Here he preached from a tent, and gave two sermons with a brief interval between them. Next day at North East, in Maryland, his audience was fifteen hundred, and at Joppa, the day after, only forty.

"Friday, December 7th.—Preached in the morning and evening to small, polite auditories. The Governor came to the morning service; I and my friends dined with him."

These journeyings were not without some hardship and adventure, as, for example, when they found the river Potomac, six miles broad, lashed to such fury by a gale that after getting half-way across they were compelled to put back. Not infrequently they went hungry, with no means of replenishing their stores, so distant were the plantations from one another. In a letter to Gilbert Tennent, Whitefield wrote:

"In these parts Satan seems to lead people captive at his will. The distance of the plantations prevents people assembling together. Here are no great towns, as in other provinces, and the community is made up of negroes and convicts; and if they pretend to serve God, their masters, Pharaoh-like, cry out, 'Ye are idle, ye are idle'."

On December 14th he reached the capital of Virginia, Williamsburg, and dined with the governor. He was much interested in "the beautiful college . . . in which is a foundation for about eight scholars, a president, two masters and professors in the several sciences. The present masters came from Oxford. Two of them were my contemporaries there. I rejoiced in seeing such a place in America." Here, too, he did some effective preaching.

Through the various little towns of Virginia and Carolina he made his way, finding audiences of one hundred phenomenal in such districts!

He arrived at Charleston on Saturday, January 5th, 1740. Preaching in one of the Dissenting meeting-houses, he tells us "the auditory was large but very polite."

At length, after a journey of five months, during which he had kindled several of the principal cities of the new world and made many firm friendships, especially among the

Presbyterians, Whitefield reached Savannah on Thursday, January 10th.

It is interesting to find that Whitefield's great project, "the apple of his eye," to erect an Orphan House at Savannah, originated in a suggestion made by that kindly spirit, Charles Wesley. Indeed, the latter, with General Oglethorpe, had actually drawn up a scheme before George Whitefield arrived on the scene. It was Whitefield, however, who found the energy and unflagging zeal to make the House a reality. The trustees of Georgia had granted him five hundred acres of land for the purpose, and by his strenuous preachings he had collected funds to the amount of £1,010, of which £80 10s. od. was from Whitefield's own pocket. With these resources, Whitefield now proceeded to put his scheme into effect. The site chosen was called Bethesda, almost ten miles to the north of Savannah, and out to which Whitefield had to make his own road—a road cut through the pine-groves—a magnificent vista nearly three miles in length![1]

Whilst busy with the Orphan House, Whitefield took up his work as priest, and preached to great audiences. William Stephens, in the *Journal of the Proceedings of Georgia*, 1742, notes the constant theme of these discourses as being "Justification and Regeneration" and he writes:

"I hope for one on good works before long."

It was not long, however, before Whitefield felt that with the Orphan House upon his hands, it was difficult for him to do justice to his priestly office, and he accordingly resigned it, an action which left him free to roam where he would.

Certain letters of Whitefield written at this time are valuable indications of his thought and disposition. Thus, to the Rev. Ralph Erskine, of Dunfermline, he wrote in a vein which aptly reveals the catholicity of his spirit—a catholicity that eventually cost him the Erskines' friendship:

"I see no other way for us to act at present than to go on preaching the truth as it is in Jesus; and then, if our brethren cast us out, God

[1] Tyerman. Vol. II. p. 155.

will direct us. God will direct us to take that course which is most conducive to His glory and His people's good. I think I have but one objection against your proceedings—your insisting only on *Presbyterian government*, exclusive of all other ways of worshipping God. Will not this necessarily lead you (whenever you get the upper hand) to oppose and persecute all that differ from you in their Church government or outward way of worshipping God? Our dear brother and fellow-labourer, Mr. Gilbert Tennent, thinks this will be the consequence, and said he would write to you about it. For my own part, although I profess myself a minister of the Church of England, I am of catholic spirit, and if I see any man who loves the Lord Jesus in sincerity, I am not very solicitous to what outward communion he belongs."

In another letter to Ralph Erskine, Whitefield gives us his conviction about war fought to defend religious principle:

"My only scruple at present is, whether you approve of taking the sword in defence of your religious rights? One of our great English Bishops, I remember, called you Cameronians. They, I think, took up arms, which I think to be contrary to the spirit of Jesus Christ and His apostles."

Another important letter of Whitefield's at this time sprang out of his experiences on that flying journey from Philadelphia to Savannah, and it pays tribute to his tenderness of heart, his honesty and his courage. It was addressed "to the inhabitants of Maryland, Virginia, and North and South Carolina," and contained the following:

"As I lately passed through your provinces I was touched with a fellow feeling of the miseries of the poor negroes. Could I have preached more frequently among you, I should have delivered my thoughts in my public discourses, but as business here required me to stop as little as possible on the road, I have no other way to discharge the concern that lies upon my heart than by sending you this letter. How you will receive it, I know not, but whatever be the event I must inform you, in the meekness and gentleness of Christ, that I think God has a quarrel with you, for your cruelty to the poor negroes. Whether it be lawful for Christians to buy slaves, I shall not take upon me to determine, but sure I am it is sinful, when bought, to use them worse than brutes, and I fear the generality of you who own negroes are liable to such a charge, for your slaves, I believe, work as hard as the horses on which you ride. These, after they have done their work, are fed and taken proper care of, but many negroes, when wearied with labour in your plantations, have been obliged to grind their own corn after their return home. Your dogs are caressed and fondled at your tables, but your slaves, who are frequently styled dogs or beasts, have not an equal privilege. They are scarce permitted to pick up the crumbs that fall from their master's tables. Nay, some, as I have been informed by an eye-witness, have been, upon the most trifling provocation, cut with knives, and have had forks thrown into their flesh, not to mention what numbers have been given up to the usage of cruel taskmasters, who by their unrelenting scourges, have ploughed upon their backs and made long furrows, and at length, brought even death itself."

The letter concludes:

"The Scripture says, 'Thou shalt not muzzle the ox that treadeth out the corn.' Does God take care of oxen? And will He not take care of the negroes? Undoubtedly He will. 'Go to, now, ye rich men, weep and howl for your miseries that shall come upon you.' Behold, the provision of the poor negroes which have reaped down your fields, which is by you denied them crieth, and the cries of them which have reaped are entered into the ears of the Lord of Sabaoth."

This letter was printed and distributed broadcast, and brought upon Whitefield a great deal of spiteful enmity.

It seems a thousand pities that Whitefield did not see his way clear, like Wesley, to take the Abolitionist attitude towards slavery, for if, with his unique power of public persuasion, he had linked this clear duty to the converted state of the soul, he might have antedated the work of Wilberforce and Wool- man, and made a bitter civil war in America unnecessary. In justice to Whitefield, however, we must recognise that his deeply humanitarian attitude was an advance upon the general callous indifference of the churches and clergy of the time. Moreover, morals altogether were sadly confused in the world of the eighteenth century, even by good evangelicals.

Thus, Whitefield is full of indignation at the prodigality of the gay life of his time, in both England and America, yet he had no condemnation for the rapidly developing liquor trade, and was not himself an abstainer.

Ninde, in his *George Whitefield, Prophet-Preacher*, reminds us very aptly that "the Puritans looked askance at the theatre, but they were extremely fond of cock-fighting, and they saw no harm in the lottery. Massachusetts went in whole-heartedly for distilleries, and then passed a law sternly forbidding kissing in the streets between the sexes as a gross indecency! As late as 1759 a Boston sea-captain, returning from a long cruise and meeting his wife on the wharf, saluted her as one would naturally expect. At once he was arrested and sentenced by the outraged magistrate to be publicly whipped!"

As we shall be invited to consider more deeply later, Conversion and the New Birth for the Evangelicalism of the period, whilst genuine experiences, were essentially mystical in character, and the vision of the true ethical state of the changed heart and life was blurred and faulty. The determination, clear and self-evident, of the poles of moral change for a soul that would be saved, had yet to be ascertained and is, indeed, only becoming more generally and finally clear in our own day.

CHAPTER V

"AMERICA'S OLDEST CHARITY"[1]

"I have aimed at nothing in founding Bethesda but His glory and the good of my country."—GEORGE WHITEFIELD.

IT will be convenient at this juncture to tell in brief the whole story of the Bethesda adventure and achievement, bringing it down to the modern, highly efficient and useful institution which still bears the honoured name.

When Whitefield returned to Savannah a visit to the neighbouring villages speedily impressed him anew with the urgency of the children's needs. Their condition, as he put it, gave him "an ocular demonstration of the great necessity and promising vitality of a future orphan house." There was a touch of statesmanship in his outlook. "It will be a great encouragement to people to go to the colony when they are assured their children will be provided for after their decease, and it will be an unspeakable comfort to the parents already there who fear nothing so much as having their children left destitute when they are dead."

It was on Tuesday, March 25th, 1740, that "with full assurance of faith," Whitefield laid the first brick of the new House, naming it "Bethesda," in the hope that it would indeed be a House of Mercy.

"The workmen attended, and with me, kneeled down and prayed."[2]

By the time the building was well started, forty children: English, Scotch, Dutch, French and American, had been placed under his care and these, with the workmen made nearly one hundred mouths to feed.

From this point onwards Whitefield's life is one continual and heroic struggle to support adequately "the oldest charity

[1] *History of Bethesda* by T. Gamble, Junr.   [2] *Journal.*

in America." With magnificent self-forgetfulness, he strained his physical powers beyond endurance to fulfil his obligation of honour to "God's little ones."

When the work on the buildings began, Whitefield had only £150 in hand in cash. This was augmented later in March, 1740, by the first collection taken in America after the erection of the Orphanage, at the Church of the Rev. Joseph Smith in Charleston, resulting in £70.

"Many thought he spoke as never man spoke," said Joseph Smith. "So charmed were the people with his manner of address that they shut up their shops, forgot their secular business, and laid aside their schemes for the world, and the oftener he preached the keener edge he seemed to put upon their desires to hear him again."

But great inroads were speedily made upon these slender resources, and Whitefield, undaunted, set off in "the Orphan House sloop, the *Savannah*," the first craft to bear that name, for Newcastle, in Pennsylvania, and resumed his work of preaching with its double objective, the saving of souls and the raising of funds. After great labours, which reduced him physically to such a condition that "thrice a day he was lifted upon his horse, being unable to mount otherwise, then rode and preached and came in and laid himself along two or three chairs," he returned to Savannah with £500 plus, if you please, a bricklayer, a tailor, two maid servants, and two more little orphan girls! By this time his family had increased to one hundred and fifty, and their needs permitted him no rest.

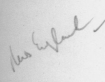

He next attacked New England,[1] and here he was well received. "Many recognised in him a worthy successor to the Puritan fathers." Twenty thousand people listened to his farewell sermon at Boston. Soon another £500 was in his coffers.

Some of his other difficulties deserve notice. On his return from New England he found the orphans removed from the temporary hired house to Bethesda.

"The great house," he wrote, "would have been finished if the Spaniards had not taken a schooner laden with bricks (10,000) and provisions to a considerable value." Later, in Britain, he was to be in danger even of arrest and imprison-

[1] *See* succeeding chapter.

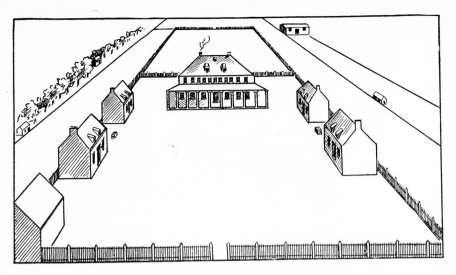

THE ORIGINAL BETHESDA ORPHANAGE,
Savannah, Georgia, of Whitefield's day

[*Face page* 90

ment because of Bethesda's financial needs and debts, but always, by the mercy of Providence, his requirements were eventually met.

In this work for the orphans, developing hand in hand with the Awakener's great spiritual work, there was surely both the prophecy and the dynamic of that mighty work for children which followed in the wake of the Evangelical Revival. Shaftesbury's deliverance of the child-slaves of commerce, Robert Raikes' struggles for child-education and his founding of the Sunday School movement, Spurgeon's and Barnardo's work for orphans in Great Britain, and the development of great educational establishments in America, these were some of the fruits, near and distant, of the new impulse to philanthropy that Whitefield associated so closely and practically with the preaching of the Gospel.

"The great house," as it was called, had a high roof and belfry and was surrounded by a colonnade. There was a cellar and a kitchen, on the ground floor the entrance hall was utilised as a chapel; on the left the library, and behind it the orphan's dining-room; on the right George Whitefield's two parlours, the staircase rising between them. On the second and third floors were Whitefield's study and bedroom, the manager's room, two bedrooms for boys, two for girls, and five others for general use.

The routine of the "house" was built on the adage, "Satan finds some mischief still for idle hands to do." "The children rose every morning at five o'clock, and spent fifteen minutes in private prayer. At six they assembled in the chapel with other members of 'the family.' There a psalm was sung and the morning lesson expounded by Whitefield or the manager. At seven a morning hymn and free prayer closed the set devotions. Seven to eight was the breakfast hour, interspersed with free hymn singing. From eight to ten they were carding, spinning, picking cotton or wool, sewing, knitting, cleaning the house, fetching water, cutting wood, not to mention other useful occupations! The boys learned the trades of shoe-making, tailoring, carpentering, etc. At ten school began until dinner at noon. From two to four the children were again in school and from four to six work once more. Supper was served at six again to the accompaniment of hymns. At eight Whitefield catechised the orphans, and at nine light refreshments prepared them for the fifteen minutes of private prayer which ended their day as it had begun." [1]

Altogether it could hardly have been a "rest cure" to be one of Whitefield's orphans, yet there were at least music, quiet and method in Whitefield's régime for them, whereas, left to the tender mercies of the world of their time, they would have been much more cruelly overworked without any compensating advantages.

Whitefield was full of a passionate zeal for the spiritual welfare of his "family." He continually yearned over their souls, and undoubtedly this explains in part his high-handed action in taking orphans out of positions where they were independent and happy and putting them in the home. He wanted them where they would get spiritual good and find their souls' salvation. General James Oglethorpe, who could be firm enough and wise enough, when he liked, put his foot down very strongly upon such action on the part of the young clergyman, arguing rightly, that Whitefield was responsible only for the "destitute" orphans of the colony, not for those who were prospering. Accordingly, he even sent to the House and arrested and restored certain orphans by main force to their former positions.

In spite of the evident self-sacrifice of Whitefield in his strenuous labours of preaching on behalf of his "family," the most abominable calumnies were set afoot by malicious people as to his use of the money raised for Bethesda. Unhappily, too, some credence was given to these slanders even in quarters from which a more generous and trustful attitude might have been expected. Thus, later on, when visiting Scotland there was a movement against him in the synod at Glasgow, one of the grounds of which was "the chimerical scheme of his Orphan House, and want of evidence that the money collected is rightly applied."

But what was intended for a reproach turned out to be for his honour, for it transpired that the magistrates of Savannah had published, three years before, in the *Philadelphia Gazette*, an affidavit not only of Whitefield's accuracy of accounts and right application of all funds, but including also a recognition

[1] See *History of Bethesda*, T. Gamble.

of his personal generosity to the cause. This latter is a remarkable fact, and is a testimony to the Methodist frugality of the evangelist. In round figures, omitting shillings and pence, the donations to Bethesda contained in those accounts were as follows:[1]

England	..	..	..	..	..	£4,471
Scotland	..	..	..	..	..	978
Georgia	..	..	..	..	..	275
Charleston	..	..	..	..	..	567
Beaufort	..	..	..	..	..	16
Northern points Boston, New York, Philadelphia, etc.						1,809
Cash from boarders and sale of produce					..	3,983
Whitefield's personal benefactions—sums expended for Bethesda and never claimed by him					..	3,299
						£15,398

A sheer gift of over three thousand pounds (£9,000 value to-day) is a sufficient guarantee not merely of Whitefield's honesty, but of his heroic self-sacrifice.

During thirty years, a succession of boys and girls numbering one hundred and forty and forty-three respectively, were "clothed, educated, maintained and suitably provided for," and over and above these, many other poor children were received for temporary periods, educated and maintained.

Whitefield himself was always deeply confident of the Divine guidance and blessing in this work. Thus, when lying ill in Bermuda, in 1748, where he had gone for a brief spell of rest, he found that God had raised up friends for his orphans even there. A group of gentlemen of the island planned to discharge for him all arrears upon the House and Whitefield writes in his *Journal*:

"Thanks be given to thy name, O God! Thou knowest all things; Thou knowest that I want to owe no man anything but love; and provide for Bethesda after my decease. Thou hast promised that Thou wilt fulfil the desire of them that fear Thee. I believe, Lord, help my unbelief, that Thou wilt fulfil this desire of my soul."

That desire was fulfilled. Before tracing, however, the subsequent history of this historic charity, we must note Whitefield's commendable firmness over his project for adding to the Orphan House a Theological College for the training

[1] *History of Bethesda*, and Tyerman, Vol. II. p. 581.

of ministers to serve in the Southern States. When his plans for this urgent scheme were ripe, the Earl of Dartmouth presented, on Whitefield's behalf, a draft of the charter proposed to the Archbishop of Canterbury. The latter, with the Lord President of the Privy Council, insisted that the head of such a College should be "a Church of England minister, and that the prayers should not be extempore but the liturgy of the Church, or some other settled and established form." Whitefield declined absolutely to accept a Charter couched in such terms. He pointed out that the greater part of the contributions to the Orphan House had come from Dissenters, and he had constantly declared that the "intended College should be founded on a broad bottom or not at all." So ended Whitefield's dream for a seminary for preachers after his own heart, but though unrealised in his form, it was not without a degree of realisation, as we shall see, in another way.

In the year 1770 Whitefield had the joy of amplifying the Orphan House for the rather more modest purposes of a school or academy. Under a new régime in the colony of Georgia, James Wright, the Governor, with the whole Council of Georgia, James Habersham being president, attended at Bethesda for the opening of the new buildings. An eye witness has left the following eloquent account of the event:

SAVANNAH. January 29, 1770, Monday morning.

"You would have been pleased to have been at the Orphan House Academy yesterday, where his Excellency our Governor, the Hon. the Council, and the Commons House of Assembly, were agreeably entertained in consequence of an invitation given them by the Founder, the Rev. Mr. Whitefield. Everything was conducted with much decency and order. His Excellency was received at the bottom door by the officers, orphans, and other domestics; and was then escorted upstairs by Mr. Whitefield through a gallery near sixty feet long, into a large room thirty feet in length, with six windows, canvassed and made ready for blue paper hangings. In a room of the same extent over against it (intended for the library, and in which a considerable number of books is already deposited), was prepared, on a long table and adjacent sideboard, cold tongue, ham, tea, etc. for the gentlemen to refresh themselves with, after their ten miles' ride, from Savannah. Between eleven and twelve, the bell rung for public worship. A procession was formed in the long gallery, and moved forward to the chapel in the following order. The orphans, in round, black, flat caps, and black gowns; the

94

chaplain in his gown; the workmen and assistants; the steward and superintendent, with their white wands; the clerk of the chapel; the Founder in his university square cap; with the Rev. Mr. Ellington, now missionary at Augusta, and designed to be chaplain, and teacher of English and elocution at the Orphan House Academy; then his Excellency, followed by his Council and the Chief Justice; then the Speaker, succeeded by the other Commons, and a number of gentlemen and strangers, among whom were the Governor's two sons. As the procession moved along, the clerk of the chapel began the doxology, the singing of which was harmonious and striking. At the chapel door, the orphans, officers, and domestics broke into ranks on the right hand and the left; and, as his Excellency with his train went up the chapel stairs, the orphans sang:

> " Live by heaven and earth ador'd,
>   Three in One, and One in Three,
> Holy, holy, holy Lord,
>   All glory be to Thee!

"The Governor being seated fronting the chapel door, and a great chair, with tapestry hangings behind, and a covered desk before him, divine service began. Mr. Ellington read prayers; and then Mr. Whitefield enlarged, for about three-quarters of an hour, on 'The hands of Zerubbabel have laid the foundation of this house; his hands shall also finish it; and thou shalt know that the Lord of hosts hath sent me unto you. For who hath despised the day of small things?' (Zech. iv., 9, 10). His whole paraphrase was pertinent and affecting, but when he came to give us an account of the small beginnings of our now flourishing Province of which he was an eye-witness; and also of the trials and hardships, obloquy and contempt, he had undergone in maintaining, for so long a term, such a numerous orphan family, in such a desert; as well as the remarkable supports and providences that had attended him in the Orphan House Academy to its present promising height; especially when he came to address his Excellency, the Council, Speaker, etc., etc.,— the whole auditory seemed too big to speak, and unable to give itself proper vent. Sermon being ended, all returned in the same manner as they came, the clerk, orphans, etc., singing as they walked:

> " This God is the God we adore,
>   Our faithful, unchangeable friend,
> Whose love is as large as His power,
>   And neither knows measure nor end.

> " Tis Jesus, the first and the last,
>   Whose Spirit shall guide us safe home;
> We'll praise Him for all that is past,
>   And trust Him for all that's to come.

H   95

"In about half an hour the bell rung for dinner. All went down, in order, to a large dining room, intended hereafter for academical exercises. It is forty feet long, with eight sash windows, and the Founder's picture, at full length, at the upper end. Two tables, the one long and the other oval, were well covered with a proper variety of plain and well-dressed dishes. After dinner, two toasts were given by his Excellency, viz., 'The King,' and 'Success to the Orphan House College.' The whole company broke up, and went away, in their several carriages, about five in the afternoon. One thing gave me particular pleasure; when the Governor drank 'The King,' Mr. Whitefield added, 'And let all the people say, "Amen"'; upon which a loud amen was repeated from one end of the room to the other.

"Upon the whole, all seemed most surprisingly pleased with their spiritual and bodily entertainment, as well as with the elegance, firmness, and dispatch of the late repairs, and additional buildings and improvements.

"The situation is most salubrious and inviting; the air free and open; and a salt-water creek, which will bring up a large schooner east and west, ebbs and flows at a small distance from the house. I suppose there might be above twenty carriages, besides horsemen; and there would have been as many more, had not the invitations been confined to the Governor, Council, and Commons House of Assembly. A strange sight this, in the once despised, deserted Province of Georgia, where, as Mr. Whitefield told us in his discourse, about thirty years ago, scarce any person of property lived; and lands, which now sell for £3 an acre, might have been purchased almost for threepence.

"But I must have done. Excuse me for being so prolix. Yesterday's scene so lies before me, that to tell you the truth, I wanted to vent my feelings. If Mr. Whitefield intends, as I am informed he does, to give a more general invitation to the gentlemen in and about Savannah, I will endeavour to be amongst them. Accept this hasty scribble (as I hear the ship sails to-morrow), as a mark of my being, dear sir, your obliged friend and servant."

Whitefield, at his death, bequeathed the orphanage property not to the magistrates of Savannah, as they expected, but to Selina, Countess of Huntingdon, recommending John Habersham, who had been his able and faithful manager throughout, as a suitable person to act for her on the spot. Habersham, by this time, as noted above, had risen to the proud position of president of His Majesty's Council for Georgia.

Right nobly did Lady Huntingdon take up her responsibility, in spite of being sixty-three years of age at the time. It was she who came near to fulfilling Whitefield's dream of a preachers' college at Bethesda.

The Countess conceived the project of making Bethesda the centre of a great mission movement to the American colonies. Several years before she had founded at Trevecca, in Wales, a seminary, with the saintly Fletcher, of Madeley, for its first superintendent. This afterwards, 1791, was merged into Cheshunt College, then in Hertfordshire, now situated at Cambridge. She now selected, from among students trained there, a number of volunteers for the work in America.

On October 9th, 1772, they were ordained to their work, and throughout all the Huntingdon Connexional Churches, the congregations assembled for prayer and fasting. On October 27th the missionaries embarked at Gravesend amid scenes of great enthusiasm. "Vast multitudes attended them to the river side." [1]

This band of devoted men had a warm welcome from Whitefield's Pennsylvanian friends, and, settling at Bethesda, did most valuable and effective preaching work, not only among the colonists but also with the negroes and the Indians.

Then suddenly disaster fell—Bethesda was destroyed by fire. Lady Huntingdon, however, "held no commerce with despair," and was so thankful that no lives had been lost that she speedily arranged, through her own generosity and that of her friends for a new Bethesda. Reared this time, however, upon an educational foundation, and doubtless affected by the atmosphere of antagonism between the two countries, it did not regain its former status. "It lived, but declined in vigour and usefulness. The war between the colonies and the mother country checked its operations." [2] It was during this period that there occurred one of the most remarkable over-rulings of Providence in the history surely of any institution. At one time during the war the governing board, *the charter of which only continued so long as three trustees met every anniversary day, which was on St. George's Day*, was composed only of a Protestant, a Roman Catholic, and an Israelite. These were not the likeliest of men to foregather with each other and to make matters worse they were all three captured by the British! By a

[1] Life of Countess Huntingdon.
[2] *History of Bethesda*, T. Gamble.

most wonderful coincidence, however, these men found themselves prisoners on board the same British man-o'-war off the Georgian coast. They secured permission of the captain to go ashore on this particular St. George's Day and they celebrated the anniversary under an oak-tree at Tunbury, Georgia, and so maintained the trust in being. The cause suffered badly, too, from the dishonesty of Lady Huntingdon's first president, named Piercy, who is severely condemned by her biographer. After the war a special Act was passed through the United States legislature regularising the Countess of Huntingdon's possession of Bethesda, and awarding £1,000 worth of "specie of confiscated property" for the use of the Academy, as it was now called.

Little, however, was done in the next ten years, and Lady Huntingdon passed away. In 1801, however, the north wing of the semi-restored building was repaired and completed, and the place was used for a school in 1802. Once again fire destroyed the building in 1805, and this being followed by a hurricane which also seriously damaged the property, the trustees determined to surrender their trust. The property was dissipated by sales of portion after portion, until, within a few years, not a trace of the original Bethesda remained. But the end was not to be so.

There was an interlude of forty years and then the original site of Bethesda came into the possession of a Society whose history was curiously parallel with Whitefield's institution. About ten years after Bethesda was founded, a group of five men of whom we have but the names of three, Benjamin Sheftall, Richard Milledge, and Peter Tonder, started the St. George's Society for the care and education of orphan children in the colony. After the war this was called "The Union Society in Savannah," and was incorporated under an Act of August 23rd, 1786. Under the auspices of this Society, in 1854, the original Bethesda was purchased, and suitable buildings erected upon it, and once again an Orphanage flourished in Savannah in continuance of Whitefield's dream!

Whitefield's influence, indeed, played no small part in this re-creation. "In choosing Bethesda," said President Fry in his report at the time, "the board of managers were influenced by the fact that upwards of a century it had been consecrated

THE BETHESDA ORPHANAGE TO-DAY

[*Face page* 98

to the same noble purpose, and that it had an unblemished reputation for health." Year after year the number of orphans in the care of the Society grew, and all was very prosperous till suddenly once again war intervened to cast its gloom over the prospect. The Civil War was a very dark period indeed, the public at large suffering too cruelly to support such institutions. Bethesda was turned into a military hospital, and again, in 1866, it lay in ruins. But nothing seemed able to hold back Bethesda from the destiny to which Whitefield had consecrated it, and a spate of wealth pouring upon the Society after the Civil War, made it possible, in 1870, for the Bethesda site to become once more the scene of building operations. The corner-stone of a noble building, better designed for Orphanage work than any before it, was laid, with Masonic ceremonies, at the celebration of the one hundred and twentieth anniversary of the Society, on April 27th, in the presence of two thousand visitors. From that day to this the institution has never looked back. In 1902 it was maintaining no less than one hundred and twenty-five boys.

The latest report (1929) of the Homes is full of rejoicing over good work accomplished, and a prospect full of the highest promise. Whitefield's dream has gained an imperishable reality.[1]

---

[1] This report opens thus:

" I beg to submit a report of the 189th year's service of Bethesda Home to the community of Savannah. It has been a gratifying year in that the friends of the home have been privileged to observe some of the fruits of their efforts in the quality and character of the boys leaving the home. Besides the three boys in higher institutions of learning, reports of whose progress are most satisfactory, a number of boys have gone into employment and are doing well.

.   .   .   .   .   .

" There is no abatement in the number of applications for admission of boys, but, rather, an increase. This is not due to hard times alone, it is partly due to the excellent reputation the home bears as a man-building institution. We have here what is really a high-class school for boys, where we assume all responsibility and give the boys the best of care.

.   .   .   .   .

" The Income of the Society for the year ending March 31st, 1929, was $40,282.99 and Expenses $47,787.16, leaving a deficit of $7,504.16."

CHAPTER VI

WHITEFIELD IN NEW ENGLAND

"On many counts, it certainly exceeds all other provinces in America; and for the establishment of religion perhaps all other parts of the world. Every five miles or perhaps less you have a meeting house. . . . I like New England exceeding well."—GEORGE WHITEFIELD in 1740.

IN certain vital respects the most important thing that happened during Whitefield's second visit to America was his impact upon the New England States, occurring, as it did, in close conjunction with the notable work of Jonathan Edwards. Before we are free to tell this fascinating part of the great story, however, we must pause to notice a few other matters.

We pass over, as comparatively unimportant, Whitefield's sharp quarrel with the Commissary of Charleston—the Rev. Alexander Garden. There were faults on both sides, for Whitefield could be a very irritating opponent. Thus, whilst Alexander Garden was preaching against Whitefield from the text, "Those that have turned the world upside down have come hither also," Whitefield was retaliating with a sermon from the text, " Alexander, the coppersmith, hath done us much harm!" But whilst Garden carried his opposition to the point of denying Whitefield the Holy Sacrament, the people of Charleston took the young evangelist to their hearts and thronged to his services. Nor need we waste time and space over Whitefield's somewhat arrogant tilting at Archbishop Tillotson and the author of *The Whole Duty of Man*. A little mental arrogance in Whitefield is not surprising considering that at this time, though famous in two countries, he was still only twenty-five years of age! Whitefield, in spite of occasional outbursts of intolerant criticism and invective against those opposed to his deeply cherished convictions, remained, on the whole, much more tolerant and sweet-spirited than his critics.

Whitefield's first essay at courtship, however, is too psychologically significant to be missed. Nothing is so pathetically eloquent of the complete concentration to the point of unnaturalness, of Whitefield and Wesley upon the salvation of the soul, than their awkwardness and lack of grace in courtship. Wesley's story, as we have already noted, has been told very intriguingly, and with a suspicion both of tears and laughter behind the telling, by Marie Conway Oemler in *The Holy Lover*. Whitefield seems to have gathered the fact that the Lord meant him to marry, not from any flutterings of his all-too-concentrated heart but from the failure of the women he brought with him from England to serve his family of orphans. Thus writing to the parents of the young lady of his rather cold-blooded choice he says:

"On board the *Savannah*,
"4th April, 1740.

"My dear Friends,

"Since I wrote last, we have buried our sister L . . . . . .; Rachel I left at Philadelphia and sister T . . . . . seems to be in a declining state; so that sister A . . . . . alone is like to be left of all the women which came over with me from England.

"I find, by experience, that a mistress is absolutely necessary for the due management of my increasing family, and, to take off some of that care, which, at present, lies upon me. Besides, I shall, in all probability, at my next return from England, bring more women with me; and I find, unless they are all truly gracious, or indeed if they are, without a superior, matters cannot be carried on as becometh the gospel of Jesus Christ. It hath been, therefore, impressed upon my heart that I should marry, in order to have a helpmeet for me in the work, whereunto the dear Lord Jesus hath called me.

"This comes (like Abraham's servant to Rebekah's relations), to know whether you think your daughter, Miss E . . . . . . is a proper person to engage in such an undertaking? If so, whether you will be pleased to give me leave to propose marriage unto her?

"You need not be afraid of sending me a refusal; for I bless God, if I know anything of my own heart, I am free from that foolish passion which the world calls *love*. I write, only because I believe it is the will of God that I should alter my state; . . . but your denial will fully convince me that your daughter is not the person appointed by God for me. He knows my heart; I would not marry but for Him, and in Him, for ten thousand worlds. But I have sometimes thought Miss E . . . . . would be my helpmeet; for she has often been impressed upon my heart. I should think myself safe in your family, because so many of you love the Lord Jesus, and consequently, would be more watchful over my precious and immortal soul.

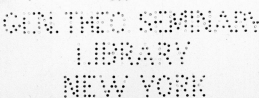

"After strong crying and tears at the throne of grace for direction, and after unspeakable troubles with my own heart, I write this. . . . Be pleased to spread the letter before the Lord; and if you think this motion to be of Him, be pleased to deliver the enclosed to your daughter; if not say nothing, only let me know you disapprove of it, and that shall satisfy, dear sir and madam, your obliged friend and servant in Christ.

"GEORGE WHITEFIELD."

The letter enclosed with this precious document was as follows:

"On board the *Savannah*,
"April 4, 1740.

"Dear Miss E. . . . . . .

"Be not surprised at the contents of this. The letter sent to your honoured father and mother will acquaint you with the reasons.

"Do you think you could undergo the fatigues that must necessarily attend being joined to one who is every day liable to be called to suffer for the sake of the Lord Jesus Christ? Can you bear to leave your father and kindred's house, and to trust in Him, who feedeth the young ravens that call upon Him, for your own and children's support, supposing it should please Him to bless you with any? Can you undertake to help a husband in the charge of a family, consisting perhaps of a hundred persons? Can you bear the inclemencies of the air, both as to cold and heat, in a foreign climate? Can you, when you have a husband, be as though you had none, and willingly part with him even for a long season, when his Lord and Master shall call him forth to preach the Gospel, and command him to leave you behind?

"If, after seeking to God for direction, and searching your heart, you can say, 'I can do all these things through Christ strengthening me', what if you and I were joined together in the Lord, and you came with me, at my return from England, to be a helpmeet to me in the management of the Orphan House? I have great reason to believe it is the Divine will that I should alter my condition, and have often thought you were the person appointed for me. I shall still wait on God for direction and heartily entreat Him that, if this be not of Him, it may come to naught.

"I write thus plainly, because, I trust, I write not from any other principle but the love of God. I shall make it my business to call on the Lord Jesus; and would advise you to consult both Him and your friends. For, in order to obtain a blessing, we should call both the Lord Jesus and His disciples to the marriage. I much like the manner of Isaac's marrying Rebekah; and think no marriage can succeed well, unless both parties concerned are like minded with Tobias and his wife.

"I think I can call the God of Abraham, Isaac and Jacob to witness that I desire to take you, my sister, to wife not for lust, but uprightly;

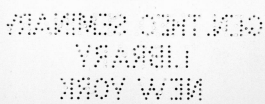

and therefore, I hope He will mercifully ordain, if it be His blessed will we should be joined together, that we may work as Zacharias and Elisabeth did, in all the ordinances of the Lord, blameless. I make no great profession to you, because I believe you think me sincere. The passionate expressions which carnal creatures use, I think, ought to be avoided by those that would marry in the Lord. I can only promise, by the help of God, to keep my matrimonial vows, and to do what I can towards helping you forward in the great work of your salvation.

"If you think marriage will be in any way prejudicial to your better part, be so kind as to send me a denial. I would not be a snare to you for the world. You need not be afraid of speaking your mind. I trust I love you only for God, and desire to be joined to you only by His command and for His sake. With fear and much trembling I write and shall patiently tarry the Lord's leisure, till He is pleased to incline you, dear Miss E. . . . . . to send an answer to your affectionate brother, friend and servant in Christ,

"GEORGE WHITEFIELD."

That is surely one of the most remarkable love-letters ever penned. From the internal evidence of these letters we can gather that although they were written from a well-disciplined heart, some severe battles had been fought out before that calmness had been reached. The ascetic note of early Methodism did not permit its devotees to approach the facts of marriage easily, and only under stress of circumstances and the very demands of the sacred cause itself, could any such concession to the flesh be contemplated. To the modern mind this attitude is so strained as to be almost ludicrous, yet we, on the other hand, have to deplore the prevalence of the other extreme in our own time—the fatal ease with which the claims and natural rights of the flesh are allowed to override and wipe out those of the soul.

Gledstone thinks that Whitefield was not in love, but there are lines in these letters which, coming from one so repressed as Whitefield, undoubtedly indicate great inner passion. We may assume safely, therefore, that, in Whitefield's case, honest and strong and highly purified love was deliberately sacrificed to a rather hard and strained conscientiousness. A higher duty rendered the young lady the merest means to an end. Perhaps the young lady felt that in such an atmosphere marital love would find it hard to live, and harder still to flourish, for very wisely she did not accede to Whitefield's request. Who was she? A little putting of two and two together brings us to a sure conclusion.[1] The editor of Whitefield's collected works applied "To Mr. and Mrs. D." for the letter to the parents. Charles Wesley's *Journal* tells us that Mr. and Mrs. Delamotte, of Blendon, with whom Whitefield stayed in the summer of 1739, and whose son, Charles, accompanied the Wesleys to Georgia, had a daughter named Elizabeth, and there is a letter of Whitefield's of February 1, 1740, written from Savannah to Miss Elizabeth D. . . . So there is little doubt but that Miss Elizabeth Delamotte was the "elect lady." This is confirmed by another letter of Whitefield's from Savannah, June 26, 1740, to William Seward in which the following highly diverting verdict is found:

"I have received many agreeable letters from England; but find, from Blendon letters, that Miss E . . . . . . D . . . . . . is in a seeking state only. Surely that will not do. I would have one that is full of faith and the Holy Ghost."

So the matter of Whitefield's marriage fell into abeyance for a while.

Other correspondence of an important nature at this time, was that with John Wesley written in view of Wesley's changing theological outlook. We may conveniently record here the story of what is commonly called the "break" between Whitefield and Wesley. Considering the generally fierce and intolerant style of theological controversy of the time, both of these men showed their essential greatness in the comparative mildness of their mutual reproaches. As far back as their common work at Bristol the trouble commenced, Wesley being accused by letter of not preaching "election." Wesley consulted his "lot" method to decide for or against publishing a sermon of his upon "free grace" and the lot he drew said, "preach and print." This he did, but at Whitefield's request he held up the printing of the sermon until Whitefield had departed for America. After Whitefield had gone Wesley published his sermon, and also began to teach his doctrine of perfection, namely, "Free, full and present salvation from all guilt, all the power, and all the in-being of sin." He then wrote and published his *Journal* from his *Embarking for Georgia to his Return to London*, and a *Life of Halyburton*, with a preface in which he expounded his

[1] Tyerman, Vol. I. pp. 370-1.

doctrine further. These came into the hands of George White-field at Savannah, together with a letter from Wesley urging his acceptance of the new doctrines.

Whitefield wrote in reply the following letter entirely beautiful in spirit if uncompromising in tone:

"I could now send a particular answer to your last; but, my honoured friend and brother, for once hearken to a child, who is willing to wash your feet. I beseech you by the mercies of God in Christ Jesus our Lord, if you would have my love confirmed toward you, write no more to me about misrepresentations wherein we differ. To the best of my knowledge, at present, no sin has dominion over me, yet I feel the strugglings of indwelling sin day by day. I can therefore by no means come into your interpretation of the passage mentioned in the letter, and as explained in your preface to Mr. Halyburton. The doctrine of election and the final perseverance of those who are in Christ, I am ten thousand times more convinced of, if possible, than when I saw you last. You think otherwise; why, then should we dispute, when there is no probability of convincing? Will it not in the end destroy brotherly love, and insensibly take from us that cordial union and sweetness of soul which, I pray God, may always subsist between us? How glad would the enemies of the Lord be to see us divided! How many would rejoice, should I join and make a party against you! And, in one word, how would the cause of our common Master every way suffer by our raising disputes about particular points of doctrine! Honoured sir, let us offer salvation freely to all by the blood of Jesus; and whatever light God has communicated to us, let us freely communicate it to others. I have lately read the life of Luther, and think it nowise to his honour, that the last part of his life was so much taken up in disputing with Zwinglius and others, who in all probability equally loved the Lord Jesus, notwithstanding they might differ from him in other points. Let this, dear sir, be a caution to us; I hope it will be to me; for, by the blessing of God, provoke me to it as much as you please, I do not think ever to enter the lists of controversy with you on the points wherein we differ. Only I pray to God, that the more you judge me, the more I may love you, and learn to desire no one's approbation but that of my Lord and Master Jesus Christ."

On August 9th, 1740, Wesley wrote Whitefield:

"My Dear Brother,

"I thank you for yours, May the 24th.[1] The case is quite plain. There are bigots both for predestination and against it. God is

[1] This was a letter written from Cape-Lopen and similar in view to the one quoted above.

sending a message to those on either side. But neither will receive it, unless from one of his own opinion. Therefore, for a time, you are suffered to be of one opinion, and I of another. But when His time is come, God will do what man cannot—namely make us both of one mind. Then persecution will flame out, and it will be seen whether we count our lives dear unto ourselves, so that we may finish our course with joy.

"I am, my dearest brother, ever yours,

"JOHN WESLEY."

Here is the severest letter Whitefield wrote to Wesley, and although its tone is irritatingly superior, yet one phrase quoted in it as used by Wesley may be sufficient to explain and condone it.

"Boston,
"Sept. 28, 1740.

"Dear Brother Wesley,

"What mean you by disputing in all your letters? May God give you to know yourself: and then you will not plead for *absolute perfection*, or call the doctrine of election a 'doctrine of devils.' My dear brother, take heed. See you are in Christ a new creature. Beware of a false peace. Strive to enter in at the strait gate: and give all diligence to make your calling and election sure. Remember you are but a babe in Christ, if so much. Be humble; talk little; think and pray much. Let God teach you and he will lead you into all the truth. I love you heartily. I pray you may be kept from error in principle and practice. Salute all the brethren. If you must dispute stay till you are master of the subject, otherwise you will hurt the cause you would defend. Study to adorn the Gospel of our Lord in all things, and forget not to pray for your affectionate friend and servant,

"G.W."

On November 24, Whitefield wrote Wesley from Bohemia, Maryland,

"Dear and Honoured Sir,

"O, that there may be harmony, and very intimate union between us: Yet it cannot be, since you hold *universal redemption*. But no more of this. Perhaps, in the spring, we may see each other face to face. This evening I propose to embark for Georgia. Wonderful things our Lord brings to pass, in these parts, every day. Here is close opposition from some of the Presbyterian clergy. The seed of the serpent is in us all, of whatever communion. I expect much more opposition every hour. The devil rages in London. He begins now to triumph indeed. The children of God are disunited among themselves. The King of the Church shall yet over-rule all things for good. My dear brother, for Christ's sake, avoid all disputation. Do not oblige me to preach against you; I had rather die. Be gentle towards the . . . (? Moravians) They will get great advantage over you if they discover any irregular warmth in your temper. I cannot pray and unite with them.

"Honoured sir, adieu!

"Yours eternally in Christ Jesus,

"GEORGE WHITEFIELD."

Such letters do honour to the two great revival leaders, and whilst, largely by the too zealous partisanship of their followings, they were pushed into increasing opposition, they never entirely lost their profound respect and affection for one another. As to which was right, who shall say? The tone of the Church to-day is more Arminian than Calvinistic, yet doubtless sound modern theology would see in each position a complementary truth to be fulfilled in a higher synthesis of thought. This we shall examine in more detail towards the end of our story.

Returning to Whitefield's American itinerary, we find him landing at Newport, Rhode Island, on Sunday evening, September 14, where he was met by "the most venerable man I ever saw," the Rev. Nathaniel Clap, then seventy-two years of age. Through Mr. Clap's good offices Whitefield officiated from the Church of England pulpit to great congregations. At the close of the afternoon service on the second day more than a thousand people followed the young Awakener to the house where he was lodging, "I therefore," says Whitefield, "stood upon the threshold and spake near an hour. . . . It was a very solemn meeting. Glory be to God's great name."

Whitefield reached Boston, the capital of New England,[1] on Wednesday, September 17, 1740. Oldmixon, the historian, thus describes the famous city as it was in those days. "There are abundance of fine buildings in it, public and private: as the Court House, Market Place, Sir William Phil's house, and others. There are several handsome streets. It contains ten or twelve thousand souls; the militia consisting of four companies of foot. There are three parish churches, a French church, and two meeting-houses in the city. The Old Church, North Church and South Church belong to the Presbyterians,

---

[1] New England comprised the northern states of the N. American Union, i.e. Maine, Vermont, New Hampshire, Massachusetts, Rhode Island and Connecticut.

who are the Church of England as by law established; the French Church belongs to the French Protestants; and the meeting-houses to a congregation of Church of England men and Anabaptists." Rather a promising ecclesiastical mixture! As Tyerman points out, these mixed religionists were doubtless all keenly Calvinistic, and so Whitefield was assured of a welcome. One doctor of divinity there was who seeing Whitefield, cried, "I am sorry to see you here," only to meet the humorous but not very complimentary retort, "So is the devil!"

"I preached to about four thousand in Dr. Colman's meeting-house," was the first impact of Whitefield on New England! That was on Friday the 19th. On the Sunday following his audience was fifteen thousand on Boston Common. Six thousand greeted him at another meeting-house next day! So the days of revival went by with meeting-house and open-air gatherings thronged by the populace. On one such occasion a meeting-house crowd was seized with unaccountable emotion and panic whilst waiting for the preacher. Some threw themselves from the galleries, others leaped out of the windows, and no less than five persons lost their lives. The moment Whitefield arrived and saw the state of the congregation he ordered them to follow him to the famous common. On Wednesday, September 24th, he preached at Cambridge,[1] "the chief college in New England for training the sons of the prophets. It has one president, four tutors and about a hundred students." Feeling that the tone of this college was, from his point of view, heretical, he preached from the text, "We are not as many, who corrupt the word of God." Many clergy had gathered from the neighbouring districts, and in the court of the college under an elm, afterwards to be known as Washington's elm because it was there the patriot raised the sword of the revolution, Whitefield met another audience of no less than seven thousand! "The Holy Spirit melted many hearts," we are told. In one of the meeting-house gatherings at Boston, Dr. Sewall's, Whitefield received no less than £550 for his Orphan-House and on the same day at Dr. Colman's church a second audience gave him £470.[2] That was a Sunday,

---

[1] In 1708 Oldmixon wrote, "Cambridge is a university, and has two colleges, Harvard College and Stoughton Hall."

[2] But the New England currency was much depreciated at this time, and this £550 was worth about £100 sterling. (Gledstone).

THE OLD SOUTH PRESBYTERIAN CHURCH,
Newburyport, Mass. (as in Whitefield's day), where Whitefield's remains are still to be
viewed in the crypt beneath the pulpit.

[*Face page* 108

and into it Whitefield compressed five such preachings whilst his correspondence reveals three letters bearing that same date. One of these letters bears witness to the extreme love of neatness and order that Whitefield had developed. "Not a paper in his room was allowed to be out of place. He thought he could not die easy if he had an impression that his gloves were mislaid." In the letter in question he is writing to one who criticised the neatness of his attire. He writes, "I could not but smile to find you wink at the decency of my dress. Alas, my brother, I have known long since what it is to be in that state you are, in my opinion, about to enter into. I myself once thought that Christianity required me to go nasty. I neglected myself as much as you would have me for above a twelvemonth, but when God gave me the spirit of adoption I then dressed decently, as you call it, out of principle, and I am more and more convinced the Lord would have me act in that respect as I do. But I am almost ashamed to mention any such thing."

In other words, clothes, being insignificant, might as well be as decent as possible rather than otherwise.

We know, too, from another letter, that, on that day of typical labour—on which nevertheless he wrote letters—his lodging was so thronged with inquirers that he could scarcely find time to eat bread!

From Boston the Awakener sped to Ipswich, forty miles away, and addressed immense gatherings there, and at Newbury, Hampton, Portsmouth, thence back, through Ipswich where he preached to still greater crowds, to Boston again. It was on this tour that on September 30th, 1740, Whitefield came for the first time to the little town on the estuary of the Merrimac, Newbury, or Newbury Port, as it was then called, in Essex County, Massachusetts, where thirty years later he was to lie stilled in death. His reception was not a happy one, the Rev. Christopher Toppan of the First Church being by no means in sympathy with the revival and even carrying, it is alleged, a whip wherewith to scourge " enthusiasts " from the " house of prayer." " The greatest pulpit orator of the age " arrived in a blinding snow-storm to find open-air preaching impossible and every pulpit closed against him save one. It was the Rev. John Lowell of the Third Church who boasted the appropriate motto: " In necessariis unitas; in non-necessariis libertas;

in omnibus, charitas " who gave the Awakener his opportunity. One hundred and forty-three persons were added almost immediately to the Third Church as a result, and later the First *Presbyterian* Church (better known as " Old South ") came into being. It is a symbolic coincidence that this little town, so bound up with Whitefield in life and in death, was the birthplace[1] of William Lloyd Garrison, the champion of the slaves and also the town in which Whittier's first poems were printed. Back at Boston in addition to more preaching services, Whitefield dealt day after day with many hundreds who sought him at home in all kinds of spiritual difficulty and moral perplexity. A brilliant specimen of Whitefield's impromptu genius in the pulpit, overwhelming in its dramatic power and deeply human appeal, is provided by a description published in Boston at this time in a work called *The Rebels*. " After he had finished his prayer, he knelt a long time in profound silence; and so powerfully had it affected the most heartless of his audience, that a stillness like that of the tomb pervaded the whole house.

"Before he commenced his sermon, long, darkening columns crowded the bright sunny sky of the morning, and swept their dull shadows over the building, in fearful augury of the storm that was approaching.

"'See that emblem of human life,' said he, as he pointed to a flitting shadow. 'It paused for a moment, and concealed the brightness of heaven from our view; but it is gone. And, where will you be, my hearers, when your lives have passed away like that dark cloud! Oh, dear friends, I see thousands sitting attentive with their eyes fixed on the poor unworthy preacher. In a few days we shall all meet at the judgment seat of Christ. We shall form part of that vast assembly which will gather before His throne. Every eye will behold the Judge. With a voice whose call you must abide and answer He will inquire, whether on earth you strove to enter in at the strait gate; whether you were supremely devoted to God; whether your hearts were absorbed in Him. My blood runs cold when I think how many of you will then seek to enter in, and shall not be able. O what plea can you make before the Judge of the whole earth? Can you say it has been your whole endeavour to mortify the flesh, with its affections and lusts?

---

[1] The house next door to the parsonage where Whitefield died!

"No!" you must answer, "I made myself easy in the world, by flattering myself that all would end well; but I have deceived my own soul, and am lost."

"'O false and hollow Christians, of what avail will it be that you have done many things? That you have read much in the sacred Word? That you have made long prayers? That you have attended religious duties, and appeared holy in the eyes of men? What will all this be, if, instead of loving God supremely, you have been supposing you should exalt yourselves in heaven by acts really polluted and unholy?'

"'And you rich men, wherefore do you hoard your silver? Wherefore count the price you have received for Him whom you every day crucify in your love of gain? Why, that, when you are too poor to buy a drop of cold water, your beloved son may be rolled into hell in his chariot, pillowed and cushioned.'

"'O sinner! by all your hopes of happiness, I beseech you to repent. Let not the wrath of God be awakened! Let not the fires of eternity be kindled against you! See there!' said the impassioned preacher, pointing to a flash of lightning, 'it is a glance from the angry eye of Jehovah! Hark!' continued he, raising a finger in listening attitude, as the thunder broke in a tremendous crash, 'it was the voice of the Almighty as He passed by in His anger!'

"As the sound died away Whitefield covered his face with his hands, and fell on his knees apparently lost in prayer. The storm passed rapidly by, and the sun, bursting forth, threw across the heavens the magnificent arch of peace. Rising and pointing to it the young preacher cried, 'Look upon the rainbow, and praise Him who made it. Very beautiful it is in the brightness thereof. It compasseth the heaven about with glory and the hands of the Most High have bended it'." [1]

When, after this tour de force, Whitefield was asked to publish the sermon he replied with that quiet humour which often flashed through his conversation, "I have no objection, if you will print the lightning, thunder, and rainbow with it."

Whitefield was succeeded at Boston in his rôle of Awakener by his remarkable disciple, Gilbert Tennent, who laboured

[1] Wakeley's *Anecdotes of Whitefield.*

for four months in the city. His preaching was searching and often terrible. Many hundreds were convinced of sin by his powerful ministry. The ministers of Boston were inspired with new faith, and life and power. "And now," records a Rev. Thomas Prince, pastor of Old South Church, "was such a time as we never knew. The Rev. Mr. Cooper was wont to say that more came to him, in one week, in deep concern about their souls, than had come in the whole twenty-four years of his preceding ministry. I can also say the same as to the numbers who repaired to me."

This kind of thing continued for a year and a half after Whitefield's departure. Thirty religious societies sprang into being. Ministers, beside officiating in their Churches preached in private houses nearly every night. Chapels were continually crowded. Says good Dr. Colman in a letter to Isaac Watts, September 15th, 1741, "Our lectures flourish, our Sabbaths are joyous, our Churches increase, our ministers have new life and spirit in their work."[1]

On October 13, Whitefield came to Concord where he "preached to some thousands in the open air, and collected about £45 for the orphans." Thence the Awakener passed to Sudbury and Marlborough. Here is an affecting note about the latter place. "Wednesday, October 15, Perceived Governor Belcher to be more affectionate than ever. After morning prayer he took me by myself and exhorted me to go on in stirring up the ministers; for, said he, 'reformation must begin at the house of God.' As we were going to meeting, he said, 'Mr. Whitefield, do not spare rulers any more than ministers, no, not the chief of them.' I preached in the open air to some thousands. The word fell with weight. After sermon, the governor remarked, 'I pray God, I may apply what has been said to my own heart. Pray, Mr. Whitefield, that I may hunger and thirst after righteousness.' Dinner being ended, with tears in his eyes, he kissed me, and took leave of me."

At length Whitefield reached Northampton, the home of Jonathan Edwards, and the source and centre of "the Great Awakening" of New England religion. Edwards was the grandson of a Rev. Mr. Stoddard, who in a ministry of fifty-

[1] Gillies' *Historical Collections.*

JONATHAN EDWARDS

He promoted a Revival at Northampton, Mass., which developed into "the Great Awakening" and prepared the way for Whitefield in New England. Jonathan Edwards was a great champion of Calvinism, and has been called "America's most original thinker in metaphysics." He was afterwards first Principal of New Jersey College, which developed into Princeton University.

[*Face page* 112

seven years in Northampton had been instrumental in reaping what he called "five harvests"—five revivals of religion. When Edwards took up his ministry the town was in a sorry moral plight, but a drastic change soon took place. Jonathan Edwards himself declares, "There was scarcely a single person in the town of Northampton, either old or young, that was left unconcerned about the things of the eternal world. Those who were wont to be the vainest and loosest, were now generally subject to *great awakenings*. The town seemed to be full of the presence of God. It never was so full of love, nor so full of joy; and yet, so full of distress, as it was then. There were remarkable tokens of God's presence in almost every house. Our public services were beautiful." [1]

The coming of Whitefield to such a centre was like applying fresh fuel to an already kindled fire. Jonathan Edwards' preaching had been of a terroristic character, its stress, like Gilbert Tennent's, being upon judgment and the darker side of the Calvinistic creed. Whitefield, with that sure touch of insight that seldom failed him, tells us "I found my heart drawn out to talk of scarce anything besides the consolations and privileges of the saints and the plentiful effusion of the Spirit upon believers." It was just the complimentary message needed to melt hearts already scorched and broken with fires of judgment. The movement started so powerfully by Jonathan Edwards and the school that gathered about his teaching would have smouldered and died after all too brief a blaze, if it had not been gathered up into the tenderer atmosphere and more positively healing revivalism of George Whitefield. Indeed, there are few features of this whole story more impressive than the sense of a "brooding spirit of Revival" hovering over the Churches of the time both in Britain and America, and which brought about the most timely human contacts in pursuit of the great end.

Thus there was the kindling of the sacred fire in the Wesleys in time to bring the great Trio together for revival purposes in London, the flowing together of the souls of Whitefield and Howell Harris in Wales, the contacts with the Tennents, of Pennsylvania, and with Benjamin Franklin, the union of

[1] *Narrative of late Surprising Conversions in New England.* (Jonathan Edwards, 1737.)

forces between Whitefield and the Countess of Huntingdon and the Earl of Dartmouth, with Jonathan Edwards and the temporary alliance with the Erskines' which brought Whitefield to Scotland. These form a kind of mosaic of inevitable ordained connection over which the electric current of revival ran with all-consuming energy.

From Northampton, where the great awakening was rendered greater still, Whitefield made his way back to New York through New Haven, Milford, Stratford, Fairfield, Newark, kindling the flame of revival in each place.

We are told that he approached New York with great diffidence and sinking of heart, yet Pemberton's Meeting-house was filled with a greatly agitated audience.

"On Sunday morning his soul was down in the depths, before going to evening service he could only cast himself on the ground before God, confessing himself a miserable sinner, and wondering that God could be so gracious to such a wretch. On his way to the meeting-house he became weaker, and when he entered the pulpit he would rather have been silent than have spoken." [1]

What experienced minister does not know that strange law, here superbly illustrated, that an abased preacher means an exalted congregation. The sermon that followed was absolutely marvellous in its effect. It had hardly begun before the congregation was visibly affected. Loud weeping and crying arose all over the building. Many were so overcome as to fall exhausted into the arms of friends. Whitefield himself was so carried away that he spoke literally till he could speak no more. Such an effect meant still larger preachings next day, but then he took farewell of them, and with another £110 for his orphans he passed on to Staten Island. There, too, the fire fell from heaven upon the crowds. Here even Whitefield's Charleston host, who had accompanied him apparently from friendship rather than from religious interest, succumbed to his power, and was so struck down and overpowered physically that his strength quite left him, and for a night he could scarcely move. From that moment he lived as a fervid Christian to his life's end!

Thus on to Philadelphia passed the now physically exhausted

[1] Gledstone, p. 157.

evangelist, arriving there exactly a year after the date of his first entry into the city. Here the same programme awaited him with similar results. But by this time a building had been erected by the citizens to house such visiting preachers as they cared to hear. It was one hundred feet long and seventy broad. When Whitefield arrived the roof was not yet on but the floor was boarded, a pulpit provided, and he had the honour of preaching the first sermon in it. Later this building became an academy for training ministers, and is now the Union Methodist Episcopal Church.

Whitefield arrived back at Savannah to find that, in spite of the money he had raised after most exhausting labours, such was the continual expense of the Orphan Home, he was still £500 in debt.

In the middle of January, 1741, Whitefield took ship in the *Minerva* from Charleston *en route* for Britain once more. Before we follow him let us hear the testimony of a keen historian [1] upon the effect which the evangelist's labours had upon American Christianity.

"The Congregational Church of New England, the Presbyterians and Baptists of the Middle States, and the mixed colonies of the South, owe their later religious life and energy mostly to the impulses given by Whitefield's powerful ministrations. The 'great awakening' under Edwards had not only subsided before Whitefield's arrival but had reacted. Whitefield restored it; and the New England Churches received under his labours an inspiration of zeal and energy which has never died out. He extended the revival from the Congregational Churches of the Eastern to the Presbyterian Churches of the Middle States. In Pennsylvania and New Jersey where Frelinghuysen, Blair, Rowland, and the two Tennents had been labouring with evangelical zeal, he was received as a prophet from God; and it was then that the Presbyterian Church took that attitude of evangelical power and aggression which has ever since characterised it. Whitefield's preaching, and especially the reading of his printed sermons in Virginia, led to the founding of the Presbyterian Church of that State, where it extended to the South and South-West. The stock, from which the Baptists of Virginia, and those of the South and South-

[1] Dr. Abel Stevens' *History of the Methodist Episcopal Church.*

West have sprung, was also Whitefieldian. And, although Whitefield did not organise the results of his labours he prepared the way for Wesley's itinerants. When he descended into his American grave, they were already on his track. They came not only to labour, but to organise their labours; to reproduce, amid the peculiar moral necessities of the new world, both the spirit and the method of the great movement as it had been organised by Wesley in the old."

Thus we see how great a debt the American Churches owe to Whitefield, the Pioneer Evangelist, as well as to Wesley, the Constructive Ecclesiastic, to the Awakener and the Fire-Bringer as well as to the Hearth-Builder.

PART III

THE REVIVAL IN FLOOD

CHAPTER I

ENGLAND, SCOTLAND—AND MARRIAGE

"Last night God brought me hither . . . welcomed in the
name of twenty-thousand. The streets were all alarmed.
By three o'clock this morning people were coming to hear
the word of God."—WHITEFIELD at Glasgow, 1742.

DURING Whitefield's absence from England the Revival had
made great progress under the preaching of Holy Club members
and others. Charles Wesley preached at Kennington, and in
the fields of Gloucester, to thousands, and also at Kingswood
and Bristol, where great numbers were converted. Howell
Harris was busy in Wales, Benjamin Ingham (with Moravian
leanings) and others were kindling the flame in Yorkshire,
whilst John Wesley had turned the old Foundry in London
into a thronged meeting-house. Everywhere the fire of a new
religious zeal was spreading.

Whitefield enjoyed a pleasant and uneventful voyage home,
arriving at Falmouth on March 11th, 1741. In letters written
on board he revealed his intention of being back in America
within a month or two. As a matter of fact, forty months
were to elapse before he could return. Upon arrival he found
himself plunged in trouble of various kinds. Methodism at
home was breaking fast into two camps—the one Arminian
with Wesley, the other Calvinistic with Whitefield—and, as
usual in such controversies, each side contained enthusiasts
who would out-Wesley Wesley and out-Whitefield Whitefield!
These caused sad mischief between the two devoted friends.
The latter had written just before leaving Bethesda a letter in
reply to Wesley's great sermon on "Free Grace." Wesley
had, somewhat mischievously, sent a copy of that sermon to
Commissary Garden, Whitefield's pet enemy, of Charleston.
Moreover, in a preface to a volume of *Hymns and Sacred Poems*,

published by John Wesley and Charles Wesley, the doctrine of Christian Perfection had been elaborately argued. As Tyerman aptly remarks:

"That doctrine he (Wesley) never set higher than in this memorable preface—indeed, in after life, he wished to modify some of its strong assertions."

In this volume there appeared a poem of Charles Wesley's of thirty-six stanzas, which had been affixed to Wesley's sermon, and which particularly aroused Whitefield's ire. Here are some of the verses that, we may judge, affected him:

" *For every man He tasted death,*
He suffer'd once for all.
He calls as many souls as breathe
And all may hear the call.

.   .   .   .   .

A power to choose, a will to obey
Freely His grace *restores*.
We all *may* find the living way
And call the Saviour ours.

Thou canst not mock the sons of men,
Invite us to draw nigh,
Offer Thy grace to all, and then
Thy grace to most deny!

Horror to think that God is hate!
Fury in God can dwell!
God could a helpless world create
To thrust them into hell!

Down there an endless death to die
From which they could not flee—
No, Lord! Thine inmost bowels cry
Against the dire decree."

To make matters worse, a long letter sent privately by Whitefield to Wesley from Boston on September 25th, expostulating with him strongly, fell into the hands of Calvinists in London, who, without the consent of either party, promptly published it—it even appeared in the *Weekly Miscellany* of March 14th, 1741! Wesley tells us in his *Journal*:

"1741, February 1st, Sunday. Having procured one of the copies, I related, after preaching, the naked fact to the congregation, and told them, 'I will do just what I believe Mr. Whitefield would, were he here himself.' Upon which, I tore it to pieces before them all. Everyone who had received it did the same. So that, in two minutes, there was not a whole copy left."

There is not the slightest doubt that Whitefield entered upon this controversy with extreme unwillingness, and there is as little but that, once entered upon it, he was both intemperate and unwise. The initial provocation lay with Wesley, but since he was breaking new theological ground, it was justifiable provocation in the sacred cause of truth. Whitefield's worst slips in retaliation were that he divulged publicly a fact known to him privately, that Wesley had used the "lot" to decide for or against printing the "Free Grace" sermon, and further, in his persistent references publicly to his protagonists by name.

But here again, we must not forget that Wesley was eleven years Whitefield's senior, and whilst that should have demanded of Whitefield gentler treatment of his old friend, yet it also accounts for rather callow blunders on the one side, and a masterly reticence on the other.

One interesting result of the cleavage was the publication of the first Methodist newspaper. J. Lewis started it under the title of *The Weekly History, or an account of the most remarkable particulars relating to the present progress of the Gospel*. Price, One Penny. It was a small folio of four pages, issued on April 11th, 1741. Whitefield was announced as a regular contributor.

For the time being, the tide of popularity flowed with the Wesleys in London and in Bristol, and Whitefield found himself treated almost as an outcast by the crowds that once had hung upon his lips. When he took up his old stand under the trees at Moorfields, the crowd passed him by with scorn and mockery, putting their fingers in their ears! Every church was closed to him, whilst his publisher, James Hutton, whose consistent principle it was to publish only what he believed to be in accordance with the Word of God, refused any longer to print for him because of his Calvinism. His important business friend, William Seward, was dead, and a bill pertaining to the Orphan House, drawn by Seward for £350, was presented to Whitefield under threat of arrest if he failed to pay it. He was at that time already a thousand pounds in debt for his charges, and his personal funds were not more than twenty!

It is a fine tribute to his piety and his grit that, amid such general failure, his courage and faith never faltered. He spent a night in prayer, and the following morning a friend called upon him to ask his advice, on behalf of a lady, about the investment of a sum of four hundred pounds. Whitefield replied, "Let her lend it to me, and in a few months' time, God willing, she shall have it again." When all the circumstances were laid before the lady in question she cheerfully loaned the evangelist the money.

On another occasion, about this time, when he found himself penniless and forsaken, a stranger approached him and thrust a guinea into his hand, and the thought flashed upon his mind, "Cannot that God Who sent this person to give me this guinea, make it up to fifteen hundred?"

Thus he turned another financial corner. The estrangement of the public was also soon surmounted. Taking the contempt and hatred visited upon him with a noble meekness, Whitefield gathered about him a "few Free Grace Dissenters," and these erected for him a great wooden partition on a piece of ground at Moorfields. This rude structure Whitefield called his tabernacle, and it became for twelve years his cathedral. That magic voice could still charm like no other, that burning sincerity still had a message vital to the hearts of men, and crowds began to throng his morning lectures. So great, indeed, was the fresh awakening that, feeling the need for help, he called a number of lay preachers to his assistance, and in this anticipated, before Wesley, one of the greatest features of Methodism. He was still the pioneer!

After a tour of revival-preaching in Wiltshire, Essex— where he visited with great effect Braintree and Halstead— and in other counties, Whitefield responded to a very earnest and cordial invitation from the Erskines to visit Scotland. These two remarkable men, Ebenezer and Ralph Erskine, brothers, had wielded powerful ministries in their Churches; thus one of them, Ralph, was able to report:

"Sabbath, July 10th, 1737. I preached at half-past seven in the morning. The (Sacramental) Tables began to be served a little before nine, and continued till about twelve at night, there being between four and five thousand Communicants."

These brothers, with other ministers, provoked by the injustices that arose from the resuscitation of the law of patronage in the Church of Scotland by Parliament in 1712, protested and were expelled. They, therefore, with others, formed "The United Secession Church," or "The Associate Presbytery."[1] For a time these ejected ministers, like Whitefield and Wesley in England, became open-air and tent missioners. Naturally, interest and correspondence arose between men so similarly concerned with true religion in their respective countries, and Whitefield's fame and the cordial spirit of his letters commended him especially to the Erskines.

"How great is our need of such awakening gales of heaven as you speak of in your last visit to Georgia," wrote Ralph, "come, if possible, dear Whitefield, come. There is no face on earth I would desire more earnestly to see."

But at the same time, Ralph Erskine made an unfortunate and unfair stipulation.

"Such is the situation of affairs among us, that unless you come with a design to meet and abide with us of the 'Associate Presbytery,' and if you make your public appearances in the places especially of their concern, I would dread the consequence of your coming, lest it should seem equally to countenance our persecutions. Your fame would occasion a flocking to you, to whatever side you turn, and if it should be in their pulpits, as no doubt some of them would urge, we know how it would be unproven against us. I know not to whom you could safely join yourself, if not with us."[2]

In reply to this, Whitefield wrote to each brother. To Ebenezer he said:

"This morning I received a kind letter from your brother Ralph, who thinks it best for me wholly to join the 'Associate Presbytery'

[1] In 1847 this amalgamated with the Presbytery of Relief originated by the Rev. Thomas Gillespie into the United Presbyterian Church, and as this present chapter is being penned, the old feud is being healed and with the United Free Church the U.P. Church has been reincorporated in the United Scottish Presbyterian Church, disestablished in all but name. A small remnant of the United Free Church continues, however, whose earnest convictions must be respected by all, under the Moderatorship of the Rev. James Barr, B.D., M.P.

[2] "Life and Diary of Rev. Ralph Erskine." p. 322.

if it should please God to send me into Scotland. This I cannot altogether agree to. I come only as an occasional preacher, to preach the simple Gospel, to all who are willing to hear me, of whatever denomination."

To Ralph he wrote:

"I cannot but think that the 'Associate Presbytery' are a little too hard upon me. If I am neuter as to the particular reformation of Church Government till I have further light, it will be enough."

Whitefield reached Scotland on July 30th, 1741, ten years before Wesley's first visit, and at once fell to preaching at Dunfermline, where Ralph Erskine lived. He tells us how surprised he was at the Meeting House by "the rustling made by opening the Bibles all at once, a scene I never was witness to before." He preached also in Edinburgh "to many thousands in a place called Orphan House Park."

On August 5th he met the Associate Presbytery there. Some idea of the debate that followed may be gathered briefly from a letter Whitefield wrote afterwards to his friend, Mr. Noble, of New York:

"The Associate Presbytery are so confined that they will not so much as hear me preach, unless I will join with them. I . . . asked them seriously what they would have me to do? The answer was that I was not desired to subscribe immediately to the Solemn League and Covenant, but to preach only for them until I had further light. I asked, why only for them? Mr. Ralph Erskine said, 'they were the Lord's people.' I then asked whether there were no other Lord's people but themselves, and supposing others were the Devil's people, they certainly had the more need to be preached to, and therefore I was the more and more determined to go out into the highways and hedges, and that if the Pope himself were to lend me his pulpit I would gladly proclaim the righteousness of Jesus Christ therein."

With such a good case it seems a pity that Whitefield referred so rashly to the Pope before men of such keen principle.

After that, the argument became sharp indeed. Ebenezer Erskine tried to impress upon Whitefield the need for organising under some definite Church policy the crowds of converts gathered by him, and Whitefield asserted that he felt called only to preach. At one time it was contended that only one form of Church government was divine. Whitefield, laying his hand on his heart, replied, "I do not find it here." Alexander Moncrieff retorted, as he rapped the Bible, "But I find it here!"

The ultimate result of these deliberations was that the Associate Presbytery turned against Whitefield as ardently as before they had been for him. Not only did they disavow him, but preached against him, and even called him an agent of the Devil.

But Whitefield had reached Scotland, and Scotland soon knew it.

"There was commotion in all classes of Society, and no small division about this new preacher. . . . He was in a flood-tide of popularity in the Scottish capital. He had the ear of the people, from the poorest to the noblest. At seven in the morning he had a lecture in the fields, which was attended by 'the common people and by persons of rank.' . . . Children's meetings sprung up all over the city."[1]

Edinburgh, Glasgow, Dundee, Paisley, Perth, Stirling, Crieff, Falkirk, Airth, Kinglossie, Culross, Kinross, Cupar of Fife, Inverkeithing, Newbattle, Galashiels, Maxton, Haddington, Killern, Balfrome, Aberdeen, was his comprehensive itinerary, and everywhere flame burst beneath his feet.

Whitefield's troubles since his return from America seem to have ripened and mellowed his disposition, though he was always a man of ardent affections and friendliness. One sign of the deepening character, however, was a letter written from Aberdeen to Wesley asking forgiveness for a wrong he felt he had done his friend (doubtless this was the making public of the privately-known "lot" decision about the "Free Grace" sermon).

Whitefield's impact upon the aristocracy of Scotland is worthy of notice—taken as it should be in conjunction with his remarkable access to similar circles in England and America. He became the spiritual guide and adviser of such notables as Lord Rae, the Marquis of Lothian, the Earl of Leven, Lady Mary Hamilton, Colonel Gardiner, Lady Frances Gardiner, Lady Jane Nimmo and Lady Dirleton. Out of such associa-

[1] Gledstone, p. 176.

tions came great good for the common people. Out of them also came for Whitefield the gifts of a horse—a very necessary instrument—and of another £500 for his orphan family!

This first visit to Scotland was suddenly broken for an interesting purpose. Was it that gift-horse that touched his imagination, I wonder? Anyway, Whitefield suddenly rode from Scotland to Wales to get married!

We have no details of his courtship, and maybe there was none. The day before the wedding he wrote to Earl Leven:

"I find a restraint upon me now, so that I cannot write. God calls me to retirement, being to enter the marriage state to-morrow. I am persuaded your lordship will not fail to pray that we may, like Zacharias and Elisabeth, walk in all the ordinances and commandments of the Lord blameless."

The register reads as follows, in the handwriting of the Rev. John Smith, Vicar of Eglwsilan:

"George Whitefield
and
Elizabeth James,
Married, November 14, 1741."

Mrs. James was a widow of thirty-six years (Whitefield himself being but twenty-six), her maiden name being Burnells,[1] Whitefield's own sentences about her are characteristic of him:

"Once gay, but for three years last past a despised follower of the Lamb of God, neither rich in fortune nor beautiful as to her person, but I believe a true child of God, and one who would not, I think, attempt to hinder me in His work for the world."

Wesley expressed his opinion about her once as "a woman of candour and humanity." Whitefield is said to have been inspired to venture on matrimony by the idyllic union that existed between the Rev. Ebenezer Jones, of Pontypool, and his wife, and the interesting speculation has been made by some that Mrs. James was Mrs. Jones' sister.

We need not accept too readily the suggestion that Whitefield's marriage was not a happy one. The general testimony

---

[1] Gillies' *Memories of Whitefield.*

of his references to the matter show that he, at least, found considerable satisfaction; whether Mrs. Whitefield was as happy and satisfied, it is hard to say. Women expected less of a husband in those days, and she was a woman of courage and resource. Perhaps the best story about her is to the effect that when on one occasion they were both caught by an angry mob and Whitefield appeared nervous, she pulled at his gown, crying, "Now, George, play the man for God!"

But his wedding did not detain Whitefield long from his task of preaching. Within seven days he was on the move once more, and arrived at Bristol to find John Wesley stricken of a fever. Neither of them mentions any conversation on this occasion, but there can be little doubt that there was something like a reconciliation. From Whitefield's subsequent letters it appears that, from this point onward, he was rather more sympathetic to Wesley's doctrine of sanctification, especially in the more modified form in which Wesley now presented it.

When he reached London on December 4th, Whitefield found good news awaiting him from America.

"Reverend and Dear Sir," wrote the Rev. Thomas Prince from Boston, "Since my last, our exalted Saviour has been riding forth in His magnificence and glory through divers parts of our land, in as triumphant a manner as hath never been seen or heard among us, or among any other people, since the days of the apostles. . . . Almost every week we hear of new and surprising conquests. . . . Amazing works of this kind are now going on at Taunton, Middlesburgh, Bridgewater, Abington, York, Ipswich, Rowley, Cape Anne, Ritting and Berwick. On a day of fasting and prayer at Portsmouth, the Spirit of God came down and seized the people by scores and hundreds, and in three days there were a thousand in that town in deep distress about their souls."

That was the kind of news to act like a tonic upon the lion-hearted evangelist—the news that the Revival was in flood in America as well as in Britain. Whitefield himself was able to write in similar terms to Lord Rae of Scotland a few days later from Gloucester.

"In England, as well as in Scotland, the Redeemer is riding on from conquering to conquer. I have preached here twice every day for some days past."

The Methodist care of the consecrated use of time is well illustrated in a letter of Whitefield's penned at this juncture:

"Bristol, December 28, 1741.
"Dear Mr. M. . . .
"My dear wife was pretty well; I expect her here on Friday. We shall bring no more goods to London than we shall use; but I know not what to say about coming to your house, for, I am told, you and your wife are dilatory, and that you do not rise sometimes till nine or ten in the morning. This will never do for us, and I am persuaded such conduct tends much to the dishonour of God, and to the prejudice of your own precious soul. . . . Labour, therefore, my dear brother, to get an abiding presence of God in your heart. . . . Be not slothful in business. Go to bed seasonably, and rise early. Redeem your precious time. Be much in secret prayer. Converse less with man and more with God. Accept this advice, given in great love."

Events were moving rapidly in Wales at this period. Howell Harris had met with such success in preaching that about half a score of clergymen of the Established Church had gathered about him and become also itinerant preachers. A numerous body of lay-preachers had sprung into being as well, and Methodist Societies were daily increasing in numbers.[1]

The closing weeks of 1741 and the opening month of the New Year found Whitefield preaching with his usual phenomenal success in Bristol. Towards the end of this visit he went to hear Charles Wesley preach and remarks in a letter:

"Yesterday, I went to hear Mr. Charles. I believe the Lord helped him in some part of his discourse. I would be free; I would meet more than half-way; but we are all too shy. The Lord fill his soul with more of the disinterested love of Jesus."

Leaving Bristol on January 22nd, the Awakener preached thrice at Tockington, a little Gloucestershire village, then "to many thousands at Stroud with wondrous power." A fortnight spent in Gloucester from January 25th was used up in constant preaching—often three times in the day. "Here there is such an awakening," he wrote to a friend, "as I never saw in these parts before. O the blessed effect of field-preaching!"

[1] *History of the Calvinistic Methodists in Wales*, p. 8, quoted by Tyerman.

WHITEFIELD IN HIS YOUNGER DAYS

[Face page 128

Then on to Bath, where a similar programme awaited him! From Bath he proceeded to London again, writing *en route* to Lady Mary Hamilton, another Scotch friend, thus:

"Honoured Madam—I am now upon the road to London. . . . I have lately seen the Redeemer riding in His Strength and getting Himself the victory in poor sinners' hearts. . . . I have heard from my orphans to-day. They have been reduced to straits; but the Lord has stirred up a wealthy friend or two to assist them. I find there has been a fresh awakening among them. I am informed that twelve negroes, belonging to a planter lately converted at the Orphan House, are savingly brought home to Jesus Christ. I am glad to hear that the work goes on in Scotland."

Finally, writing from London, April 6th, 1742, he is able to say:

"I believe there is such a work begun as neither we nor our fathers have heard of. The beginnings are amazing; how unspeakably glorious will the end be! In New England, the Lord takes poor sinners by hundreds, I may say thousands. In Scotland the fruits of my poor labours are abiding and apparent. In Wales the Word of the Lord runs, and is glorified, as also in many places in England. In London our Saviour is doing great things daily!"

Thus in whichever direction the Evangelist turned those eager, glowing eyes of his, the spate of revival greeted his vision, and poured forth in tidal strength wherever he passed. Before we follow him North again, let us see him settled at his work for a while in London. For from this time, except for his visits to America, it became a general policy of Whitefield's to work in London at his Moorfields' centre (and later at Tottenham Court Chapel as well), throughout the winter, and tour the Provinces throughout the summer—the kind of methodical rhythm into which so true a Methodist was bound eventually to bring so great a work. After two months of wintry weather spent preaching to great crowds at the Tabernacle, Whitefield, with the early breath of Spring, stepped into the original arena of his Moorfields preachings, and took his stand once more beneath the trees of God's out-of-doors. Commencing on Easter Monday, April 19th, Whitefield preached seven sermons where "Satan's children keep their annual rendezvous." It is best to give an account in his own graphic words, culled in brief from certain letters written afterwards to friends:

"I must inform you that Moorfields is a large spacious place given, as I have been told, by one Madam Moore for all sorts of people to divert themselves in. For many years past, from one end to the other, booths of all kinds have been erected for mountebanks, players, puppet shows and such-like. With a heart bleeding with compassion for so many thousands led captive by the Devil at his will, on Easter Monday at six o'clock in the morning, attended by a large congregation of praying people, I ventured to lift up a standard amongst them in the name of Jesus Christ of Nazareth. Perhaps there were about ten thousand waiting, not for me, but for Satan's instruments to amuse them. . . . I mounted my first pulpit[1] and almost all flocked immediately around it. I preached on these words. 'As Moses lifted up the serpent in the wilderness,' etc. They gazed, they listened, they wept. All was hushed and solemn and I believe many felt themselves stung with deep convictions of their past sins. Being thus encouraged, I ventured out again at noon; but what a scene! The fields, the whole fields, seemed, in a bad sense of the word, all white, ready not for the Redeemer's but for Beelzebub's harvest. All his agents were in full motion, drummers, trumpeters, merry-andrews, masters of puppet-shows, exhibitions of wild beasts, etc., etc., all busy in entertaining their respective auditories. I suppose there could not be less than twenty or thirty thousand people. My pulpit was fixed on the opposite side and immediately, to their great mortification, they found the number of their attendants sadly lessened. Judging that, like St. Paul, I should now be called, as it were, to fight with beasts of Ephesus, I preached from these words, 'Great is Diana of the Ephesians.' You may easily guess that there was some noise among the craftsmen, and that I was honoured with having stones, dirt, rotten eggs, and pieces of dead cats thrown at me, whilst engaged in calling them from their favourite but lying vanities. My soul was indeed among lions; but far the greater part of my congregation seemed to be turned into lambs. This encouraged me to give notice that I would preach again at six o'clock in the evening. I came, I saw, but what? Thousands and thousands more than before, still more deeply engaged in their unhappy diversions; but among them, some thousands waiting as earnestly to hear the Gospel. This

---

[1] This was on view at the Centennial Exhibition in Philadelphia, U.S.A., as the property of the American Tract Society. "The portable pulpit of George Whitefield . . . is made of pinewood, and is so contrived that it can be easily taken apart and put together. The great preacher delivered more than two thousand sermons from this pulpit in the fields of England, Wales and America; and he once remarked that the Gospel had been preached from it to more than ten millions of people." From the *London Watchman and Wesleyan Advertiser*, June 14th, 1876.

was what Satan could not brook. One of his choicest servants was exhibiting, trumpeting on a large stage; but as soon as the people saw me in my black robes and my pulpit, I think, all of them to a man left him and ran to me. For a while I was able to lift up my voice as a trumpet. God's people kept praying, and the enemy's agents made a kind of roaring at some distance from us. At length they approached nearer, and the merry-andrew (who complained that they had taken many pounds less that day on account of my preaching) got upon a man's shoulders and, advancing near the pulpit, attempted many times to strike me with a long, heavy whip, but always with the violence of his motion, tumbled down. Soon afterwards they got a recruiting sergeant, with his drum, etc., to pass through the congregation. I gave the word of command and ordered that way might be made for the King's officer. The ranks opened, while all marched quietly through, and then closed again. Finding these efforts to fail, a large body on the opposite side of the field assembled together, and having got a large pole for their standard, advanced towards us with steady and formidable steps, till they came very near the skirts of our congregation. I saw, gave warning, and prayed to the Captain of our salvation for support and deliverance. He heard and answered; for just as they approached us, with looks full of resentment, they quarrelled among themselves, threw down their pole, and went their way, leaving, however, many of their company behind. I think I continued in praying, preaching and singing (for the noise at times was too great to preach) about three hours. We then retired to the Tabernacle. My pockets were full of notes from persons brought under concern. I read them amid the praises and spiritual acclamations of thousands who joined with the holy angels in rejoicing that so many sinners were snatched, in such an unlikely place and manner, out of the very jaws of death. This was the beginning of the Tabernacle Society. Three hundred and fifty awakened souls were received in one day and, I believe, the number of notes exceeded a thousand."

That was Easter Monday, and Whitefield repeated his daring programme on the Tuesday in the Marylebone fields, a similar resort. Here he had a still narrower escape, for "passing from the pulpit to the coach, I felt my hat and wig to be almost off. I turned about, and observed a sword just touching my temple. A young rake, as I afterwards found, was determined to stab me, but a gentleman, seeing the sword thrust near me, struck it up with his cane. The enraged multitude seized the man, and had it not been for one of my friends, who received him into his house, he would have undergone a severe discipline."

The next day he assailed the Moorfields task again, and this time the merry-andrew proved himself a sorry one indeed by behaviour too indecent to be described.

"I must own," says Whitefield, "that at first it gave me a shock . . . but recovering my spirits, I appealed to all since now they had such a spectacle before them, whether I had wronged human nature in saying with good Bishop Hall that 'man when left to himself, is half a devil and half a beast'."

Here, in conclusion of these memorable and unique scenes, is a characteristically tender reference of Whitefield's to the children. He writes:

"I cannot help adding that several little boys and girls were fond of sitting round me on the pulpit while I preached and handing me the people's notes. Though they were often struck with the eggs, dirt, etc., thrown at me, they never once gave way, but on the contrary, every time I was struck, turned up their little weeping eyes, and seemed to wish they could receive the blow for me."

Thus did Whitefield carry the holy war into the very heart of the enemy's forces and bring the Gospel of New Life back to the common people.

CHAPTER II

THE PREACHING BRAES OF CAMBUSLANG

"Last Lord's Day I believe, there were here thirty thousand people and above two thousand five hundred communicants."—GEORGE WHITEFIELD at Cambuslang.

WHITEFIELD'S first visit to Scotland had been attended by such fire of revival that it was not surprising to find an eager desire expressing itself that he should return. Whitefield arrived in Edinburgh on June 3rd, 1742, and good news greeted him immediately, "scarcely one of his converts," he was told, "had fallen back either among old or young." He found, too, that in his absence the good work which his coming had so mightily stimulated, had gained still further momentum and the spirit of revival was manifesting itself in a quite remarkable degree.

The centre of the new fire was Cambuslang, a small suburb of Glasgow. Its minister, the Rev. William McCulloch, is described as a man of "genuine piety, and of considerable capacity; but had nothing particularly striking either in the manner or substance of his preaching." [1] As a matter of fact he was in considerable trouble with his flock before the time of which we write. Then, in 1740, finding reports of the wonderful work of George Whitefield in America published in booklet form in Edinburgh and Glasgow he began the habit of reading to his congregation of the revival and its triumphs overseas. Many Cambuslang people were, accordingly, to be found in Whitefield's audiences at Glasgow on the occasion of his first visit. Then later the Rev. William McCulloch began to preach upon the New Birth, and after about twelve months of such preaching the fire of God fell upon the people.[2] He was soon preaching every day, and spending the rest of the day with

[1] From *Life of John Erskine, D.D.*, quoted also by Tyerman.
[2] *Revivals of Eighteenth Century*, D. Macfarlan.

133

penitents. In less than three months three hundred persons were converted! The flame spread to Kilsyth—twelve miles from Glasgow—and again the great change coincided with the minister's preaching upon the New Birth, although we note also in this instance the part played by "societies for prayer." On May 16th the minister, the Rev. James Robe invited penitents to come after his service into his barn, but the numbers were so great that the barn had to be exchanged for the Church. The neighbouring parishes of Kirkintilloch, Auchinloch, Campsie and Cumbernauld, caught fire too.

Then dramatically into this spreading heat of enthusiasm stepped Whitefield. The arrangements for his work at Edinburgh were original, and a tribute to Scottish financial perspicacity. In the park of Heriot's Hospital seats were erected for two thousand people, some of them being covered over, and these were let at various prices for the sermon. " The money thus raised . . . amounted to £260 5s. od. Out of this expenses were paid, including a £60 expenses fee to Whitefield, leaving £87 4s. od. profit for the hospital.[1] Here Whitefield preached twice every day to "great multitudes" and regularly visited the three hospitals. From Edinburgh he set out, on June 15th, upon a tour including Paisley, Irvine, and other places in the West Country, and " everywhere the greatest commotion followed his preaching."[2]

At last he reached Cambuslang, the heart of the great "Wark" as the Scots called it. A characteristic letter to Rev. William McCulloch preceded his coming,

"Edinburgh,
"June 8, 1742.

"Reverend and very dear Brother,

"I heartily rejoice at the awakening at Cambuslang and elsewhere. I believe you will both see and hear far greater things than these. I trust, that not one corner of poor Scotland will be left unwatered by the dew of God's heavenly blessing. The cloud is now only rising as big as a man's hand; in a little while, we shall hear a sound of an abundance of gospel rain. God willing, I hope to be with you at the beginning of next week."

There followed one of the most amazing fortnights of this eventful life.

[1] *The Scots Magazine*, 1742, p. 580.
[2] *Cambuslang*, by J. T. T. Brown.

WHITEFIELD PREACHING IN SCOTLAND

[*Face page* 134

"At noon," says Whitefield himself, "I came to Cambuslang, the place which God had so much honoured. I preached at two o'clock to a vast body of people, again at six in the evening, afterwards at nine. Such a commotion was surely never heard of, especially about eleven o'clock at night. It far outdid anything I ever saw in America. For about an hour and a half there was such weeping, so many falling into deep distress, and manifesting it in various ways, that description is impossible. The people seemed to be smitten in scores. They were carried off and brought into the house like wounded soldiers taken from a field of battle. Their agonies and cries were deeply affecting. Mr. McCulloch preached after I had done, till past one o'clock in the morning, and even then the people could scarcely be got to retire. Throughout the whole of the night the voice of prayer and praise might still be heard in the fields."

On Saturday, July 9th, Whitefield preached to twenty thousand people on what are still known as "The Preaching Braes." On the Sunday over thirty thousand persons were present. Scarce ever was such a sight seen in Scotland! Seventeen hundred souls took the Holy Sacrament, which was served in two great tents erected on the braes. The local historian already quoted writes: "The great multitudes that had gone away homewards from our quiet valley carried with them a report of the proceedings to places where the name of Cambuslang was before unknown. The Revival became the topic of conversation even in remote parts of the Kingdom; and when there seemed to be a subsidence of the excitement people still looked to this village to begin the work again."

On the 15th August a second Communion was held, and such a multitude gathered as had never been seen before in Scotland. Twelve ministers officiated, and the Sacrament was again served in tents, three this time, erected in the Glen. Referring to the audience of that memorable day, Mr. McCulloch writes, "that so far as I can hear, none ever saw the like in Scotland from the Revolution down, or anywhere else on a sacramental occasion. Some have called it fifty thousand, some forty thousand, and the lowest estimate, with which Mr. Whitefield agrees, makes them to have been upwards of thirty thousand. Three thousand of these took Communion. Of these some were from England

and even from Ireland and many were Episcopalians and some even Quakers."

"To us, living on the spot where everything was transacted, it is easy to fill in the colouring needed to give life to the varied pictures presented to our imagination. The overhanging cliffs topped by the God's acre 'where human harvests grow,' the green slopes and the little brook, are as they ever were; and lingering there the summer twilight still lends the sublimity of calmness which, no doubt, often seemed to the vast congregations on our Preaching Braes, like a realisation of devotion within the eternal temple itself." [1]

The Cambuslang revival shook the whole of Scotland, and sent its fire over all the country. Moreover, there is not the slightest doubt from the foregoing that this "great awakening" in Scotland was nursed by and enveloped in the personality and work of George Whitefield.

Dr. Gillies, in his *Historical Recollections*, gives us two valuable little pen-pictures of Whitefield in Scotland. He writes: "There was something exceedingly striking in the solemnity of his evening congregations, in the Orphan-house park at Edinburgh and the High Church-yard at Glasgow, especially towards the conclusion of his sermons, when the whole multitude stood fixed, and, like one man, hung upon his lips with silent attention, and many under deep impressions of the great objects of religion and the concerns of eternity."

We must pause a moment in this record to glimpse the great heart of the evangelist as it yearns over its most distant charges. In a letter addressed to Mr. Habersham, the superintendent of the Orphan House, we find an illuminating revelation of some of Whitefield's difficulties and the spirit in which he met them.

"Edinburgh,
"24th September, 1742.

"My most endeared Friend and Brother,

"With this, I send you a 'continuation of the Orphan House Account' which I have printed to satisfy the public and to promote future collections. I yet owe upwards of £250 in England, upon the Orphan House account, and have nothing towards it. How is the world mistaken in my circumstances! worth nothing myself, embarrassed for others, and yet looked upon to abound in riches!

[1] *Cambuslang*, J. T. T. Brown.

Our extremity is God's opportunity. O faith! then trust all-conquering power. I put my trust in God, and through His mercy, I shall not miscarry. I pray for you. I think and dream of you almost continually. I long, I long to be with you, and methinks, could willingly be found at the head of you, though a Spaniard's sword should be put to my throat.[1]

"Some of my friends in Philadelphia, are suspicious that I am joined to the Moravian Brethren; but indeed I am not. My principles are still the same; only as I believe many of them love the Lord Jesus I would be friendly to them, as I would be to all others who bear the image of our common Master, notwithstanding some of my principles are as far distant from their's as the east is from the west."

Meanwhile the revival continued to spread. At Kilsyth on Sunday, October 3rd, one of the most remarkable sacraments of the revival was observed. A dozen ministers officiated and the solemnities began at eight-thirty in the morning and continued without intermission till the same hour at night. Twenty-two distinct services were held. "The work in the west goes on and increases," Whitefield wrote to a friend, "there is a great awakening also at Muthel." In a sermon delivered in London in 1769, Whitefield declared "Once when I was preaching in Scotland, I saw ten thousand people affected in a moment, some with joy, some with crying, 'I cannot believe,' others 'God has given me faith' and some fainting in the arms of friends. Seeing two hardened creatures on a tombstone, I cried out 'You rebels come down,' and down they fell directly, and exclaimed before they went away, 'What shall I do to be saved?'"

The malice and prejudice that continually pursued Whitefield wherever he went was certainly not absent from his Scottish tours and it is well illustrated by the comments of the *Scots Magazine* of 1742 (pp. 459–464). Whitefield had succeeded in raising for the funds of Bethesda no less than £300 from various audiences in Edinburgh and Glasgow.

"By his affecting comments on the widow's throwing her two mites into the treasury, many, who live on charity, have literally given him the whole of their living, and been obliged to beg their next meal. At his diets for collecting, where he

---

[1] To Whitefield's natural concern, the Spaniards had lately invaded Georgia with a fleet of 76 small ships and an army of 24,500 men. Oglethorpe, however, repulsed the attempt.

has raised the passions of his audience by a suitable sermon, his next care is to ply them while in a right frame. For this purpose, he makes his last prayer very short—thereafter pronounces the blessing without singing psalms; and then immediately falls on collecting, in which he shows great dexterity."

But alas! it was not only from secular quarters that prejudice and criticism rose to attack him. Religious people looked askance at such an extremely youthful leader—he was still but twenty-seven years of age! The Erskines and their Secessionist followers also were still bitterly hostile, and one of them, Adam Gib, published "A Warning against the Ministrations of Mr. George Whitefield." The following letter from Whitefield to a friend reveals his spirit under such provocation:

"The Messrs. Erskine and their adherents, would you think it? have appointed a public fast to humble themselves, among other things, for my being received in Scotland, and for the delusion, as they term it at Cambuslang, and other places; and all this because I would not consent to preach only for them, till I had light into, and could take, the Solemn League and Covenant. But to what lengths may prejudice carry even good men! From giving way to the first risings of bigotry and a party spirit, good Lord, deliver us!"

Whitefield's divine spirit of charity prevailed to overcome this opposition in some degree. Ralph Erskine met Whitefield shortly afterwards at Dunfermline, and was so overcome by Whitefield's magnanimity and the proofs of the Spirit's power with him, that he embraced Whitefield crying, "We have seen strange things!"

Whitefield left Scotland for London on November 1st, 1742, proceeding by road and reaching his winter quarters at the Tabernacle, Moorfields, in five days. From a letter written just after his return we learn that his wife travelled by boat and had a distressing journey. "The ship was in imminent danger, but the Lord gave her much of his presence. I trust she will be ready shortly for another voyage." The discomforts of sea-travel in those days must have been disagreeable enough for a man, and Mrs. Whitefield is doubtless deserving of our utmost admiration for her courage and her devotion to such a globe-trotting husband!

The effects of Whitefield's work in Scotland were very profound and far-reaching. Undoubtedly his labours refreshed the fountains of religious zeal for all the Churches and his catholicity of spirit was a great healing-factor amid the bitter diversions of the time concerning Church-polity. It must have been an education in Christian temper for men like the Erskines and others to meet George Whitefield. Gledstone remarks very truly upon the mellowing of Whitefield's spirit from this time onwards. The trouble and discipline he had endured and had accepted with such genuine and beautiful meekness of spirit chastened him into a noble self-mastery and self-abnegation. Writing to Wesley with whom he was now on the best of terms again he says: "Let the King live for ever, and controversy die," whilst to another friend he writes, "I care not if the name of George Whitefield be banished from the world, so that Jesus may be exalted in it."

"He went," says Gledstone, "chastened and humbled to Scotland; he returned in the power of quietness and confidence, persuaded that his was not the task of doing anything but preach the Lord Jesus, as he knew and loved Him. He had tried the disputing way in the Arminian struggle, and the quiet way in the Scotch contendings, and found the latter far preferable to the former."

Upon his return to London, Whitefield's heart was greatly uplifted to find a still further awakening in progress—the revival was in flood indeed. So great was the pressure of audiences that speedily he was compelled to enlarge the Tabernacle. Howell Harris, the great lay-preacher of Wales, was at this time in London, and preaching with great power.

During the four months which Whitefield now devoted to the Tabernacle his ministry again drew numbers of the highest personages in the land. The Countess of Huntingdon was indefatigable in leading her fellow-peeresses to hear her favourite preacher. Catherine Duchess of Buckingham; Sarah Duchess of Marlborough; and the Ladies Hastings were among those thus beguiled for their good. But Whitefield possessed a strong attraction for men, too, and such well-known figures as Lord Hervey, keeper of the privy-seal;

Charles Duke of Bolton, The Earl of Oxford, Lord Sidney Beauclerk, son of the Duke of St. Albans, and even scions of the royal house itself, such as Frederick Prince of Wales and William Augustus Duke of Cumberland, youngest son of King George II and "hero" of Culloden, were to be seen in his audiences.[1] The presence of these latter, together with the influence of the Countess of Huntingdon, undoubtedly accounts for the tolerant attitude of King George II to the Dissenting bodies. One impressive instance of the monarch's generous attitude relates to Dr. Philip Doddridge, the famous Northampton Dissenter, who, as already noted, befriended Whitefield when Dissent generally was very shy of him. Doddridge was cited to appear before the Consistory Court at Northampton, under the Five Mile Act, to answer to the charge of keeping an Academy without license of the Bishop. Doddridge refused to appear, and the case went to a Civil Court at Westminster Hall, London. There the judges decided in favour of Doddridge. The ecclesiastical authorities, however, pressed for the case to be reopened, whereupon the King himself intervened to prevent it, ordering "that in his reign there should be no prosecutions for conscience' sake." This was a definite step towards full liberty for Nonconformist educational institutions, and without doubt it was the influence of Whitefield that underlay the happy result.

Indeed, Whitefield was frequently engaged directly in the defence of the Methodist movement from legal and ecclesiastical attack. We may note two such instances about this time. One of the Methodist lay preachers had been cited for holding a conventicle in Wales, and Whitefield, upon hearing of it, at once opened a correspondence with the Bishop of Bangor. One letter read thus:

> "London,
> "Nov. 19, 1742.

"My Lord:—
"I received your Lordship's letter this evening. It confirms me in the character given me of your lordship's spirit. I verily believe you abhor everything that has a tendency to persecution; and yet, in my humble opinion, if Mr. C. . . . is not redressed, he is persecuted.

[1] *Life and Times of the Countess of Huntingdon.*

"My lord, the whole of the matter seems to be this: In Wales, they have fellowship meetings, where some well-meaning people meet together, simply to tell what God has done for their souls. In some of these meetings, I believe, Mr. C. . . . used to tell his experience, and to invite his companions to come and be happy in Jesus Christ. He is, therefore, indicted as holding a conventicle; and I find this is the case of one, if not two more.

"Now, my lord, as far as I can judge, these persons, thus indicted, are loyal subjects of his Majesty and true friends of the Church of England service, and attendants upon it. You will see, by the enclosed letters, how unwilling they are to leave the Church; and yet, if the Acts, made against persons meeting together to plot against Church and State, be put in execution against them, what must they do? They must be obliged to declare themselves Dissenters. I assure your lordship it is a critical time for Wales. Hundreds, if not thousands, will go in a body from the Church, if such proceedings are countenanced. I lately wrote them a letter, dissuading them from separating from the Church, and I write thus to your lordship, because of the excellent spirit of moderation discernible in your lordship and because I would not have (to use your lordship's own expression) 'such a fire kindled in or from your diocese'."

That last quotation—using the bishop's own words—is a master-stroke. Whitefield knew the power of the Methodist Movement, and thus subtly warned the bishop against a cleavage such as the Established Church might live to regret.

The other instance was that of John Cennick[1]—a lay preacher of the early days of the movement in Bristol who had somewhat violently espoused the Calvinistic side of the dispute between Whitefield and Wesley, and who had laboured hard as a Revival-preacher in Kingswood and London and elsewhere, particularly in Wiltshire. In the latter district he had framed for himself a preaching circuit including Lyncham, Chippenham, Avon, Langley, Hullavington, Malmesbury, Littleton-Drew, Fosham, Brinkworth, Stratton, Somerford, Tytherton and Swindon.

Cennick's experience at Swindon illustrates the frequent sufferings of the early Methodists at the hands of the populace. He was with Howell Harris and twenty-four others singing and praying in the streets of Swindon when, before he could preach, the mob "fired guns over our heads, holding the

[1] Author of the well-known " grace ", " Be present at our table Lord."

muzzles so near our faces that Howell Harris and myself were both made as black as tinkers with the powder. We were not affrighted, but opened our breasts, telling them we were prepared to lay down our lives for our doctrine. They then got dust out of the highway and covered us all over; and then played an engine upon us, which they filled out of the stinking ditches. While they played upon Brother Harris I preached; and when they turned the engine upon me, he preached. This continued till they spoiled the engine; and then they threw whole buckets of water and mud over us. Mr. Goddard, a leading gentleman of the town, lent the mob his guns, halberd and engine, and bade them use us as badly as they could, only not kill us; and he himself sat on horseback the whole time, laughing to see us thus treated. After we left the town, they dressed up two images, and called one Cennick and the other Harris, and then burnt them. The next day, they gathered about the house of Mr. Laurence, who had received us, and broke all his windows with stones, cut and wounded four of his family, and knocked down one of his daughters." [1]

A while later, when Cennick was preaching at Stratton a mob from Swindon arrived armed with "swords, staves and poles." "Without respect of age or sex they knocked down all who stood in their way, so that some had blood streaming down their faces and others were taken up almost beaten and trampled to death." In spite of such treatment, however, Cennick's persistence told on the people, and he was able to form several societies. The persecution in these villages continued, however, and at last Cennick wrote to Whitefield describing the sufferings his followers were undergoing. Whitefield thereupon wrote to the Bishop of Sarum, whose name was Sherlock, and who was a prelate of learning and real piety. Although the bishop could not do much to restrain the mob, he could prevent the clergy from inciting the crowd to violence. The result of Whitefield's appeal does not transpire, but we find Whitefield himself a few months later in this district seeking, with his innate chivalry, to share the hardships of his disciple.

Whilst Whitefield was labouring in London and planning a

---

[1] From *Cennick's Diary*, quoted by Tyerman.

great tour of the West as soon as the spring arrived, his old friend, Benjamin Ingham, was winning crowds of converts in Yorkshire and Lancashire and had founded there no less than fifty Religious Societies under Moravian ministers.

Thus the Revival, like a river in flood, sped on, gathering momentum every day.

CHAPTER III

WALES AND THE WEST

"Wales is upon my heart."—WHITEFIELD.

WHITEFIELD had used this sentence in a letter to Howell Harris written from Scotland on September 3rd, 1742. Now in January, 1743, Whitefield set out for the Principality to make a vital and lasting contribution to its religious future.

We may tarry awhile in our story here to look more closely at Howell Harris, one of Whitefield's dearest friends, and one who exercised a great influence upon him. Harris, by a curious coincidence, was born on January 23rd, 1714, on the very spot afterwards occupied by the Calvinistic Methodist Theological College at Trevecca, Breconshire. Trained and educated for the ministry of the Established Church, his prospects were suddenly ended by the death of his father, and he opened a school in Trevecca. His father's death became the occasion of religious doubt, and for a while he led a fast and gay life. His spiritual pilgrimage back to faith and Methodism was characterised by the main theological feature of that time—the gradual working through the barrenness of self-reformation and strenuous obedience to Divine command into the peace of "free grace," and a relation of such trust and submission to Christ in His redeeming love that the "dynamic" of grace became his possession. His record of this experience is valuable.

"June 18th, 1735. Being in secret prayer, I felt suddenly my heart melting within me, like wax before the fire, with love to God my Saviour; and also felt, not only love and peace but a longing to be dissolved and be with Christ, and there was a

cry in my inmost soul which I was totally unacquainted with
before, Abba, Father! Abba Father![1] I could not help calling
God my Father; I *knew* I was His child, and that He loved me
and heard me. My soul being filled and satiated cried, 'It is
enough; I am satisfied. Give me strength and I will follow
Thee through fire and water!'"

Desiring now to enter holy orders, he was refused on the
ostensible ground of extreme youth, but really because he had
begun preaching and lecturing. "Since you are advanced,"
wrote his vicar, "as far as to have your public lectures from
house to house, and even within the limits of the church, it is
full time to let you know the sin and penalty you incur by so
doing." Thus one of Wales' greatest sons and preachers was
excluded from the regular ministry. Whitefield having
initiated a correspondence, refers thus to their first meeting.
"When I first saw him my heart was closely knit to him. I
wanted to catch some of his fire, and give him the right hand
of fellowship with my whole heart." It was from Harris' bold
conduct at a country fair that Whitefield received the inspiration
to make similar attacks upon the pleasure-grounds of the people.
The story is worth repeating. Being with Harris at such a
place near Bristol, Whitefield was much troubled in his preaching
by the pranks of a merry-andrew who, possessed of unusual
talent, actually succeeded in reducing the redoubtable George
to silence by his mockery. Whitefield requested Harris to
mount the platform and try what he could do. Taking for his
text the words, "The great day of His wrath is come, and who
shall be able to stand?" he was answered by the poor buffoon,
"I am able." Whereupon Harris exclaimed in a tremendous
voice, looking at him with piercing eyes, "What! such a poor
contemptible worm as thou art!" The words were no sooner
uttered than the clown fell to the ground helpless, overcome
by a peculiar tremor, from which it is said he never recovered.[2]
This incident seems to have settled Whitefield in his courage
for such occasions for on a later occasion he declared, "I told
my fellow-travellers that I was resolved to follow the example
of Howell Harris in Wales, and to bear my testimony against

---

[1] *Life of Howell Harris*, by Hugh J. Hughes. Psychologists will be interested in this naïve confession in view of Harris' recent loss of his father.
[2] *Life of Howell Harris*, by Morgan, p. 58.

such lying vanities let the consequences to my own private person be what they would."[1]

The inspiration that passed between these two men was perfectly mutual, iron sharpening iron, and Howell Harris became one of Whitefield's preachers.

Harris was a man of superb courage, and he needed it all, for the mob was merciless to him, yet in spite of the often calculated mischief plotted against him, of which the rabble were but the tool, his work proceeded apace. The Revival was soon in flood in Wales. "The people are wounded by scores and flock under the word by thousands," wrote Harris to Whitefield in Scotland.

It was because the revival had now assumed such proportions, and that divisions were appearing among the converts, that Whitefield hastened to Wales to attend the first Calvinistic Methodist Conference held at Waterford on January 5th, 1743. That memorable conference was made up of four clergymen, George Whitefield, Daniel Rowlands, Rector of Llangeitho, J. Powell and William Williams, curate of Llanwithiel; and of three lay-preachers, Howell Harris, Joseph Humphreys and John Cennick. The choice for Moderator fell upon Whitefield. This was a great tribute to the evangelist. But it is plainly remarkable that whilst Howell Harris took the initiative in founding Societies and launching this first Conference, it was to his bosom-friend, George Whitefield, that he turned when requiring a leader for the new régime. It is the most eloquent kind of testimony to the supreme value and prestige of Whitefield in the total Revival situation on its Calvinistic side. Whitefield is so laden with honour as the pioneer evangelist of the Evangelical Revival that there is no need to snatch at any dubious extra dignity for him. Under Whitefield's guidance a series of wise regulations were devised for the new Societies and their ministries, the lay-preachers being divided into Superintendents and Exhorters, each superintendent being given a certain district. Each public exhorter was given twelve or fourteen Societies to overlook. The headquarters of the new organisation was to be the Moorfields' Tabernacle, London. In these particulars we have defined for us very clearly and emphatically,

[1] *Life of Whitefield*, Phillips.

146

HOWELL HARRIS

Co-founder with Whitefield of Welsh Calvinistic
Methodism (Photograph supplied by Rev. Elvet
Lewis, M.A.).

[*Face page* 146

Whitefield's large share in the founding of Welsh Calvinistic Methodism.

It was no mere figure-head Moderator that Whitefield became either, as the preaching-tour which followed speedily made manifest. It was indeed as "The Awakener" that the newly-appointed Moderator travelled the length and breadth of his new diocese.

Saturday, April 9th.—Preached at Cardiff, and at Fonmon. At Cardiff the congregation large; and the greatest scoffers quiet.

Sunday, April 10th.—Preached twice at Lantrissaint, where Howell Harris also preached in Welsh (and also, according to Harris, at Penmarc.)

Monday, April 11th.—Preached from a balcony, in the street, at Neath, to about three thousand people.

Tuesday, April 12th.—Preached once at Harbrook, and twice at Swansea, the congregations at the latter place consisting of four thousand persons. (In all these visits, he was accompanied by Howell Harris, who generally preached in Welsh, after Whitefield's sermon was concluded.)

Wednesday, April 13th.—Preached twice at Llanelly, and once at Abergwilly.

Thursday, April 14th.—Preached twice at Carmarthen, "one of the greatest and most polite places in Wales"; in the morning from the top of the cross; in the evening, from a table near it. It was the Great Sessions. The Justices desired I would stay till they rose, and they would come. Accordingly they did, and many thousands more, and several people of quality.

Friday, April 15th.—Preached at "Narberth, to some thousands, with great power."

Saturday, April 16th.—Preached at Newton, and at Jeffreston to "several thousands, very like the Kingswood colliers."

Sunday, April 17th.—"Preached at Llys-y-fran, and had, as it were, a Moorfields' congregation, 'also to about the same number near Haverfordwest.'"

Wednesday, April 20th.—"Preached, at eight in the morning, to about eight thousand people at Carmarthen; and in the afternoon, to several thousands, at Narberth."

Thursday, April 21st.—"Preached this morning at Larn, and coming over the ferry, had an unexpected compliment paid me, of one ship firing several guns, and of some others hoisting their flags. The afternoon I preached at Kidwelly, to a large congregation. One of the ministers preached against me last Sunday, and mentioned me by name; but, like my other opposers, and like the viper biting the file, he only hurt himself."

Friday, April 22nd.—"Preached twice at Carmarthen, to about ten thousand people. We had another blessed Association, and have now settled the counties in Wales."

And so, according to the Awakener's own testimony,[1] on to Llangathan and Llandovery, Brecon, Trevecca and Guenfithen, Builth and Gore and, as he crossed the border, Leominster, Hereford, Ross, whence he sped to Gloucester. In three weeks Whitefield had travelled four hundred miles, spent three days in attending Associations, preached forty times, visited thirteen towns and covered seven counties.

Thus was Methodism in its Calvinistic aspect soundly rooted in the religious life of Wales.

There is little doubt that the reason why Whitefield postponed his proposed return to Georgia at this time was because of the duties and responsibilities thrust on him by his Moderatorship, and it is certainly interesting to reflect that had George Whitefield cared to exert his powers in this more constructive kind of work he might have rivalled even John Wesley in his capacity for organisation.[2]

Whitefield found that the "barn," his favourite preaching place in Gloucester, had been turned in his absence, into a "commodious chapel." After preaching there three or four times he departed for London and his beloved Moorfields. Staying just over a month in London the Awakener set out once more for the West, preaching all the way from London to Gloucester, then at Fairford, Burford, Bengeworth, Stroud, Hampton, Bristol and Kingswood. Thence he went through John Cennick's "danger-zone" in Wiltshire, much to that worthy's delight. Wednesday, June 29th, 1743, saw him in Trevecca opening another Association of the Calvinistic Methodists.

"About eight we opened the Association with great solemnity.

---

[1] The above itinerary is quoted by Tyerman from Whitefield's letter to his secretary, Syms.
[2] A fact which gives weight to the observation on page 23.

Our Saviour was much with me, teaching and helping me to fill my place in a particular manner. About midnight, we adjourned, but several of the Brethren sat up all night and ushered in the morning with prayer and praise. About eight we met again, and were greatly delighted at the simple accounts the superintendents brought in of their respective Societies. . . . Indeed, Jesus has done great things in Wales. The work is much upon the advance. I was surprised to find so much order. Brother Howell Davies has been blessed to the conversion of a young clergyman,[1] rector of St. Bartholomew's, London."

On his return journey, Whitefield had an exciting time at Hampton. One of his preachers, Thomas Adams, whose name will ever be revered in that district, had recently been disgracefully persecuted there by the mob. Hence Whitefield, as was his custom, deliberately visited the place.

"On Thursday last, I came here, expecting to be attacked, because the mob had threatened that if I ever came again they would have my black gown to make aprons with. No sooner had I entered the town than I heard the signals, such as the blowing of horns and ringing of bells, for gathering the mob. My soul was kept quite easy. . . . As it happened I finished my sermon, and pronounced the blessing, just as the ringleaders of the mob broke in upon us. One of them, as I was coming down from the table, called me a coward; but I told him they should hear from me in another way. I then went into the house and preached upon the staircase to a large number of serious souls; but the troublers of Israel soon came in to mock and mob us. As you know, I have very little actual courage; but I leaped downstairs, and all ran before me." If the mischief-makers did not damage Whitefield, however, they seriously hurt some of his helpers, and poor, brave Adams was thrown "a second time into the pond"—the Bourn Brook —receiving a "deep wound on the leg."

Finding such experiences all too common, especially in Wiltshire, Whitefield and his preachers decided to invoke

[1] The Rev. Richard Thomas Bateman—"a man of high birth and great natural endowments." After preaching for four years with great power in Wales he returned to St. Bartholomew's in London, in 1747, and threw it open to Whitefield and Wesley. He was a member of Wesley's 1748 Conference. (Journals of J. and C. Wesley).

the aid of the law. In view of this decision, Whitefield set out upon his return to London, preaching all the way.

He carried, eventually, a particularly glaring instance to the Gloucester Assizes on March 3rd, 1744. The action was brought against five of the ringleaders of the mob. The day of trial was observed as a day of fasting and prayer by all the Societies in England and Wales and Scotland. The case was triumphantly successful. "I then retired," says Whitefield, "to my lodgings, kneeled down, and gave thanks, with some friends. Afterwards, I went to the inn, prayed and returned thanks, with the witnesses; exhorted them to behave with meekness and humility to their adversaries; and sent them home rejoicing. In the evening I preached on these words, "By this I know that Thou favourest me, since Thou has not suffered mine enemy to triumph over me."

From Hampton, *en route* for London, the Awakener passed through Bristol where "he preached four times in the fields, to congregations as large as those at the beginning of his career."

At Exeter his audience on the Southernhay Green numbered upwards of ten thousand, "just like a Moorfields' congregation," says Whitefield—his frequent standard of comparison.

At Northampton, it is gratifying to record, he found a good friend in one of the most outstanding Dissenters of the period, Philip Doddridge. There was at this period an extraordinary diffidence in all religious circles, Dissenting and Established, regarding emotion. A paralysis of timidity and caution lay upon Nonconformity—perhaps due in part to the exhausting struggles of a previous time. "Enthusiasm" was regarded with pious horror, and the word actually became a synonym for disorder and irreverence. This curious use of the word is well illustrated in a letter written by Doddridge in defence of Methodists:

"In some extraordinary conversions there may be and often is a tincture of enthusiasm, but, having weighed the matter diligently, I think, a man had better be a sober, honest, chaste, industrious enthusiast, than live without any regard to God and religion at all. I think it infinitely better that a man should be a religious Methodist than an adulterer, a thief, a swearer, a drunkard, or a rebel to his parents, as I know some actually

JOHN WESLEY

CHARLES WESLEY

PHILIP DODDRIDGE

ISAAC WATTS

[*Face page* 150

were who have been wrought upon and reformed by these preachers."

The following letter to Doddridge on behalf of the famous Coward Trust is not without humour in view of the reverence with which, to-day, both Doddridge and Methodists are viewed:

"It was with the utmost concern that I received the information of Mr. Whitefield's having preached last week in your pulpit, and that I attended the meeting of Coward's Trustees this day, when that matter was canvassed, and that I now find myself obliged to apprise you of the very great uneasiness which your conduct herein has occasioned them. . . . The Trustees are particularly in pain for it with regard to your academy as they know it is an objection made to it by some persons in all appearance seriously, and by others craftily; and yet they are afraid of giving their thoughts even in the most private manner concerning it, lest it should be made an occasion of drawing them into a public opposition to the Methodists as they are likely to be in some measure by your letter to Mr. Mason (excusing your prefixing a recommendation of a book of theirs, without the advice of the Trustees) which latter they have desired me to inform you has given them great offence."

In spite, however, of such censure, Doddridge continued his support of Whitefield. It was a support given more, perhaps, on the ground of that principle of liberty which was to Doddridge the highest good, than out of great love for Whitefield, of whom he wrote in one of his replies to Neal: " I am not so zealously attached to him as to be disposed to celebrate him as one of the greatest men of the age, or to think that he is the pillar that bears up the whole interest of religion among us "—a sober judgment that can be excused in so notable a contemporary. Doddridge's opinion of Wesley seems to have been equally sober.[1]

The people of Northampton, however, seemed to have plenty of use for "enthusiasm" in religion, for Doddridge's chapel was so overcrowded that two windows had to be taken out to let fresh air in, and Whitefield's sermon *out* to the multitude that besieged the building.

Whitefield was in haste to return to London for another reason beside the impending appeal to the law. He was expecting the birth of a son. In view of this delightful event

[1] *Philip Doddridge*, by Stanford.

Whitefield endeavoured to play the part of an attentive and considerate husband settling in London and tearing himself away from his great work sufficiently, for example, to take his wife for a drive one day acting upon advice. But fine rider as he was, he was not very skilled in driving, and he landed them both in a ditch fourteen feet deep! Mrs. Whitefield, with great presence of mind, by stretching her arms across the chaise and gripping the further side, managed to prevent their being actually thrown out of the vehicle. They were hastily and with some difficulty rescued by passers-by, Whitefield having, eventually, flung himself on the back of the horse to prevent its struggling and kicking. He writes about it with husbandly equanimity. "But, oh amazing love! We were both so strengthened, that the chaise and horse being taken up, and our bruises washed with vinegar in a neighbouring house, we went on our intended way and came home rejoicing in God our Saviour." But probably sad mischief had been wrought, as the sequel shows. A month afterwards his son was born—October, 1743, and when a week old the infant was baptized in the Tabernacle before a large congregation.

Whitefield and his wife were very poor at this time—supreme religious orator of two nations though he was—and this child was born into a home furnished only with a few borrowed "sticks." He wrote to an old friend about it in these words: "This afternoon I received your kind letter, and thank you a thousand times for your great generosity in lending me some furniture, having little of my own. I know who will repay you. Next week, God willing, my dear wife and little one will come to Gloucester, for I find it beyond my circumstances to maintain them here." But within three weeks Whitefield was penning from the Bell Inn, his brother's house, news of the little one's death, hiding a broken heart beneath a brave faith. Was that unhappy ride the cause of so untimely an end? Or was it the risks of travel from London to Gloucester in those difficult days in the depth of winter?

"Last night," he writes piteously, "February 8th, 1744, I was called to sacrifice my Isaac—I mean to bury my own child and son, about four months old. Many things occurred to make me believe he was not only to be continued to me, but to be a preacher of the everlasting gospel. Pleased with the thought, and ambitious of having a son of my own so divinely employed, Satan was permitted to give me wrong impressions, whereby, as I now find, I misapplied several texts of Scripture. . . . Upon these grounds, I made no scruple of declaring 'that I should have a son, and that his name was to be John.' I mentioned the very time of his birth, and fondly hoped that he was to be great in the sight of the Lord! . . . the child was even born in a room which the master of the house had prepared as a prison for his wife, on account of her coming to hear me. Upon my coming here, without knowing what had happened, I inquired concerning the welfare of parent and child, and by the answer found that the flower was cut down. Immediately called all to join in a prayer, in which I blessed the Father of mercies for giving me a son, continuing it to me so long, and taking it from me so soon. All joined in desiring that I would decline preaching till the child was buried; but I remembered a saying of good Mr. Henry, 'that weeping must not hinder sowing,' and therefore preached twice the next day, and also the day following, on the evening of which, just as I was closing my sermon, the bell struck out for the funeral.

"At first, I must acknowledge, it gave nature a little shake, but looking up, I recovered strength, and then concluded with saying that this text on which I had been preaching, namely, 'All things work together for good to them that love God,' made me as willing to go to my son's funeral as to hear of his birth.

"Our parting from him was solemn. We kneeled down, prayed, and shed many tears, but I hope tears of resignation; and then, as he died in the house wherein I was born, he was taken and laid in the church where I was baptized, first communicated and first preached. . . ."

It was said that ever afterwards there was one sermon of Whitefield's which, whenever he preached it, was so laden with pathos and power that it never failed to melt vast audiences into tears—the subject being, "Abraham's offering up of Isaac." "Adieu! adieu! my son," Whitefield would cry in agonising tones. "The Lord gave thee to me and the Lord calls thee away; blessed be the name of the Lord. Adieu, Isaac! my only son, whom I love as my own soul! Adieu! Adieu!"

And when all hearts were in the hollow of his hand:—
"But! .behold! I show you a mystery hid under the sacrifice
of Abraham's only son which, unless your hearts are hardened,
must cause you to weep tears of love and that plentifully too.
I would willingly hope you even prevent[1] me here and are ready
to say, 'It is the love of God in giving Jesus Christ to die for
our sins.' Yes, that is it!"

[1] 'Prevent' namely 'anticipate'.

CHAPTER IV

THE AWAKENER'S FIFTH VOYAGE

"Here are thousands and thousands in these parts of America who, as to spiritual things know not their right hand from their left; and yet are ready to hear the Gospel from my mouth."—GEORGE WHITEFIELD at Philadelphia, 1747.

A CONTROVERSY into which Whitefield entered at this time, with the Bishop of London, is worthy of record in view of the attitude it reveals, on the part of the Revival leaders, to their standing in the Established Church. Certain anonymous papers against the Methodists were circulated among the Religious Societies, and the Bishop of London was suspected of being their author. Whitefield endeavoured by advertisement and by a direct appeal, to ascertain their authorship before replying and then, fairly sure of their origin, he addressed a trenchant reply to the Bishops as being responsible, at least, for the further publication of the papers.

In this letter Whitefield charged the writer with seeking to prove that Methodism was dangerous to Church and State in order to force the Methodists to turn Dissenters. "As yet," Whitefield wrote, "we see no sufficient reason to leave the Church of England and turn Dissenters; neither will we do it until we are thrust out." In order to reply to the charge of the pamphlet that Methodists were breaking statute law by field-preaching, Whitefield made a special study of all the Acts of Charles II in which the term "field" was mentioned, and asserted as his conclusion that only seditious conventicles were condemned thereby—an offence of which Methodists were not guilty. Whitefield followed this up by a defence of his plan of field-preaching as being but a following of the example of the Lord and His Apostles. "What if the Methodists,"

155

he burst forth, "do incite the rabble . . . ? These rabble, my lord, have precious and immortal souls, for which the dear Redeemer shed His precious blood, as well as the great and rich. These, my lord, are the publicans and harlots that enter into the Kingdom of Heaven while self-righteous professors reject it. To show such poor sinners the way to God . . . and to pluck them as firebrands out of the burning, the Methodist preachers go out into the highways and hedges. If this is to be vile, by the help of my God, I shall be more vile."

It was a powerful and convincing reply.

Strong appeals now began to reach Whitefield from America to return, not only to Savannah, but also to his great itinerant ministry among the American Churches. Accordingly he took passage in a ship that was to sail from Portsmouth in June, 1744. The captain, however, took fright at the evangelist's reputation lest he should "spoil his crew," and cancelled the booking. Incidentally this turned out well, for it brought Whitefield to Plymouth, which had need of him. A number of the "baser" sort there had determined to make things as hot as possible for the "enthusiast," and as it was supposed that Whitefield might preach in the Hoe immediately on arrival they had a performing bear and a drum there in readiness. But the Awakener did not arrive till the next evening. He was not permitted to be long in doubt as to the character of his welcome, for a gang of men broke into his room, without, however, doing him any bodily harm. The next incident in this exciting reception was that he actually entertained his own appointed murderer to supper. An attempt was made to decoy him out to supper at a tavern in the town by a man who represented himself as the nephew of a friend in New York. Whitefield invited the man to sup with him instead. "He came, we supped, I observed that he frequently looked around him, and seemed very absent; but having no suspicion I continued in conversation with him and with other friends till we parted. I now find that this man was to have been the assassin; and, that, being interrogated by his companions as to what he had done, he answered that being used so civilly, he had not the heart to touch me." A crony of this man's, however, did actually assault George Whitefield in his room with a golden-headed cane, but the evangelist's stentorian voice brought speedy aid. Whitefield quotes in comment:

> "Thus Satan thwarts and men object
> But yet the thing they thwart effect."

Whitefield refused to prosecute his assailant. As was so often the case elsewhere, so at Plymouth, great antagonism was accompanied by great success. Over a period of about six weeks, whilst detained by the presence of French men-o'-war in the Channel, Whitefield preached with stirring effect in Plymouth and its neighbourhood.

"There is a ferry over to Plymouth, and the ferrymen are now so much my friends, that they will take nothing of the multitude that came to hear me preach, saying 'God forbid that we should sell the word of God.'"

One of the fruits of this preaching at Plymouth was the remarkable conversion of Henry Tanner, afterwards Minister of the Tabernacle at Exeter, built in 1769 through his exertions. A youth of twenty-six, he was working in a shipwright's yard when he heard Whitefield's voice from a great distance. Deeming the Awakener mad, he, with half-a-dozen friends, stuffed stones into their pockets and set off to assault the preacher. Whitefield's text was Acts xvii, 19, 20, "May we know what this new teaching is." Tanner was arrested by the coincidence of the text with his own amazed curiosity and decided to hear Whitefield again the next evening. On that occasion conviction of sin laid hold of his soul, and he cried out in agony of mind, and, coming yet a third time to hear the great preacher, he found the peace of God. Tanner at once joined the Society Whitefield had started in Plymouth, and in spite of persecution from his wife as well as others, began preaching the truth he had found.

Whilst Whitefield was incurring such risks and achieving such triumphs in Plymouth, the Methodists of Exeter who were at this time all Whitefieldian, were passing through a storm of mob-persecution. The scandalous and terrible treatment meted out to them, especially to the Methodist women, was exposed fully by Whitefield in a publication that deserves our notice—the *Christian History*, the organ of the Revival on its Whitefieldian side. This had been developed from the *Weekly History*, and whilst still printed and sold by J. Lewis, of Bartholomew's Close, it was under Whitefield's control, and was doubtless his property.[1] It was discontinued upon White-field's return to England in 1748. Here again, this time in religious journalism, Whitefield is pioneer.

Whitefield sailed from Plymouth on August 10th, 1744, and, after a terribly dangerous and rough voyage reached York in New England on October 26th. England and France were at war and showing no mercy to each other's shipping. Helped perhaps by the prevailing nervousness, Whitefield rapidly organised religious services on board, and a curious sequel occurred to the praying and preaching that became the every day routine. A collision occurred between the vessel White-field was on, the *Wilmington*, and another, to the damage of the latter. When this was reported to the convoying ships the comment was all too readily forthcoming, "this is your praying and be d . . . to you." Whitefield took the blasphemy as a challenge, and lifting up his mighty voice he cried dramatically, "God of the sea and God of the dry land, this is a night of rebuke and blasphemy; show Thyself, O God, and take us under thy own immediate protection; be Thou our convoy, and make a difference between those who fear Thee and those who fear Thee not." The next day the *Wilmington*, during a furious gale, was parted from the convoy for the rest of that voyage, and made the journey in perfect safety! One day they had a false alarm. Deeming themselves pursued by two enemy ships, the alarm was sounded, guns were sighted, arms distributed, chains put about the masts, decks cleared! "All," says Whitefield, "except myself, seemed ready for fire and smoke. My wife, after having dressed herself to prepare for all events, set about making cartridges, whilst I wanted to go into the holes of the ship, hearing that was the chaplain's usual place. I went, but not liking my situation, I crept upon deck, and for the first time in my life, I beat up to arms, by a warm exhortation."[2] The pursuers turned out to be harmless friends who had also been separated from the convoy!

Arrived at last at York, New England, Whitefield was prostrated by an attack of nervous colic due to a surfeit of potatoes

---

[1] Mr. Whitefield had *ordered* it to be printed in a pocket volume as judging it less cumbersome. *Cf.* No. 5. Vol. VI.
[2] *Cf.* letter to Ralph Erskine, p. 122.

eaten when he and his company were all but starved. Whitefield says he "could have gnawed the very boards." For four days his life hung in the balance. A friend, with a physician, hurried from Boston, "either to take care of me or attend my funeral; but to their great surprise they found me in the pulpit." Whitefield always declared that the pulpit was his "grand catholicon," his panacea for every ailment!

The following day he crossed the ferry to Portsmouth, New England, for the same purpose, renewed his cold and was disabled again. A substitute was found, but at the time of the service Whitefield suddenly exclaimed to the three doctors attending him "my pains are suspended; by the help of God, I will go and preach, and then come home and die." The rest of the incident is told in his own words:

"With some difficulty I reached the pulpit. All looked quite surprised. I was as pale as death, and told them they must look upon me as a dying man; and that I came to bear my dying testimony to the truths I had formerly preached amongst them, and to the invisible realities of another world. I continued an hour in my discourse and nature was almost exhausted, but O, what life, what power, spread all around! All seemed to be melted, and were in tears. Upon my coming home, I was laid on a bed upon the ground, near the fire; and I heard them say, 'He is gone', but God was pleased to order it otherwise. I gradually recovered, and soon after, a poor negro woman came, sat down upon the ground, looked earnestly in my face, and said, 'Master, you just go to heaven's gate; but Jesus Christ said, Get you down, get you down; you must not come here yet. Go first, and call more poor negroes.' You will find by this, I am still alive; and if spared to be made instrumental in making any poor dead soul alive to God, I shall rejoice that the all-wise Redeemer has kept me out of heaven a little longer."

Whilst his health was thus affected Whitefield was also the subject of a series of hostile attacks by pamphlets and sermons. There is no need to enter into the unprofitable discords of these letters excepting to say that Whitefield gave as good as he received. Some famous men tilted against him, including Dr. Timothy Cutler, president of York, in 1719, and afterwards rector of Christ Church, Boston, the Rev. Charles Chauncey, D.D., pastor of the First Church in Boston from 1727-1787, and the Rev. Edward Igglesworth, D.D., professor of Divinity at Harvard.

Whitefield preached in the neighbourhood of Boston, and in the city itself for three months. Great crowds hung upon his utterances every day, and all the scenes of commotion that attended his previous visit to the city were repeated. The audiences at his morning lectures alone achieved an average of two thousand in number.[1] His presence in Boston at this time proved to be the turning point in a picturesque and striking development of the colonial empire. The island of Cape Breton—the key to Canada—had till now been a French possession—a centre of great fishery enterprise and other commercial undertakings. Moreover, English ships were greatly exposed to privateers and men-of-war issuing from the island. A plan was formed to attack and appropriate the place. Colonel Peperell raised a force of six thousand men and personally begged Whitefield to bless the expedition, but the evangelist, to his credit, was very loath to do so. The general then became insistent that with Whitefield's tremendous public influence for him to refuse was to seriously affect recruiting both of men and resources. After much prayer and thought Whitefield yielded to the extent of providing a motto, "*Nil desperandum. Christo duce.*" "Upon this great numbers enlisted," and Whitefield preached a sermon before the expedition embarked. It was entirely successful, though only after a stern and desperate struggle.

Whitefield seems always to have shown a commendable hesitancy in sanctioning the process of war, which is some compensation for his deplorable blind-spot on slavery.

The Awakener's subsequent itinerary from Boston to Bethesda is a little obscure. "As his bodily strength increased, he began to move further southward; and after preaching eastward as far as Casco Bay and North Yarmouth, he went through Connecticut, Plymouth and Rhode Island preaching to thousands, generally twice a day."[2]

"Though there was much smoke, yet every day I had convincing proof that a blessed gospel fire had been kindled in the hearts both of ministers and peoples."

In the neighbourhood of Philadelphia he was the subject of many tempting financial offers—one gentleman inviting him to preach at a certain centre for six months only of every year

---

[1] Andrews' *Life of George Whitefield*.   [2] Dr. Gillies.

at £800 a year. There were other similar requests but, writes the Awakener to his mother, "as yet the Lord Jesus keeps me from catching at the golden bait." "On my way to Philadelphia," he also records, "I had the pleasure of preaching, by an interpreter, to some converted Indians, and of seeing nearly fifty young ones in a school near Freehold, learning the Assembly's catechism. A blessed awakening had been begun among the Delaware Indians by the instrumentality of Mr. David Brainerd." Brainerd was a great missionary genius— a Yale man who was expelled in 1742 because of outspoken criticism of the irreligiousness of a tutor. The following year he began work among the Indians, living as nearly as possible as one of themselves. Unhappily, a great career was cut short in early life, and he died at Jonathan Edwards' house at the age of only twenty-nine.

After a very successful tour of Maryland, and with a gap of three months unaccounted for, but probably spent in "ranging and hunting" for souls in the great forests, Whitefield reached Bethesda in January, 1746. There he was speedily busy on the audit and presentation of the Orphanage accounts in order to silence and dumbfound his malicious critics. A visitor to the Orphanage who had come with hostile intent at this time, has left the following testimony: "It gave much satisfaction to have an opportunity to see Mr. Whitefield's Orphan House, as the design had made such a noise in Europe, and the very being of it was so much doubted everywhere, that even no farther from it than New England, affidavits were made to the contrary. . . . Prepossessed with a bad opinion of the institution, I made all the inquiries I could, and, in short, became a convert to the design which seems very conducive to the good of the infant colony. . . . I could not here perceive anything of that spirit of uncharitableness and enthusiastic bigotry for which their leader is so famed, and of which I heard shocking instances all over America."

One cannot repress something like a shudder at such an exclamation on the part of a good man as the following: "God has put it into the heart of my Carolina friends to contribute liberally towards purchasing a plantation and slaves, in that province, which I purpose to devote to the support of Bethesda." And later, "Blessed be God, the purchase is made. One negro has been given me; some more I purpose to purchase this week." All one can say, in fairness to Whitefield's blind-spot, is that at least the frankness of his association of God with slavery shows his utter sincerity. His position was largely due to the influence of the equal flat-rate value given to all parts of Scripture by the view of the Bible prevailing at the time whereby the slavery of the Old Testament was made as authoritative as the freedom of the New. Whitefield's argument in defence of his position reveals this mischievous but all too common attitude. He says:

"As for the lawfulness of keeping slaves I have no doubt, since I hear of some that were bought with Abraham's money, and some that were born in his house and I cannot help thinking that some of those servants mentioned by the apostles in their epistles were, or had been, slaves. It is plain that the Gibeonites were doomed to perpetual slavery; and though liberty is a sweet thing to such as are born free, yet to those who never knew the sweets of it, slavery may, perhaps, not be so irksome."

What is the significance one wonders of that "perhaps?" Were there some lurking spasmodic workings of doubt in his profoundly human heart?

During the succeeding months of 1746 the Awakener again visited Maryland and also toured Virginia where a remarkable revival had sprung up, due solely to the mere reading of a volume of his sermons.

His health, however, began now to give him fresh trouble. The convulsions, that had brought him so near death at Portsmouth, returned. "My body is weak and crazy," he wrote, and later under date, May 21st, 1747, "I have now been upon the stretch preaching constantly for almost three weeks. My body is often extremely weak but the joy of the Lord is my strength, and by the help of God I intend going on until I drop. These southern colonies lie in darkness and yet, as I find, are as willing to receive the Gospel as others." In 1747 Whitefield was again in New England and at Boston where he wrote, "I have been in New England nearly three weeks. The Lord is with me. Congregations are as great as ever. I could gladly stay in New England, but I must return to the southern provinces. Though faint, I am still pursuing, and, in the strength of Jesus, hope to die fighting."

Being weighed down at the same time with a burden of debt for the Orphan House, he retired to Bermuda for a season of complete rest. Before he went he wrote a delightful letter to John Wesley containing the following:

"My heart is ready for an outward as well as an inward union. Nothing shall be wanting on my part to bring it about; but I cannot see how it can possibly be effected till we all think and speak the same things. I rejoice to hear that you and your brother are more moderate with respect to *sinless perfection*. . . . As for *universal redemption*, if we omit on each side the talking for or against reprobation, which we may do fairly and agree, as we already do, in giving an universal offer to all poor sinners that will come and taste of the waters of life, I think we may manage very well. . . . There is a debt, rev. sir, I shall never be able to discharge to you or your brother. Jesus will pay you all. For his sake I love and honour you very much and rejoice as much in your success as in my own."

Whitefield spent a month in Bermuda, but it could not be all rest for so ardent a spirit as his, and often he was preaching two or three times a day.

He found the gentlemen of Bermuda very generous towards his Orphanage and was able soon to remit £100.

Finding that a vessel was shortly to leave Bermuda for England, Whitefield decided to return, more especially because the season was becoming too hot for him to return with safety to the Southern States. He intended to come back the following year and rejoin his wife at Bethesda.

His brief visit to America had not, however, been in vain, though beset by bodily trials. Once again he had carried the sacred torch of Revival through the American Churches, kindling thousands of hearts to a purer flame, and he had extended the work of God by at least one whole state, namely Virginia.

During his absence from England he had received varied reports of the work in the homeland. Howell Harris had rekindled Wales once more. Cennick had succeeded Whitefield for a while at Moorfields, and had introduced "choirs" following the example of the Moravians but in December, 1745, he had seceded entirely to the Moravians. Unhappily Cennick took many people with him. This defection, accompanied by trouble over the Antinomianism which is the constant shadow upon Free Grace, had somewhat thinned out the followers of Whitefield in London. These difficulties, however, vanished like mist before the sun upon the Awakener's return.

His homeward voyage was, as usual, a period of heart-searching and deep study. With that fearless candour which was one of his most attractive traits, he acknowledges in a letter to a clergyman of South Carolina, "I have been too bitter in my zeal. Wild-fire has been mixed with it, and I find I frequently wrote and spoke in my own spirit when I thought I was writing and speaking by the assistance of the Spirit of God. . . . By these things I have given some wrong touches to God's ark, and hurt the blessed cause I would defend, and also stirred up needless opposition. This has humbled me."

The voyage was, happily, a short one, and in four weeks the Awakener was at Deal. It was in July, 1748, two days after landing, that he was received in London "by thousands with a joy that almost overwhelmed both them and me." He is soon writing to a friend; "Moorfields is as white as ever unto harvest and multitudes flock to hear the Word. The old spirit of love and power seems to be revived amongst us."

CHAPTER V

THE LADY OF THE REVIVAL

"A word in the lesson when I was at your ladyship's struck me, 'Paul preached privately to those who were of reputation'."—(GEORGE WHITEFIELD in letter to LADY HUNTINGDON.)

IN every age the moral and spiritual progress of the world has owed much to one or other of "God's good women," and the Eighteenth Century Revival was no exception to the rule.

Among the earliest of notable events that occurred upon Whitefield's return to England was a summons to wait upon the Lady Selina, the Countess of Huntingdon, at her home in Chelsea. It is time that we looked at this remarkable woman, without whose aid the work of Whitefield and Wesley would have been rendered much more difficult. From youth to the extreme age of over four score years, this brilliant and high principled woman worked alongside the leading figures of the revival, unobtrusively but with a profound consecration and a noble consistency of purpose. The Countess was born, probably at Stanton in Leicestershire, her father's house, in the reign of Queen Anne, in 1707, the year of the union of the English and Scotch Parliaments. By both parents, Washington Shirley, the second Earl Ferrers, and Mary Levinge, daughter of Sir Richard Levinge, Solicitor-General for Ireland, and Speaker of the House of Commons, she was of ancient and noble descent. Her childhood was marked by an early piety, prophecy of the passionate religious devotion of her later life.

In June, 1728, Lady Selina Shirley married Theophilus Hastings, Earl of Huntingdon, who could boast of Royal descent from the Plantagenet Duke of Clarence, brother of Edward

165

IV. The Earl was as renowned for his high moral principle and liberal temper as for his intellectual attainments and fine judgment of men and life. The intimate associate of Lord Chesterfield and Lord Bolingbroke, he easily surpassed them in worth of character. With such a husband, Lady Selina found herself constantly in the society of the highest ladies in the land. One episode from her association with these will disclose that in her earlier years she was a woman of spirit, of independent action, and bold enterprise.[1] Lady Mary Wortley Montague has told the story of how, in company with the eccentric Duchess of Queensbury (Prior's "Charming Kitty") and the Duchess of Ancaster and Lady Mary Granville (afterwards Lady Pendarvis and later still wife of Dean Delaney), they played the part of "bold asserters of liberty."

"They presented themselves at the House of Lords at nine o'clock in the morning, when Sir William Sanderson respectfully informed them that the Chancellor had made an order against their admittance. The Duchess of Queensbury, piqued at the ill-breeding of a mere lawyer, desired Sir William to let them up privately.

"After some modest refusals, he swore he would not admit them; Her Grace, with a noble warmth, answered they would come in, in spite of the Chancellor and the *whole House*. This reported, the Peers decided to starve them out; an order was made that the doors should not be opened till they had raised the siege. These Amazons now showed themselves qualified for the duty of post soldier; they stood there till five in the afternoon, without sustenance, every now and then playing volleys of thumps, kicks and raps with so much violence against the door that the speakers in the House were scarce heard.

"When the Lords were not to be conquered by this, the two Duchesses, very well apprised of the use of strategem in war, commanded a silence of half-an-hour, and the Chancellor, who thought this a certain proof of their absence (the Commons also being impatient to enter) gave orders for the opening of the door. Upon which they (the ladies) all rushed in, pushed aside their competitors and placed themselves in the front row of the gallery. They stayed there till after eleven, when the House rose, and during the debate gave applause and showed marked signs of dislike, not only by smiles and smirks (which have always been allowed in these cases) but by noisy laughter and apparent contempt, which is supposed to be the reason why Lord Hervey spoke so miserably."

[1] *The Countess of Huntingdon and Her Circle*, by Sarah Tytler.

What an interesting anticipation of the Suffragette struggles of a later century!

Undoubtedly the factor that occasioned Lady Huntingdon's interest in the Revival was the marriage of her husband's two sisters, Lady Margaret and Lady Catherine, to two English clergymen of Methodist opinions—the former to Benjamin Ingham, of the Holy Club, the founder of Yorkshire Methodism, and the latter to a Mr. Wheeler. Incidentally, too, here is eloquent testimony to the Earl's breadth of mind.

It was Lady Margaret's evident spiritual joy, gained, she declared, through "believing the Methodist doctrine," that aroused a deep concern in Lady Selina's mind as to her own condition. She was conscious beneath all her straining for the good life, of a lack of peace and harmony and well-being. A serious illness followed, during which she entered into the experience of rest and peace in Christ after a signal act of surrender and trust. John and Charles Wesley happened just then to be in the neighbourhood preaching in private houses, barns, etc., and Lady Huntingdon sent them a message of good-will. This identified her with the Methodists, and aroused a storm of indignation and insult.

In the Countess of Huntingdon's social situation, it must have taken considerable courage to be classed with the Methodists. Cæsar's household is never an easy place for saints. The aristocracy surrounding her was as worldly and vicious as it was brilliant intellectually, and this godly woman found it no easy task to bring up her children in innocence and faith amid the pitfalls and snares of Court life. The Earl of Huntingdon died in 1746, and his son Francis, the new Earl, came under the influence of his godfather, Lord Chesterfield, with whom he made the Grand Tour. It was a dangerous alliance this—between the blasé, cynical aristocratic roué, and the sheltered, well-bred, innocent youth. On the young Earl's return, we are told, "he was found to have the grace of a foreign courtier (of a 'petit maître,' in fact) but though bland and plausible, as might have been expected from the adopted son of the worldling of worldlings, Chesterfield, the young Earl lacked his father's solid worth and virtue." From that time the mother had the bitterness of seeing her son estranged by a deepening infidelity from the faith that was life itself to her.

As a further instance of her difficulties we may note that the Countess secured for her elder daughter, Lady Elizabeth Hastings, a place at Court as Lady of the Bedchamber to the two little daughters of the Prince and Princess of Wales.

Presently, however, Lady Elizabeth resigned and retired into private life. The reason has been stated by Horace Walpole:

"The Queen of the Methodists got her daughter named for Lady of the Bedchamber to the Princesses, but it is all off again as she will not let her play cards on Sundays."

A touch of principle on that chronic carelessness of life was unendurable to the cynical statesman, and a source only of mirth!

Nor was Lady Huntingdon's life without the shadow of even darker tragedy still than these. Her cousin, and her father's heir, Laurence Shirley, Earl Ferrers, came to the ghastly fate of the murderer's scaffold. A man of hot temper, he destroyed the balance of his reason still further by hard drinking. He treated his Countess—the sister of Sir William Meredith—with such habitual cruelty that at last a special Act of the two Houses of Parliament had to be passed, with the consent of the King, to secure her separation from him. That the Acts might be administered, receivers were appointed to draw his lordship's rents and apply them to the required maintenance. One of these was a Mr. Johnson—Earl Ferrers' land-steward, associated with the family from boyhood. On a certain afternoon in January, 1760, Lord Ferrers summoned Johnson to Stanton to explain his remittance of a sum of £50 to her ladyship, a circumstance which had flung the Earl into a terrible rage. The Earl sent the menservants out of the way that afternoon, and when Johnson arrived he locked the door of the room they had entered, and at the point of a pistol demanded Johnson's signature to a confession of villainy in the misappropriation of funds. Johnson obeyed the order to kneel meekly in the hope of appeasing the mad Earl's wrath, being all too used to these outbursts of passion. But the woman-servants, listening, heard the Earl shout, "Your time has come, you must die!" There was the crack of a pistol shot and then silence. The alarmed women beat upon the door and the Earl, with perfect indifference, permitted medical assistance to be summoned and Johnson's daughter to be brought. The poor girl found her father desperately wounded in the side. As the night wore on the Earl, excited further by drink, returned again and again to the room where the wounded man lay, and loaded him with abuse, being restrained with difficulty from tearing the bandages off him. In view of this persecution, the doctor removed Johnson in the middle of the night to the man's own house, where he died before morning. The Earl was immediately arrested and lodged in Leicester Gaol, whence he was presently removed to the Tower of London.

There, through the long period of the trial, he was repeatedly visited both by Lady Huntingdon and by George Whitefield. Horace Walpole waxes indignant over these visits, declaring that Lord Ferrers was "not mad enough to listen to my lady's sermons," and that Whitefield was "an impertinent fellow" for describing the Earl's heart as being "hard as a stone." The fact remains, however, that after he had refused to see his nearest relations, the doomed man admitted the Lady of the Revival, and when at last with seeming bravado and perfect equanimity he mounted the scaffold, dressed in a light suit with fittings of silver, it was to offer the prayer, "O God! Forgive me all my errors. Pardon all my sin!" Possibly Whitefield's ministrations had pierced more deeply than so proud a heart would show. Certainly Walpole's gibe, "The Methodists have nothing to brag of in his conversion . . . though Whitefield prayed for him and preached about him," is quite unproven.

Lady Huntingdon, however, wrestled bravely with her environment and one method she adopted was to fling open her drawing-room for religious services. To these she succeeded in drawing, however unwillingly they may have come, not merely the brilliant and cynical, but also the riotously vicious and notoriously unbelieving elements of her set. Indeed, there could be no more impressive tribute to the sterling character of the Lady of the Revival than the profound respect in which she was held by these elements, with one or two exceptions, such as Horace Walpole, who condemn themselves in slighting her.

It was for these drawing-room gatherings that Lady Hunting-don wanted the golden-tongued Awakener, and, obtaining his consent, she speedily appointed him one of her chaplains. This was the beginning of an alliance fraught with great consequences, and which yielded a strong impetus to the spreading Revival.

In a few days a most brilliant galaxy of aristocracy gathered about Whitefield in the home of the Countess, and once more we must pay tribute to his amazing adaptability, for he was perfectly at home with his audience. The wife of Lord Chester-field and his two sisters became consistent, life-long followers of his teaching. Even the Earl was impressed to a degree, declaring, "Sir, I will not tell you what I shall tell others, how I approve of you!" The great Bolingbroke himself would sit in these intense little assemblies "like an arch-bishop" and rather patronisingly tell Whitefield afterwards that "he had done great justice to the Divine attributes." But in a letter to his hostess he takes a warmer tone, "Mr. Whitefield is the most extraordinary man in our times. He has the most commanding eloquence I ever heard in any person." David Hume, the philosopher, was there and described White-field as "the most ingenious preacher he had ever heard." It is to this sceptical yet earnest and able thinker that we owe the following description of one of Whitefield's flights of apostrophe:

"Once, after a solemn pause, he thus addressed his audience, 'The attendant angel is just about to leave the threshold of this sanctuary and ascend to Heaven. And shall he ascend and not bear with him the news of one sinner amongst all this multitude reclaimed from the error of his ways?' To give the greater effect to this exclamation, Whitefield stamped with his foot, lifted up his hands and eyes to Heaven, and cried aloud, 'Stop, Gabriel, stop! ere you enter the sacred portals, and yet carry with you the news of one sinner converted to God!' This address was accompanied with such animated, yet natural action, that it surpassed anything I ever saw or heard in any other preacher."

It was not all Lady Selina's visitors who heard Whitefield gladly. One notorious beauty of unenviable reputation, Lady Suffolk, came to hear him. He knew nothing of her presence, though he was always peculiarly telepathic in regard to his audiences—and yet his bow, drawn at a venture, pierced the proud beauty's armour. After he had retired Lady Suffolk flew into a violent passion, abused her hostess to her face, and denounced the whole service as a personal attack upon herself. After a terrible storm of fury, she eventually apologised to Lady Huntingdon, but never again ventured into the hall of judgment.

Lady Huntingdon was in close touch with Dissent as well as Methodism, being a correspondent of Philip Doddridge and Isaac Watts, and her work now, under Whitefield's quickening interest, began to take on a richer form. Deeply concerned, by the divisions that appeared in the ranks of the new Methodist converts and by the exclusion of Methodist clergymen from the Churches of the Establishment, Lady Huntingdon, with remarkable determination and foresight, applied her great fortune and her equally great prestige to the task of securing more order and harmony in the new movement by the provision of Chapels or preaching centres. Thus originated the famous Connexion.[1] She had already promoted various schools and an orphanage at Kingswood. Later she founded the College for Methodist students at Trevecca, South Wales.[2] Now she began to build, repair and maintain many churches in different parts of the country—York and Huddersfield in the north, Gloucester and Worcester in the Midlands, Lewes and Brighton in the South, Swansea in the West, and Margate and Norwich in the East. So great was her expenditure that to build the Church at Brighton she had to part with many of her jewels. Moreover, with shrewd judgment, she provided preaching centres at Bath, Bristol, Tunbridge Wells, and Cheltenham, so that the aristocratic invalids who frequented these places might be brought under the influence of the new movement.

The men, sixty in number, placed in charge of all these centres, and who rotated in Circuits, were all Calvinistic Methodist in teaching, and were under the oversight of George Whitefield. In London, too, the Lady of the Revival helped generously to maintain Whitefield's buildings, Moorfields and Tottenham Court Chapel and others at which he preached

[1] *The Countess of Huntingdon and Her Circle*, Tytler.
[2] Subsequently Cheshunt College.

more occasionally such as Long Acre and Spa Fields. Moreover Lady Huntingdon was one of the first to see, with Whitefield, the need for lay preachers, and had some influence in eventually persuading the reluctant Wesley to agree to the idea.

It must not be imagined that the lady took only a benefactress' part in all this. No one took a greater personal interest in all organising details than the Countess. Whilst she does not seem to have spoken much in public, nevertheless "she did the work of a bishop" and took upon herself the burden of a keen personal oversight of all these causes. One snapshot of the Lady's home-life at Ashby may suffice us from the pen of Whitefield. "Good Lady Huntingdon goes on acting the part of a mother in Israel more and more. In a day or two she has had five clergymen under her roof which makes her ladyship look like a good archbishop with his chaplains around him. Her home is indeed a Bethel. To us in the ministry, it looks like a College. We have the sacrament every morning, heavenly consolation all day, and preaching at night. This is to live at Court indeed!"

That the nobility of the Countess consisted in more than her title is attested by one story at least. Learning that Mrs. Charles Wesley, away in Bristol, (in the absence of Charles Wesley, who had taken John's place in London—the latter himself being at death's door) was stricken down with smallpox, the Lady of the Revival at once set out from Bath for the infected house. Well she knew that dreadful scourge, for she had buried two of her own dear sons through it, but she did not hesitate to install herself as chief nurse. She then sent for Whitefield to relieve Charles in London so that the latter might return to his wife before, as they feared, the end came. Although there had been the great theological dispute between himself and the Wesleys, nevertheless Whitefield put all his big heart into his mission.

Mrs. Charles Wesley happily recovered after twenty-two days of fearful suspense and danger, and actually lived to the great age of ninety-six, many years longer than her aristocratic nurse. From which we see that Lady Huntingdon could be a good friend.

Another proof of that delightful trait was her bold bearding of David Garrick in his den at Drury Lane Theatre in regard

SELINA, COUNTESS OF HUNTINGDON

The Lady of the Revival (note symbolism—foot on coronet, crown of thorns in hand).

[*Face page* 172

to a play called *The Minor*, which cruelly lampooned the Methodists in general and George Whitefield in particular. The greatest mimic and comedian of that time, Foote, played the part of "Dr. Squintum" in this vile production. David Garrick, who was an admirer of Whitefield's, listened patiently to the lady's protest and promised to withdraw the play. This, however, did not happen at once, either because Foote raised powerful objections, or because box-office receipts were too tempting. At last, however, it was taken off and never played again.

The influence of Lady Huntingdon at Court was a further contribution to the Great Revival. It secured for Whitefield particularly, and the Methodists in general, a degree of royal protection and interest. When informed once of Whitefield's incorrigible misbehaviour and that of his companions, according to the episcopal mind, King George II is reported to have made the suggestion, with a chuckle, "Make bishops of 'em! Make bishops of 'em!"

Lady Huntingdon's preachers, other than Whitefield, were a notable group, but one in particular must be mentioned for his whimsical turn of mind—John Berridge, of Everton, one of her closest allies. The following letter to Lady Huntingdon ought to have been read by the parishioners to whom it refers:

"As for myself, I am now determined not to quit my charge again in a hurry. Never do I leave my bees, though for a short space only, but at my return I find them casting a colony, or fighting and robbing each other, not gathering honey from every flower in God's garden, but filling the air with their buzzing, and darting out the venom of their little hearts in their fiery stings. Nay, so inflamed they often are, and a mighty little thing disturbs them, that three months tinkering afterwards with a warming-pan will scarce hive them at last and make them settle to work again."

A more famous letter, here given in brief, reflecting the early Methodist attitude to calamity and death, is one that Berridge wrote to the Countess at the time of the death of her daughter, Lady Selina Hastings.

"My Lady,
"I received your letter from Brighthelmstone and hope you will soon learn to bless your Redeemer for snatching away your daughter so speedily. . . . Oh! what is she snatched from? Why,

173

truly, from the plague of an evil heart, a wicked world and a crafty devil—snatched from all such bitter grief as now overshadows you, snatched from everything which might wound her, afflict her eye, and pain her heart. But what is she snatched to? To a land of everlasting peace, where the voice of the truth is ever heard, where every inhabitant can say, 'I am no more sick . . .'

"She is gone to pay a more blessed visit, and will see you again by and by, never to part more. Had she crossed the sea and gone to Ireland" (to her sister, Countess Moira) "you could have borne it; but now she is gone to heaven 'tis almost unbearable.

"Wonderful strange love this! Such behaviour in others would not surprise me, but I could almost beat you for it, and I am sure Selina would beat you too, if she was called back for one moment from heaven to gratify your fond desire. I cannot soothe you, I must not flatter you. I am glad the dear creature is gone to heaven before you. Lament if you please, but glory, glory, glory be to God, say I.

"JOHN BERRIDGE."

The freedom of such address shows what confidence Lady Huntingdon's friends had in the gentleness that lay beneath her somewhat imperious bearing.

The character of the good Countess had the defects of its qualities. Strenuous and purposeful, she was necessarily impatient and sometimes tyrannical, but the utter selflessness of her motives was patent to all, and turned the edge of her masterfulness so that it seldom wounded.

The Lady of the Revival was honoured with a life of many years, filled to the end with good works. She outlived the main figures of the great movement by twenty-six years in the case of Whitefield, and four in the case of Wesley. Her final message to the world was a fitting comment upon a life of singular consistency in Christian devotion. "My work is done; I have nothing to do but to go to my Father." On June 17th, 1791, she passed over, and surely for her "the trumpets sounded on the other side." The churches that this good woman of God built have carried on her witness, and her spirit over nearly two centuries, and are fulfilling their ministry effectively in our own day.

CHAPTER VI

THE LAST PERIODS IN BRITAIN

"Multitudes flock to hear and many seem to be quickened."
—George Whitefield, letter to J. Hervey.

Whitefield was yet to make four more visits to America and to experience three more periods of toil in Great Britain. To tell their story in as much detail as the foregoing would be to risk a considerable degree of repetition and monotony. Whitefield was engaged throughout these years in the same tasks, and was achieving repeatedly the same kind of triumph, "cross-ploughing the land," he called it. It seems fitting, therefore, rather to select the outstanding incidents in the remainder of his amazing career and so leave space for a fuller attention to the man himself and to the challenge his story presents to ourselves.

Whitefield's influence upon the aristocracy at this time was ably seconded by the writings of his friend, James Hervey, whose *Meditations* were just published. Writing to him, Whitefield exclaims:

"Blessed be God for causing you to write so as to suit the taste of the polite world. Oh, that they may be won over to admire Him Who is altogether lovely . . .! Our Lord makes it exceedingly pleasant to me to preach His unsearchable riches. Multitudes flock to hear and many seem to be quickened."

The new work entailed by his association with Lady Huntingdon, coupled with a fresh determination, to which Whitefield committed himself in a letter to John Wesley, not to spend time in creating Societies, but to prosecute his itinerant ministry in Britain and America compelled Whitefield to surrender the Moderatorship of the Calvinistic Methodist Association. Before doing this, however, Whitefield endeavoured to

N
175

overtake some of the disorder that had arisen during his absence in America.

It is a little ironical to discover Whitefield, who had been such a thorn in the side of bishops and clergymen, playing the rôle of authority to disorderly young preachers, but the Minutes of the "Conference Book" of the Association contain the following account:

"Association held in London, July 20, 1745. Present: Whitefield (Moderator), Bateman, Harris, and others. Whitefield, after prayer and singing, opened his mind on several points. He told the exhorters and preachers present that 'he had seen so much confusion occasioned by young men going out rashly beyond their line that he was resolved not to labour with any who did not show a teachable mind and a willingness to submit.' He admonished them 'to use all means for improving their talents and abilities.' And added that 'though he hated to affect headship, yet he must see everyone acquainted with his own place, and that they must consider themselves as candidates on approbation'."

The Awakener's administration, however, was brief—his true work called him too insistently. After a quarterly "Association" at Waterford in Wales and another in London in April, 1749, he surrendered his Moderatorship to Howell Harris, a successor worthy in every way. Whitefield did not cease his co-operation with the Societies, however, and ever and anon we find him engaged in conference over their affairs.

Whitefield was now free to give more attention to a task which was very dear to the heart of the good Countess—that of raising up an evangelical ministry in the Established Church. Tyerman's eulogy of this idea, and of its prosecution by Whitefield and the Lady of the Revival, is entirely justified. He writes:

"The idea was grand—perhaps inspired—and the working it out was unquestionably the principal means of effecting the marvellous change which has taken place since then in the Established Church. Wesley created a great Church outside the Church of England. Whitefield and the Countess of Huntingdon were pre-eminently employed in improving the Church of England itself. . . . Where were the converted clergymen of the Church of England previous to the year 1748? A few, a very few, might be mentioned but even these were nicknamed Methodists. No one can estimate the service rendered to the cause of Christ outside the Church by Wesley and his 'assistants' and it is equally impossible to estimate the service rendered to the Church by the despised Whitefield, and his female prelate, the grand, stately, strong-minded, godly and self-sacrificing Countess of Huntingdon."[1]

A very good instance of Whitefield's influence in this regard is the case of Dr. James Stonehouse. The latter was a practising physician at Northampton. The death of his young wife inclined his thoughts to religion, and reading Philip Doddridge's *Rise and Progress of Religion*, he was converted.

Under Whitefield's guidance and advice he took Holy Orders, and was made Lecturer at All Saints, Bristol. A man of great ability as a poet as well as a preacher, he fulfilled a strong evangelical ministry till his death in 1795. Four years before his death he succeeded to a baronetcy. At this particular time, however, in Whitefield's career (1748) he was advising the Evangelist on matters of health. The following letter from the Awakener illustrates their intimacy, and Whitefield's common frankness in admonition of his friends:

"London,
"August 22nd, 1748.

"Very dear Sir,
"I thank you for your concern about my health. If it should please God to bring me back from Scotland to winter in Town I have thoughts of submitting to some régime or other. At present I think it impracticable. I heartily wish that you and Dr. Doddridge and Mr. Hervey would be pleased to revise my *Journal* and my last five sermons. I intend publishing a new edition soon. I always do as you desire in respect of Mr. Wesley's sermon. My prayer for him, for myself and for my friends, is this: 'Lord, give us clean hands and clean hearts. . . .' By your excellent letter you have publicly confessed Him (your Master). The eyes of all will now be upon you to see whether the truths you have delivered to others are transcribed in your own heart and copied in your life. . . . Dear sir, let me now entreat you to keep from trimming, or so much as attempting to reconcile two irreconcilable differences, God and the world, Christ and Belial. You know me too well to suppose that I want you to turn cynic. No, live a social life, but beg of the Lord Jesus to free you from love of the world. Thence arises that fear of man which now shackles and disturbs your soul. Dare, dear sir, to be singularly good. . . . I make no apology for this. You say you are my friend."

[1] Tyerman, Vol. 2, p. 192.

The Awakener's visit to Scotland was not a long one. A dozen days were spent in Glasgow, and in ever-memorable Cambuslang, but the major visit was to Edinburgh where "Moorfields' congregations," his favourite description, attended his preaching. He reports "some of the ministers were shy, many of his friends were dead, others were backsliders, the weather was boisterous," but we find him writing cheerily to the Countess:

"Ill-nature shows itself in Edinburgh, but I feel the benefit of it. Congregations are large, and I am enabled to preach with greater power. My hoarseness is quite gone and my bodily health much improved."

Later: "Thanks be to the Lord of all Lords for directing my way to Scotland. I have reason to believe some have been awakened, and many, many, quickened and comforted. . . . Two synods and one Presbytery brought me upon the carpet; but all has worked for good."

Some idea of the opposition Whitefield had to encounter may be gathered from the fact that six hundred of the followers of the Erskines, members of the Associate Presbytery whose narrow-minded behaviour we have already recorded[1] assembled in Edinburgh on November 16th and swore to observe the League and Covenant; and "solemnly engaged to strengthen one another's hands, in the use of lawful means to extirpate Popery, Prelacy, Arminianism, Arianism, Tritheism, Sabellianism and *George Whitefieldism*." What a collection of heresies!

Very shortly after his return to the south, Whitefield intervened in the persecution of certain Welsh Methodists who had been heavily fined by a bigoted magistrate. Through Lady Huntingdon's influence with the Government, the fines exacted were actually restored. Presently, on November 25th, 1745, we see Whitefield standing by the death-bed of good Isaac Watts[2] asking "how he found himself?" "I am one of Christ's waiting servants," was the dying Doctor's reply. Whitefield raised him up in bed to enable him to be more comfortable, and Watts apologised for the trouble. "Surely," replied Whitefield, "I am not too good to wait on a waiting servant of Christ!" Half-an-hour later the famous hymn-writer was dead.

[1] See page 123.
[2] *Gospel Magazine* of 1776 quoted by Tyerman.

A five weeks' tour in the West of England followed, with preaching triumphs in Gloucester, Bristol and Exeter. At Kingsbridge there were "A thousand people in the street," and a young man who had perched in a tree to see Whitefield in the midst of the crowd was summoned with a reminder about Zacchæus to "come down and be the Lord's." He came down and made his surrender to Christ, and afterwards became a minister. At Plymouth, the Awakener was greeted ten miles from the city by a great cavalcade and he preached there for a week to thousands every night.

Upon his return to London, Whitefield found himself engaged in a fierce controversy with the Bishop of Exeter, Dr. Lavington, in which Whitefield defended Methodism very ably. The argument is remarkable as much for Whitefield's developed humility and brave acknowledgment of faults and mistakes, as for the Bishop's ungracious capacity for ignorant slander and gratuitous insult.

Dr. Lavington had the effrontery to claim that the Methodists were defended by ruffian guards armed with clubs, browbeating any that opposed their spokesmen. Here is a portion of Whitefield's reply on this count.

"You add 'I have heard it often affirmed,' and so might the brethren have said that they heard it often affirmed, that when the primitive Christians received the blessed sacrament, they killed a young child, and then sucked its blood. But was there any reason why they should believe it? It is true, indeed, some of the Methodist preachers have more than once been attended with a sturdy set of followers, armed with clubs and other weapons, not as their guards, but opposers and persecutors; and who have not only menaced and terrified, but actually abused and beat many of those who came to hear him whom you, I suppose, would call their apostle. Both Methodist preachers and Methodist hearers, too, for want of better arguments, have often felt the weight of such irresistible power, which literally speaking, hath struck many of them dumb, and I verily believe, had it not been for some superior invisible guard, must have struck them dead. These are all the sturdy set of armed followers the Methodists know of."

Whitefield's reply goes on to make free and frank admission of several faults in his past behaviour, confessions made in a spirit of profound humility and penitence. For example he expresses regret for the onslaught he and Seward had made upon the writings of Archbishop Tillotson, and then goes on:

"Whatever can be produced out of any of my writings to prove that I have desired or prayed for ill-usage, persecution, martyrdom, death I retract it with all my heart, as proceeding from the overflowings of an irregular, though well-meant, zeal."

But the greatest and most valuable admission that breaks from this deeply humbled spirit is that he was wrong in making public the "lot" Wesley had cast in private. As Gledstone remarks "it is a perfect atonement for his fault." There is a touch of pathos in Whitefield's apologia:

"I came soon into the world; I have carried high sail whilst running through a whole torrent of popularity and contempt and by this means I have sometimes been in danger of oversetting; but many and frequent as my mistakes have been, or may be, as soon as I am made sensible of them, they shall be publicly acknowledged and retracted."

Whitefield's reply was so far effective as to draw from the Bishop the acknowledgment:

"Yes, Whitefield writes like an honest man, and has recanted several things; but he goes on in the same way yet."

The Bishop was to have ocular demonstration later on concerning the "armed followers" of the Methodists. The Awakener was preaching at Exeter to an audience of ten thousand people with the Bishop and his Clergy looking on, when suddenly a great stone struck Whitefield with stunning force upon the head and "almost rolled him off the table." It is to be feared that this was the work of some belonging to a ruffianly gang in Exeter known as the Church Rabble or the "God-damn-me-crew," who treated the Methodists with the utmost violence and with every obscenity short of outrage and death. These were responsible for the great riot of 1745 when the Methodists were most terribly ill-used.[1] It is not likely that the Bishop was personally responsible for the behaviour of this gang, but it is quite certain that he did not make any chivalrous protest against their action on this occasion.

[1] "An account of a later riot at Exeter," by John Cennick, quoted by Tyerman, Vol. II, p. 265.

THE LAST PERIODS IN BRITAIN

Back in London again, it became henceforth a regular feature of the Awakener's ministry in London to preach to aristocrats in Lady Huntingdon's drawing-room and to crowds of the poor in her kitchen! Later he is in the West again taking Gloucester and Bristol on his way, but preaching with marvellous effect for a whole fortnight in Portsmouth. It is to the labours of Whitefield and his followers that Independency in Portsmouth owes its origin. It was in 1739 that Whitefield first commenced his preaching in the open air at Portsmouth. But after this visit in 1749 a small society was formed. With great energy this little community entered upon its work, arranging for the expenses of the preachers who visited them by collecting weekly subscriptions. The efforts of the preachers were crowned with success, the members of the Society increased. Being greatly helped by three further visits from Whitefield, they purchased a site in Orange Street, Portsmouth Common, upon which they erected in the year 1754 a church which they called " The Tabernacle," measuring fifty-three feet by thirty, though it was neither ceiled, plastered, nor floored. Thus arose the first Independent Church of the town and the mother-church of all the other Congregational churches existing in the borough.[1] From thence he went to Wales to spend forty-eight hours in retirement at his wife's house at Abergavenny. " Sweet, sweet retirement," he exclaims. " So sweet that I should be glad never to be heard of again. But this must not be. A necessity is laid upon me, and woe is me, if I preach not the Gospel." Fourteen preachings in eight days succeeded that retirement, and for a glorious month Whitefield roused Wales once more.

A witty letter on "reformations" was received by Whitefield about this time from Benjamin Franklin, part of which is worth quoting:

" Philadelphia,
" July 6, 1749.

"Dear Sir,
    "Since your being in England, I have received two of your favours, and a box of books to be disposed of. It gives me great pleasure to hear of your welfare, and that you propose soon to return to America. . . . I am glad to hear that you have frequent opportunities of preaching among the great. If you can gain

[1] See "The Story of the Congregationalists" by Rev. J. Watkin Davies, pastor of the "mother-church," Edinburgh Road, in *The Illustrated History of Portsmouth*.

them to a good and exemplary life, wonderful changes will follow in the manners of the lower ranks; *ad exemplum regis*, etc. On this principle Confucius, the famous Eastern reformer, proceeded. When he saw his country sunk in vice, and wickedness of all kinds triumphant, he applied himself first to the grandees: and having, by his doctrine, won them to the cause of virtue, the commons followed in multitudes. The mode has a wonderful influence on mankind; and there are numbers who perhaps fear less the being in hell than out of the fashion. Our more western reformations began with the ignorant mob; and when numbers of them were gained, interest and party-views drew in the wise and great. Where both methods can be used reformations are likely to be more speedy. O that some method could be found to make them lasting! He who discovers that will, in my opinion, deserve more, ten thousand times, than the inventor of longitude.

"My wife and I join in most cordial salutations to you and good Mrs. Whitefield.

"I am, dear sir, your very affectionate friend, and most obliged and humble servant,

"BENJAMIN FRANKLIN."

Whitefield, however, could give Franklin as good as he received, and in a letter written some time later we find the Awakener striving to awaken his friend thus:

"I find you grow more and more famous in the learned world. As you have made a pretty considerable progress in the mysteries of electricity I would now honestly recommend to your diligent unprejudiced pursuit and study the mysteries of the new birth. It is a most important and interesting study, and, when mastered, will richly answer and repay you for all your pains. One, at whose bar we are shortly to appear, hath solemnly declared that without it 'we cannot enter the "Kingdom of Heaven" '."

It was during a tour in Yorkshire and the North that Whitefield became involved in the second love-affair of John Wesley, which was as unhappy almost as the first.

A very gifted and good woman, Grace Murray, some thirteen years younger than himself, had engaged Wesley's affections very deeply, and in Dublin he had gone so far as to make a *contract de praesenti* with her.[1] According to Ker in *The Students' Blackstone*, such a contract "was before the time of George II so far a valid marriage, that the parties might be compelled in the spiritual courts to celebrate it in *facie ecclesiae*."[2]

[1] See *John Wesley's last love*, by Prof. J. A. Leger.
[2] Quoted by Tyerman, Vol. II. p. 235.

Unfortunately, Charles Wesley took a violent objection to the marriage, the reason for which is obscure, and set himself with great determination to marry Grace Murray to another Methodist preacher who was in love with her, John Bennett. Whitefield was naturally interested in the matter, for Grace Murray (*née* Norman) was one of his own most renowned converts to Methodism. Writing of her first impression of Whitefield, whom she heard for the first time at Moorfields, Grace Murray says: "When Mr. W. stood up and looked round on the congregation, I fixt my eyes upon him, and felt an inexpressible Conviction that he was sent of God." When, however, her husband, who was a sailor, returned, and found his wife converted and a Methodist, he was so alarmed that he threatened to clap her into a mad-house. Relenting of his purpose, he went off to sea again in a temper "to go as far as ships will sail," and was lost at sea a few months later. So Grace Murray, a widow, became free to join Wesley's itinerating group, a fact which pays eloquent tribute to her ability and piety in Wesley's judgment at least. For ten years she pursued that course of life, so that Wesley's decision to marry her, as Mr. Arnold Lunn points out, was no sudden whim. Charles Wesley's opposition, however, was no mere sentiment but a strenuous activity to secure her union elsewhere, and the following record written by Wesley tells the rest of a pitiful story:

"October 4, 1749. At Leeds I found, not my brother, but Mr. Whitefield. I lay down by him on the bed. He told me my brother would not come till John Bennett and Grace Murray were married. I was troubled; he perceived it; he wept and prayed over me, but I could not shed a tear. He said all that was in his power to comfort me; but it was in vain. He told me it was his judgment that she was my wife [1] and that he had said so to John Bennett, that he would fain have persuaded them to wait and not to marry till they had seen me, but that my brother's impetuosity prevailed and bore down all before it. On Thursday, October 5th, one came in from Newcastle and told us 'They were married on Tuesday.' My brother came an hour after. I felt no anger, yet I did not desire to see him; but Mr. Whitefield constrained me. After a few words had passed he accosted me with 'I renounce all intercourse with you but what I would have with heathen men or a publican.' I felt little emotion, it was only adding a drop of water to a drowning man; yet I calmly accepted his renunciation and

---

[1] Because of the *de praesenti* contract.

acquiesced therein. Poor Mr. Whitefield and John Nelson burst into tears. They prayed, cried and entreated, till the storm passed away. We could not speak, but only fell on each other's neck."

At Sheffield in 1749 Whitefield by his eloquent preaching completely won over a public that had taken a strong prejudice against the Wesleys, and had actually stoned Charles in 1743. Writing from Sheffield some months after the Awakener's work in the city, Charles Wesley generously admits, "The door has continued open ever since Mr. Whitefield preached here, and quite removed the prejudices of our first opposers. Some of them were convinced by him, some converted and added to the Church."

In the winter of 1749-50, Whitefield enjoyed "golden seasons" in his London Tabernacle. Huge congregations assembled as early as six a.m. morning after morning before the day's business began—whilst the nobility also was treated to a continuous and vigorous bombardment.

To seal the closer relationship of the Wesleys, Whitefield offered to preach in Wesley's Chapel. His friendly overture was accepted, and he and Wesley freely exchanged pulpits and took each other's Communion Services as well. The result was an immediate rise of enthusiasm in both camps.

The visitation of London by earthquake at this time gave to the people a tremendous emotional mobility, which provided a unique opportunity for the message of the evangelist. Great darkness and the rocking of a few houses and the fall of a few chimneys were the only outward results but "men's hearts failed them for fear" at such unusual portents, and they were ripe grain for the sickles which Whitefield and Wesley wielded with such vigour. Enormous masses of people waited upon their ministry, whilst Whitefield with his customary "flair" for an "occasion" went boldly into Hyde Park at night to wrestle with the multitude.

Whitefield was a very sick man throughout these strenuous labours and was indeed fast qualifying for the rôle of religious suicide. For years he had utterly refused to spare himself in his great task, scarcely finding time to eat even, and now as he says he could "scarce drag the crazy load along." Preaching was at one and the same time a relief and a strain. Often it would act upon him as a tonic, but again as often he would

GEORGE WHITEFIELD IN LATER LIFE

By Hone—the best known picture, the original of which is to be seen at Whitefield's Central Mission, London. (It is said Whitefield disclaimed the habit of raising both hands together.)

preach with such passion and fury of energy as to "vomit blood" afterwards. He welcomed the spring so that he might leave the confined atmosphere of London for his beloved "ranging" in the country, and very soon we read of his being at Plymouth preaching twelve times in six days to ever greater audiences. "More tongues, more bodies, more souls," he wanted, so he declares, "for the Lord Jesus."

One of Whitefield's most interesting contacts was with the moorland village of Haworth, famous later for its association with the Brontés, but famous at this time for its incumbent, William Grimshaw, an ideal village pastor and preacher. It was nothing unusual for Grimshaw to preach thirty times a week, riding over his scattered parish and using cottage and hillside and field indifferently for a pulpit. So effective was his ministry that in so sparsely populated a district as the Yorkshire moors he could present the Awakener on his first visit with an audience of no less than six thousand persons. Over a thousand remained to the service of Holy Communion that followed.

More than once did Whitefield return to this most interesting and thriving parish and occupy for a while the old parsonage (not the one at which the Brontés afterwards lived). On one such occasion Whitefield, suddenly realizing how unrelentingly stern Grimshaw invariably was in his preaching to his flock, decided to preach himself in terms of great tenderness and hope, but he had reckoned without his host. As he proceeded to tell his audience that "as they had long enjoyed the ministry of a faithful pastor they must surely be a sincerely Godly people," Grimshaw suddenly broke in "Oh sir, for God's sake do not speak so; I pray you do not flatter them; I fear the greater part of them are going to hell with their eyes open!" If that was the case, Grimshaw must have been more successful with them later on, for he told Romaine eventually that no less than 1,200 people were in communion with his Church. "Most of them, in the judgment of charity, he could not but believe to be one with Christ."

Certainly, however, that congregation knew the terrors of judgment-preaching. Once, as Whitefield was about to preach from the scaffold erected out of doors for the purpose, he stopped and most solemnly invited the presence of the Holy Spirit. Then opening his Bible he read his text "It is appointed unto men once to die, but after that the judgment." As he proceeded to preach a wild shriek of terror arose from the midst of the crowd. Grimshaw plunged into the crowd to see what had happened and presently cried "Brother Whitefield, you stand amongst the dead and the dying, an immortal soul has been called into eternity; the destroying angel is passing over the congregation. Cry aloud and spare not." One of the audience had fallen dead! Once again Whitefield began, and read his solemn text once more. Immediately from a spot close by Lady Huntingdon and Lady Margaret Ingham who were in the crowd, a second dreadful shriek arose. Imagine the awe that swept over those thousands as they learned that another soul had been called to its account. Yet Whitefield calmly continued and finished his sermon in a strain of tremendous eloquence.

It is an indication of the high prestige that Whitefield enjoyed among many Methodists at this time that the Wesleyan Societies founded in Ireland at Dublin and Cork, finding themselves caught in cruel persecution, appealed to him for his aid, and especially for his presence. Whitefield was unable to go immediately, but his sympathy was readily forthcoming, and by correspondence and advice, and by his influence with high authorities, he did all he could to help.

In a letter to Lady Huntingdon, dated March 21st, 1750, from Exeter, the Awakener reports something of his important work for Cornwall where Methodism owes its founding much more to Whitefield than to Wesley.

"Immediately after writing my last, I preached to many thousands at Gwennap. In the evening I went to St. Ives. . . . On Monday I preached at Redruth at ten in the morning to near ten thousand . . . an unexpectedly wide door is opened in Cornwall."

From Land's End to Exeter the Awakener spread the revival fire.

In the next few months we find Whitefield literally "cross-ploughing the land." He is at Portsmouth, Olney, "great multitudes," Northampton, "Dr. Doddridge's family," at Kettering "several thousands," at Sutton, Mansfield, Rotherham, Leeds, "many thousands," at Haworth "Pentecost, Sunday, June 3rd," at Manchester, in Ingham's Yorkshire Circuit, "mountainous tract of country," thence to Edinburgh once more on July 6th, having preached, since he left London two months before, over ninety times to about 240,000 people. "Greater crowds than ever flock to hear Mr. Whitefield," was the report of a letter written by Lady Jane Nimmo on his Edinburgh visit.

Back to London, thence to Canterbury, afterwards via Exeter through Wales to Dublin! Thus sped the Awakener!

He writes from Ireland:

> " Dublin,
> "June 1, 1751.

"After being about five days on the water I arrived here on the 24th ult. I have now preached fourteen times. . . . Last Lord's Day upwards of ten thousand attended. It much resembled a Moorfields' auditory."

Athlone, Limerick, Cork, Bandon, "the largest congregations seen in Ireland," Kinsale, welcomed him in turn. "The cry now is 'Methodism is revived again,'" he wrote to Lady Huntingdon. At Belfast, which he took *en route* for Scotland, the Awakener had such a colossal and enthusiastic hearing that he regretted he had not come to that city sooner and could not make a longer stay.

Glasgow greeted him with many thousands of hearers, and Edinburgh did the same. "For nearly twenty-eight days together in Glasgow and Edinburgh, I preached to near ten thousand souls every day."

He reached London about the middle of August, and was on the high seas bound for Georgia by the end of the month, arriving there in November. This fourth visit (seventh and eighth voyages) was only a brief one and he was back in England by May, 1752. His wife had spent the time with friends in Scotland, and there is deep affection evident in Whitefield's letter of thanks to them:

"Ten thousand thanks," he wrote, "for caring so friendly for my dear wife in my absence."

He was speedily preaching again at Moorfields:

"Thousands and thousands hear the Gospel gladly, Lord, what am I to do? Not unto me, not unto me, but unto Thy free grace and unmerited mercy be all the glory."

187

Speedily he is on tour again. Bristol, where all the old time fervour was aroused again! Wales once more! Then again up through the Midlands back to Bristol and off to Scotland, preaching on the way at Wyclif's town, Lutterworth.

On his return to London a scheme was set on foot to rebuild the Moorfields' Tabernacle, and very soon a new building arose, eighty feet square, more adequate to the multitudes that sought to attend it.

The following year, 1753, saw the Awakener again "cross-ploughing the land," visiting most of the towns of his former tours and repeating his now regular triumphs of popular success for the Gospel. Wherever he went still greater crowds assembled, until we read of audiences of twenty thousand in Leeds and Glasgow. Norwich, Bradford, Birmingham, Coventry, Wolverhampton, where he addressed a "vast multitude at night in the open air," were other points in his itinerary. In November, 1753, he opened his first Tabernacle in Bristol. "It is large," he wrote, "but not half large enough. Would the place contain them, I believe near as many would attend as in London."

His tour was interrupted by a sudden call to London occasioned by the dangerous illness, thought by the doctors to be galloping consumption, of John Wesley. But great as was everyone's anxiety for a time, the great constructive evangelist of the Revival was destined to live another forty years—many years beyond the death of the Awakener.

It was in March, 1754, that Whitefield embarked on his fifth visit to America (and ninth voyage). (He took with him this time twenty-two poor, destitute children.) On his journey he visited Lisbon, and he has left a most interesting account of his observations there. He was not above learning from the Roman Catholic preachers of the city. He writes:

"The preachers here have also taught me something; their action is graceful. Surely our English preachers would do well to be a little more fervent in their addresses. They have truth on their side; why should superstition and falsehood run away with all that is pathetic and affecting?"

Whitefield was deeply impressed by the grossness of superstition and spiritual tyranny that he saw on every hand, and praised God fervently for the "great wonder of the Reformation."

THE LAST PERIODS IN BRITAIN

Just after Whitefield's return to England on May 5th, 1755, the Seven Years' War broke out between France and England, and by this and other causes the Awakener was severed from his American circuit and friendships for eight years.

The story of those eight years is a repetition of what has gone before, excepting for the great enterprise of the Tottenham Court Road Chapel, the account of which is elsewhere. He was much tried, too, with the unfaithfulness of some of his Bethesda staff, who deserted him when his need was great. In 1757 the Awakener visited Scotland for the ninth time. On this occasion the Church of Scotland was in General Assembly, and a number of its ministers invited Whitefield to a public dinner. He was also the guest of the King's High Commissioner, who turned a very deaf and indignant ear to the complaints his constancy to Whitefield aroused.

In July he was in Ireland, and this time a crowd of "Papists" in conflict with some Protestants at Oxmantown Green, two miles from Dublin, stoned him within an inch or two of his death.

"Volleys of stones came from all quarters, and every step I took a fresh stone struck and made me reel backwards and forwards till I was almost breathless and all over a gore of blood. My strong beaver hat served me for a skull cap for a while, but at last that was knocked off and my head left quite defenceless. I received many blows and wounds, one was particularly large near my temples."

He took refuge in a house but found his presence unwelcome. A carpenter induced him to put on a wig and coat for a disguise. "I accepted, and put them on, but was soon ashamed of not trusting my Master to secure me in my proper habit, and threw them off in disdain." He was almost immediately rescued by a group of Methodists who had hired a coach. He bore the scar of his temple-wounds for the rest of his days. Yet the fruit of the sermon preached on this occasion was rich indeed. A man named John Edwards, concealed from the intrepid preacher's view, was smitten to the heart. He surrendered to Christ and became a most powerful itinerant preacher over the greater part of England, Ireland and Scotland. He himself had marvellous escapes from enraged mobs, being saved on one occasion by being let down from a window in a basket after the fashion of St. Paul.

I will spare my readers a fresh list of the dozen towns or so visited by Whitefield on his return from Ireland. He must have been a remarkable rider to have covered the ground so quickly in those days of bad roads and clumsy sailing vessels. "This spiritual hunting," he declared, "is delightful sport when the heart is in the work. How soon does the summer fly away!" All these journeyings and labours, moreover, were achieved and endured by a man whose racked and tortured body was only held to its task by an indomitable will and a flaming spirit.

His winter preaching in London saw thousands turned away from the new chapel, unable to obtain entrance, but the cost of such audiences is reflected in the fact that in 1758 illness compelled Whitefield to "a short allowance of preaching—once a day except thrice on Sunday."

The usual campaign in the country of the following summer was marked by Whitefield's discontinuance of riding, and his use of a "one-horse chaise," because of the state of his health. He found this, however, too wearisome; the roads were bad and he could not read while travelling, so he exchanged it at last for a four-wheeled carriage which cost him about thirty or forty pounds.

Round the United Kingdom he toured again, his Scotch visit being characterised by the remarkable offer to him from a Scotch lady, a Miss Hunter, of money and lands worth seven thousand pounds. Whitefield, desperately poor as always, felt he could not touch the gift, not even when it was offered for the Orphan House. The temptation must have been very great, and equally great must have been Whitefield's reason for refusing it. It is a sufficient answer, however, to the charges of greed and self-interest that were preferred against him in Scotland.

In 1763 Whitefield made his sixth visit to America, but in two years he was back again.

In 1768 he is in England, defending a Methodist student expelled from Oxford University for nothing but Methodism, and busy also in collecting and editing his letters, to which we are indebted, with his *Journals*, for most of the information about his life.

In June and July the Awakener visited Edinburgh for the last time. Congregations as great as ever before gathered to hear him in the Orphan House Park, and he was in great danger of "being hugged to death" by old friends and converts of long standing. He was particularly fond of Edinburgh, and longed to die preaching there, but it was "too great, too great, an honour to be expected."

Upon his return to London he found his wife ill of an inflammatory fever, and she passed over to the other side on August 9th, 1768. Whitefield himself preached the funeral sermon, and bore eloquent tribute to her courage and faithfulness, referring to her as his "right hand." He narrowly escaped joining his wife in death immediately, for through hard riding and harder preaching in Wales he burst a blood vessel. The ardour of the Welsh temperament always tempted Whitefield to over-excitement in preaching. This was upon the occasion of the opening of Trevecca College on the Countess of Huntingdon's birthday, August 24th, 1768. The last winter but one of Whitefield's life was spent in London, 1768–69, and we may enjoy a glimpse of him there before following him through the last periods in America.

The Holy Trio, John and Charles and George, seemed to have met fairly frequently in a happy social way at Whitefield's house beside the Moorfields Tabernacle, and also at the Tottenham Court Road Chapel. How one would have loved to be an eavesdropper at those conversations! Wesley records in his *Journal* of Monday, February 27th, 1769:

"I had one more agreeable conversation with my old friend and fellow-labourer, George Whitefield. His soul appeared vigorous still, but his body is sinking apace; and unless God interposes with His mighty Hand, he must soon finish his labours."

Charles Wesley, too, in a letter to his wife, sketches the little group of ageing and now grey-headed evangelists, in their last meeting at Tottenham Court Road.

"Last Friday I dined with my brother at George's Chapel. Mrs. Hermitage was mistress, and provided the dinner. Hearty Mr. Adams was there and to complete our band, Howell Harris. It was, indeed, a feast of love. My brother and George prayed, and we all sang a hymn in the chapel."

They were never all together again in this world.[1]

---

[1] Quoted by Gledstone, p. 335.

CHAPTER VII

THE STORY OF WHITEFIELD'S CHURCHES

"And all the people shouted with a great shout, when they praised the Lord, because the foundation of the house of the Lord was laid."—Ezra iii. 11.—WHITEFIELD's text at founding of Tottenham Court Chapel, 1756.

To many readers of this book it will be a matter of keen interest to trace something of the history of the churches that the Awakener founded. For one reason such a record will show how virile still is the work that he launched two centuries ago, and how green is his memory in certain centres at least.

Not counting the numerous chapels more closely associated with the Countess of Huntingdon's foundation, though Whitefield often supplied the initiative for these, nor reckoning certain churches at which he preached frequently, such as Spa Fields and Long Acre, Whitefield planted more personally a number [1] of causes many of which are flourishing to-day. Several of these will engage our attention, Moorfields and Tottenham Court Road in London, Kingswood and Penn Street in Bristol, and the Tabernacles at Dursley and Rodborough, with those known as the Rodborough Connexion in Gloucestershire and Wiltshire. All these churches are to-day Congregational in polity, and all but one in denominational allegiance. This is a relationship which has attracted thus far very little attention, and yet has had far-reaching results. It marks the impact of the great Revivalist, not merely upon Methodism and the Church of England, but also upon one of the most potent religious strains, culturally and politically in Great Britain—that of Independency.

The English-speaking peoples are as much indebted for their social emancipation to the tradition of personal and civic freedom associated with religious Independency, embodied in the

[1] It is difficult to ascertain the exact number. By 1747 Whitefield had over thirty societies in being beside preaching stations.

history of the Congregational and Baptist Churches,[1] as they are to the kindred tradition of humanitarianism drawn from the rise of Methodism. Both of these noble strands of social energy were fused together in the churches that Whitefield founded.

Undoubtedly this bond with Methodism and with the spirit and atmosphere of the great Revival[2] has meant the kindling of a stronger evangelical passion in Modern Independency than would otherwise have been the case, and has also deeply affected its social outlook.

The first Church founded in London by the evangelist was, of course, Moorfields Tabernacle, built in 1741, and without doubt it remained the spiritual hearth of his whole career to which he ever returned with eager love. No congregation, as we have seen, could earn from Whitefield greater praise than that it was a "Moorfields' auditory." Perhaps the generous attitude of the London crowd, so notoriously good-humoured, to his first audacious approaches endeared the people and the district specially to him. It would be interesting to know just why Whitefield favoured the term "Tabernacle." He himself remarked once, " I have called it a Tabernacle because we may be called upon to move our tents," and it is believed that he never meant the Society to be permanent. It was not always easy in those days to feel secure in the tenure of a site or building for any religious cause that was not entirely orthodox. Possibly, too, Whitefield was influenced in his choice of name by the "booths" of the Moorfields' Fair, and again he may have welcomed a term that did not commit him, an Anglican clergyman, to the use of the word Church. Whitefield was always insistent that he did not desire to form societies or sects. It was by sheer force of circumstances and the obtuseness of the Established Church that his Tabernacles became Churches.

The first wooden meeting-house on the Moorfields' site erected in 1741 was at best only a huge, ugly shed. It had stood the storms natural and human of a dozen winters, and was much too small to hold the crowds that waited upon the Awakener's ministry. It was in 1752 that Whitefield, yielding to pressure

[1] ' Independent ' is the former name of the ' Congregational ' Church from which the Baptist Church arose.

[2] Illustrated also in the close relation of the Countess of Huntingdon's Churches to-day with Congregationalism.

from Lady Huntingdon, though he himself had long desired it, began to collect money towards rebuilding. He resolved not to begin without £1,000 in hand.[1] The funds, however, were speedily available, and the first brick of the new building was laid on March 1st, 1753. The new Tabernacle was built around and over the old one so that congregations continued to meet in their usual place until the shell of the new edifice was complete.

It was at Moorfields' that Whitefield gathered about him a great company of preachers, most of whom were of the "lay" variety, that is ministers without episcopal ordination. They were John Cennick, Thomas Adams, Jenkins, Smith, Stevens, Benjamin Ingham (an original member of the Holy Club), Reynolds, Edwards, Kelly, Middleton, Seagrave, Humphries, Godwin, Howell Harris, Daniel Rowland, Torial Joss. These were joined later after Whitefield's death by Rowland Hill and Matthew Wilks. It was Howell Harris who at first mostly took Whitefield's place, in his absence, but later Torial Joss became immensely popular and used to preach at both Moorfields' Tabernacle and Tottenham Court Chapel. This band formed a noble galaxy of talent; and their choice reflects credit on Whitefield's judgment.

Behind most of these names there is a fascinating story of spiritual quest and discovery, but Torial Joss was perhaps the most romantic figure of them all. Born September 29th, 1731, at Auck-Medden, a little sea-coast village twenty miles north of Aberdeen, he ran away to sea from a mother who neglected him, his father having died. Captured by the French, he suffered terribly in prison. At the age of only fifteen, when he returned to Scotland he was the victim of the press-gang and sent to a man-of-war. He escaped and reached Sunderland. There he bound himself to a ship's captain belonging to Robin Hood's Bay. A while later, by overhearing a religious conversation and through reading Bunyan he was converted. He began to pray and preach, and John Wesley, who visited the Bay, encouraged him. Appointed first mate of his captain's vessel, he tried to preach in every port they visited, and involved himself in terrible persecution. Through many such adventures he arrived at last at a captaincy, and his preaching by this time was so effective that a friend wrote

[1] *Whitefield's Works*, Vol. II. p. 477.

MOORFIELD'S TABERNACLE AND HOUSE, AS IN 1753

[*Face page* 194

to Whitefield advising him that Torial Joss was coming to London in a vessel called the *Hartley Trader* nicknamed "The Pulpit." On his arrival Joss was astounded to find himself announced by Whitefield to preach at the Tabernacle. Torial Joss made such an impression that Whitefield begged him to leave the sea and take to preaching altogether. Thus, in 1766, Torial Joss became one of Whitefield's assistants, and great crowds waited upon a ministry full of converting power and ripe with chequered and tragic experience. Four or five months each year, like Whitefield himself, Joss would be on itinerating work. In Wales the people followed him in multitudes. He became known later as the "Archdeacon of Tottenham" because of his powerful ministry at Tottenham Court Chapel. There he died and was buried in 1797.

The most notable ministers of Moorfields, as already remarked, were also ministers of Tottenham Court Chapel. This practice was kept up for many years, until 1862, when the connection between the two causes was severed. In later years Moorfields had the renown of being the church that ministered to the moral and spiritual development of one of the greatest leaders of nineteenth century Free Church life—the brilliant Congregational divine, Dr. R. W. Dale, and also to that of one of the most devoted and successful of modern missionaries, John Williams, of Erromanga. Young Dale came to Finsbury from Bocking, and settled down at the Tabernacle as a Sunday School teacher. He was particularly keen on the theological class conducted by a Mr. William Stroud, who influenced him greatly. Here, too, Dale made his first appearance in print with an article over the *nom de plume* "Gaius," in the *Christian Witness*, edited by Dr. Campbell, who was joint pastor of the two churches, from 1829 to 1865, and to whose ministry Dale owed much, but who nevertheless discouraged Robert Dale's early aspirations towards the ministry!

The historic cause was represented until quite recently by the "Whitefield's Tabernacle," in Leonard Street, City Road, Finsbury. A tablet in the wall of the present building bears the following inscription:

"Near this spot stood the tabernacle built by the Rev. George Whitefield in 1753. One hundred and fifteen years afterwards it was taken down, and in its place this building was erected."

This stone was laid by J. Remington Wills, Esq., M.P., on September 11th, 1868.[1]

The building now, alas, is used as a printing works on the ground floor and as a joinery and cabinet store at the level of the old galleries!

Next in historical sequence was the commencement by Whitefield of two Tabernacles at Bristol—the first in 1752 at Kingswood, the second in 1753 at Penn Street. The Kingswood cause has unique fame, for strictly it goes back to the meeting-room of 1741 which sprang directly from that first attempt of Whitefield's at open-air preaching, which took place at Rose Green, only a stone's throw from Hanham Mount, the scene of the second preaching. Whitefield was not the first to inaugurate open-air services for the poor savage colliers of Kingswood. Just a year before a Bristol divine, Morgan by name, had made the attempt almost on the same spot, but had not continued the practice.

A very accurate and interesting historian of Bristol Congregationalism has written in the following eloquent strain of the historic glory imparted to Kingswood by Whitefield:

"For there he broke the deadly decorum and the spiritual lassitude of his day; there he began a new era in the religious life of his native land; and there he laid the foundation for the beginning of modern foreign missionary enterprise. Thus it ranks with Athelney in the story of Alfred the Great; with Runnymede and the signing of Magna Carta; with Lutterworth and the closing days of John Wycliffe's life; with North Nibley and the birth of William Tyndale; with Kidderminster and the preaching of Richard Baxter; or with Bedford and the imprisonment of John Bunyan."[2]

When, in 1740, George Whitefield handed over his work in Bristol to John Wesley,[3] his way back to London lay through Kingswood. There he found awaiting him a crowd of colliers anxious to pay him a loving farewell. These men had gathered out of their pitiful earnings the sum of £20, and with promises of £40 more they begged Whitefield to lay a foundation stone for the Charity School he had suggested for their children. Whitefield promptly chose a stone, and kneeling upon it dedicated

---

[1] At that time the pastorate was occupied by the Rev. W. Grigsley.
[2] G. Hoskin Wicks, in *Whitefield's Legacy to Bristol and the Cotswolds*.
[3] See page 67.

the project in heartfelt prayer. That was the first foundation stone, as Mr. G. H. Wicks points out, ever laid and consecrated for Christian purposes within a radius of twenty miles of that hill of Kingswood, which had previously been a beautiful Royal Chase, and was at this time a dismal tragic mining area. Whitefield handed over the actual building of the school to the care of John Wesley,[1] and the spiritual care of the colliers was undertaken by good John Cennick. On June 8th, 1741, however, Whitefield wrote to Cennick from London, "I was resolved to send you £20 to begin the Society Room at Kingswood. I would have you lay the foundations immediately but take care of building too large and too handsome." On December 7th, 1741, the Awakener records, "In Wiltshire and at Kingswood there are many good souls and two new houses built."

In the *school-room* of the present Kingswood Tabernacle, Bristol,[2] there is to be seen a tablet with the inscription:

"This building was erected by George Whitefield, B.A., and John Cennick, A.D. 1741. It is Whitefield's first Tabernacle, the oldest existing memorial of his great share in the Eighteenth Century Revival."

This tablet was placed there on Saturday, May 3rd, 1913. Part of this building now used as a Sunday School was Mr. Whitefield's "room."

Thus the very first meeting-room he caused to be built, and the one associated with the outstanding feature of his work— the "aeration of religion"—is the only original building still standing, and it is still being used for the great original purpose.

On July 13th, 1753, the foundation stone was laid of Penn Street Tabernacle, more familiarly known as the Bristol Tabernacle. From a recently discovered diary of a Mr. Dyer, of that time, we cull the following:

"Friday morning seven o'clock, went to Smith's Hall from where the preacher (George Whitefield) and congregation repaired to the Orchard, where he laid the foundation stone of a building soon to be erected and afterwards called the Tabernacle."

[1] This is a capital instance of the sub-conscious bias in favour of Wesley's fame shown by his earlier biographers, for until Tyerman, they are all quite silent about Whitefield's share in founding the Kingswood School. (See *Life and Times of the Countess of Huntingdon*, Vol. II. p. 361.)
[2] The present minister is Rev. W. G. Stacey.

The followers of Whitefield had been meeting in Smiths' Hall, now Cutlers' Hall, and originally a Dominican Priory, for some fourteen years. The site itself of this new church was already famous as an old Friars' orchard, and the name Penn Street was associated with the famous Penn family, from which sprang William Penn, whose "holy experiment" in peaceful Quaker Government founded that city of Philadelphia and that province of Pennsylvania with which George Whitefield was destined to be so closely allied.

Here Whitefield and his preachers, including specially Cornelius Winter and William Jay, and later Rowland Hill, drew crowded audiences over a long period of years. Lady Huntingdon, a frequent resident in Bristol and in Bath, was often in attendance. One of these preachers, Matthew Wilks, is particularly to be noticed as the link between Whitefield's evangelistic zeal and the glorious extension of the work of the British churches to the foreign field. It was at Bristol that largely under Matthew Wilks's inspiration and leadership, aided by men like Dr. Bogue, Dr. Ryland and Mr. H. O. Wills, the first meeting was held out of which grew eventually the London Missionary Society. Thus the Tabernacle has become known as the cradle of the London Missionary Society. On the same spot was initiated later the Bristol Missionary Society and the Bristol Itinerant Society. There was founded also from this Church the first Sunday School in Bristol in the year 1801.

Thus we see how amazingly fruitful Whitefield's work was here as elsewhere. Nor is this the whole story, for after the Tabernacle became definitely Congregationalist in 1855, other Congregational Churches were founded and fostered from this centre in various parts of the city. Gideon Church, Anvil Street Church, Kingsland, Highbury and Arley Churches are some of these later fruits.

Part of the original Church-house still stands on this historic site, though the church building has been changed, and until to-day a vigorous though increasingly difficult work has been carried on, a new chapter in which, however, is about to open.[1]

[1] At the time of going to press the author learns from the Rev. Stanley Edwards, the present pastor, that a proposal was made by the Bristol City authorities to clear the whole district around the Tabernacle to make way for new Markets. This has led to the consideration of the desirability of preserving

RODBOROUGH TABERNACLE
THE LITTLE CHAPEL
(Originally Stable and Coach-house)

[*Face page* 198

Whilst we are in the provinces we may glance at the fact that Whitefield started certain other causes in this district. The other "house" in Wiltshire to which he refers in the letter written to Cennick in 1741 was Brinkworth. This cause afterwards seceded with Cennick to the Moravians (1745). Of late years, however, it has become Congregationalist, and is now worked by the Silver Street Church, Malmesbury. At Dursley, near Stinchcombe Hill, where he preached to "thousands," Whitefield took over and revived the Water Street meeting-house, which had been built by Joseph Twemlow in 1715, and turned it into a Tabernacle.

A group of Societies founded by Whitefield and comprising Minchinhampton, Freke's Mill (at Rodborough in the Valley), and Morston Farm near Randwich, combined to erect a preaching station at Rodborough in 1750. This, the Rodborough Tabernacle, is also a Congregational church to-day, and is as vigorously alive as ever it has been. A favourite chair of Whitefield's is preserved here, bearing appropriately enough the lines:

> "If love of souls should e'er be wanting here,
> Remember me, for I am Whitefield's chair;
> I bore his weight, am witness to his fears,
> His earnest prayers, his interceding tears.
> This holy man was filled with love divine,
> Art thou the same? Sit down and call me thine."

This Church to-day is pointing the way, in a highly original manner,[1] for other Churches particularly in the development and enrichment of the Church Meeting and in Young People's Work. From the Rodborough Tabernacle four other causes have arisen, Ebley (Countess of Huntingdon), Ruscombe (Congregational), Frampton and Stonehouse also both Congregational. What was known as the Rodborough Connexion covered Wiltshire, and included and eventually comprised

---

the Whitefield tradition in a Memorial Church in the suburbs of the city. At present, however, the municipal scheme is held in abeyance, and the work of the Tabernacle is to continue on the present site.

The pulpit originally used by Whitefield in the Bristol Tabernacle has since been removed to Marshfield Congregational Church, where it is in use at the present time.

[1] See article by present pastor, Rev. C. E. Watson in *The Congregational Quarterly*, Vol. I. No. 1. The author is much indebted to Mr. Watson for valuable information for this chapter.

Dursley, Wotton-under-Edge, for a period Gosport and Portsea, and more or less closely Haverford West and Narbet. It arose during the later years of Whitefield's life and continued for twenty or thirty after his death.

All these causes have exerted a profound influence on the religious life of the country in the past two centuries. By an interesting chain of circumstances, however, the Whitefield tradition has been focused most powerfully into the Tottenham Court Chapel. This somewhat aristocratic title is interesting. "Tabernacle" is not used here by Whitefield, possibly because he had the court in mind in building it. If so, the choice of district was shrewdly made. Until quite recently there could be seen in the Euston Road[1] two pillars which marked the entrance to King John's Palace. The road in front of this, now Euston Road, is marked in the engraving mentioned below "Tottenham Court." Without doubt here is the origin of "Tottenham Court Road."

In 1756, when Whitefield founded the Chapel, what is now a crowded business centre was then open fields on the outskirts of London, and the building was curiously isolated—a huge edifice in rustic surroundings. In 1758 twelve almshouses and a chapel-house were added. Crowded from its opening, with aristocracy and poor alike, it had speedily to be enlarged, and became with a seating capacity of 5,000, the biggest Nonconformist church then in the world.[2] The enlargement was effected by the addition to the first building of an octangular front which became known as the "oven gallery." In 1828 the lease expired, and the chapel was closed till 1831, when the trustees bought the freehold, thoroughly renovated the building, and opened it in its former *smaller* form which seated three to four thousand persons, the length being one hundred and twenty-seven feet, the breadth seventy, and the height to dome one hundred and fourteen.[3]

[1] Where Messrs. Maple, Ltd. have their garage. See engraving in British Museum.

[2] An interesting confirmation of this fact is found in the life of the painter, J. Russell, R.A., by Williamson. "In the previous August there had been . . . a general sacrament at the Tabernacle in Tottenham Court Road, *several thousands* had communicated, and Hannah Faden amongst the number for the first time" (p. 21).

[3] *Life and Times of the Countess of Huntingdon*, Vol. I. p. 207.

A Prospect of the CHAPPLE in Tottenham Court Road Built A D 1756 by Voluntary Subscription for the Revd Mr GEORGE WHITEFIELD Chaplain to the R^t Honble the Count^efs of Huntingdon.

W.G. Bowden del.

TOTTENHAM COURT CHAPEL, ORIGINAL BUILDING

[Face page 200

In that greater building of Whitefield's heyday there must have been some wonderful preaching, and some most remarkable services. Audiences of five thousand and more at five and six o'clock in the morning must have been exhilarating enough. At that time Whitefield was preaching *fifteen times a week*. Two little snapshots of the kind of work he was doing must suffice us. One of his most frequent hearers in these great services was Shuter, the famous comedian of his time (we are not told how many lesser aspirants to stage honours than Garrick and Shuter waited on this most dramatic of preachers). Shuter's chief character on the stage at this period was "Ramble." On one occasion the comedian was seated in Tottenham Court Chapel right opposite the pulpit, where the preacher could hardly fail to see him. Suddenly the flaming eye of Whitefield met that of the actor and the evangelist swept away into a flood of tenderness by an all too apt simile cried, "And thou, *poor Ramble*, who hast long rambled from Him, come thou also. Oh end thy ramblings by coming to Jesus!" Shuter was overwhelmed, and afterwards coming to the preacher he said, "I thought I should have fainted— how could you serve me so?"

How nearly Shuter was to the great change may be judged by his reply to a friend who chaffed him with being a Methodist, "A precious method is mine," he replied, "no, I wish I were; if any be right they are."

On another famous occasion the faultlessly correct Lord Chesterfield was occupying Lady Huntingdon's pew, listening to the Awakener. Whitefield was describing a blind beggar led by a little dog. The dog had broken the string and the blind man groping with his stick was approaching a precipice. Suddenly his stick struck nothing and slipped from his grasp into the abyss. Whitefield went on to describe the beggar, groping forward for the stick he had dropped and hovering unwittingly over the dreadful brink. It was more than even the cynical worldling could stand. Chesterfield leapt to his feet crying, "By heaven, he's gone!"

It is quite impossible, taking Chesterfield's character into consideration, not to feel that the judgment of this shrewd man of the world regarding Whitefield is a considerable testimony to the intellectual as well as the emotional calibre of the preacher. When the evangelist was raising funds for his new tabernacle, Chesterfield sent him twenty pounds through Lady Huntingdon, remarking, "Mr. Whitefield's eloquence is unrivalled, his zeal inexhaustible."

The subsequent history of the Tottenham Court Chapel is no less noteworthy than its commencement. A succession of brilliant, though very varied, preachers have occupied its pulpit. Torial Joss, chosen by Whitefield himself, and as we have seen, a retired sea-captain, exercised for many years a most powerful ministry. Matthew Wilks, ministered in this centre for no less than fifty years. Other famous ministers were Dr. Llewellyn Bevan, afterwards Principal of Adelaide University, Australia; and the Rev. J. Jackson Wray, whose writings also were very popular in his time.

The Tottenham Court Chapel became a "Mother" of Churches in Central London—"from this venerable sanctuary" writes Tyerman, "sprang separate congregations in Shepherd's Market, Kentish Town, Paddington, Tonbridge Chapel in the Euston Road, Robert Street, Crown Street and Craven Chapel." This last, on closing as a Congregational Church in 1894, voted the residue of its funds to the new building in Tottenham Court Road, one of the foundation stones being laid by the senior deacon, Mr. A. Bywaters.

The old building, which had stood for about one hundred and fifty years, collapsed in 1889, and after ten years spent in two temporary iron buildings the present church was erected, being opened by Dr. Joseph Parker, of the City Temple, who for a short time, 1852 to 1853, had acted as assistant to Dr. Campbell.

It was through the patient and strenuous labours of the Rev. George Suttle, with the invaluable co-operation of Mr. Harry E. Gaze,[1] that the present building was erected in 1899, and the way prepared for a new outburst of fame. This came when Charles Silvester Horne, M.A., was called by the London Congregational Union who had acquired the property, to commence a great new experiment in Christian evangelism,

[1] It was by the active interest of Mr. Harry E. Gaze, the present Organising Secretary of Whitefield's, that a seven-years Chancery suit was sustained and won, delivering the church from a fair that occupied the adjoining ground and securing the latter as recreation gardens for the people.

TOTTENHAM COURT CHAPEL WITH THE ADDITION OF OVEN GALLERY

[*Face page* 202

the Institutional Church, as one of the Central Missions of the Congregational body. The district at the time contained many large business houses, whose assistants lived upon the premises, and the new organisation, with suitable halls and rooms provided at the rear of the Church,[1] was meant to provide a social and spiritual "home away from home" for these crowds of young people.

Very appropriately Charles Silvester Horne was not only a forceful preacher and magnetic personality, but he was also one of the great political forces of his day, a keen Radical, seeking to make social legislation a channel of the spirit of the Gospel. The Educational controversy of the early years of the century, against the bill of 1902, brought him most prominently into the leadership of the Free Churches [2] where his amazing platform eloquence swept audiences like a breath of flame. The institutional work he founded, and to which he imparted a unique atmosphere and with which he started a new tradition of socialised evangelism, is still maintained at a high level and is adapting itself to the new needs of a new age.

The personality and genius of Charles Silvester Horne so perfectly exemplify the plea of this book that we might well sit at his feet for a while. The more this passionately sympathetic soul came into contact with the pressures of social environment, under which the people he sought to save were suffering, the more emphatic grew his belief in the need for both individual and social rescue. He saw very plainly that social legislation was a handmaid of the Gospel. Never, therefore, since Puritan days, did the Free Church life of this country become so frankly and directly a political force as under the influence of Silvester Horne and his older, but also very brilliant, contemporary, Dr. John Clifford, of the Westbourne Park Baptist Church. It was the educational controversy that actually forced their hand, yet behind their action there was a clearly thought-out relation between religion and politics. To render social legislation Christian it was necessary, in their judgment, for Christian people to exercise their franchise religiously, and hence to think as religious people in terms of

---

[1] By the generosity of Mr. W. H. Brown, of Woodford.
[2] *Life of C. Silvester Horne*, Selbie, p. 127.

politics. Said Dr. Clifford on one occasion, "The New Testament Christian will go to the polling-booth as he goes to a prayer-meeting, and work in the election room in the same spirit of subordination to the will of God as he teaches in the Sunday School or directs Church affairs in the diaconate; excepting that his sense of responsibility for his judgment, temper, speech, and vote will be intensely quickened by the recollection that he is shaping issues religious and social not for tens of thousands but for hundreds of millions of his fellow-men."

Silvester Horne would have said Amen and Amen to that. In his volume, *Pulpit, Platform and Parliament*, he made his apologia for this strong alliance of evangelical religion and politics. Whilst passionately devoted to personal evangelism, he realised the wickedness and futility of leaving great numbers of humanity, already handicapped by bad heredity, to fight an unequal battle on an individual basis against giant environing social evils. We cannot do better than put his case in his own eloquent words.

"The dissolution of the greatest of all democratic parliaments in the year 1910 forced Free Churchmen and social reformers to face the constitutional issue. . . . The claim of the Peers to determine the financial policy of the country carried us back to the days when John Hampden broke the power of absolution in this very question of the hereditary right to tax England apart from the consent of her representatives. No good Independent could be out of that fight. Besides this claim of the Lords meant the defeat of every proposal to give Nonconformists equal rights with Churchmen to promotion in the teaching profession.

"All the reforms which experience had taught one were most urgently needed if Christian righteousness was to be more than a pulpit phrase and was to become an established fact, were jeopardised by the predominance of the House of Lords in the national counsels. It seemed to me then, and it seems to me now, to be at least as much a part of my business as a democrat and a social reformer to seek to perfect the machinery through which the national conscience can express itself, as to endeavour to educate and stimulate that conscience. . . . Christianity is bound up with democracy."

"No Church has ever yet perished of too great a zeal for the poor, or too sacrificial a love of freedom.

"Churches will survive the mistakes they make in trying to help their fellows; what they will not survive is the attitude of detachment when the destinies of peoples are in the balance." [1]

[1] *Pulpit, Platform and Parliament*, by Charles Silvester Horne, M.A., M.P.

REV. MATTHEW WILKS

REV. LL. D. BEVAN, LL.D.

REV. J. JACKSON WRAY

REV. CHARLES SILVESTER HORNE,
M.A., M.P.

[*Face page* 204

Silvester Horne fought two elections brilliantly and with overwhelming triumph, one within a year of the other, and on the second occasion he was Chairman of the Congregational Union of England and Wales.   Brilliant successor to the pulpit of George Whitefield, and highest official of Congregationalism, he was at the same time Member of Parliament—were ever the two streams of tradition—Evangelical and Social so perfectly blended?

In view of the ultimate contention of this book, and indeed the ultimate evolution of this twofold tradition of Christian activity, we may quote further from the crowning chapter of Silvester Horne's apologia.   In the chapter entitled, "A Possible Programme," he writes

". . . the one thing to be said is that the cry of 'No Politics' is always hollow and unintelligent and dishonest.   The people who use the cry only mean that they do not like to hear the other man's politics. . . . To the Free Churchman the principle of a Free Church in a Free State is not politics, it is 'New Testament Christianity'.

"Let us agree that politics is a great and noble science, and that no Christian citizen can afford to despise it.

"Let us agree that there are in front of our nation big political questions in regard to which the Church must let her mind be human, or else abdicate all claim to moral leadership.

"If the Church is uninterested in Education, Licensing Reform, Housing, the Reconstruction of the Poor Law, a Living Wage, Divorce, the arrest of Gambling, the abolition of Slavery and, above all, International Peace, the Church may as well disband her forces and make an ignominious exit from the society she can no longer inspire and guide."

Then comes a concrete and perfectly practical proposal which unfortunately has fallen thus far on deaf ears among the Free Churches.

"My suggestion is that the Churches should agree to carve out, as it were, of the general body of political questions certain problems as to whose social and moral character there can be no dispute, and frankly claim and freely exercise the right and the duty to deal with these questions in the light of Christian ethics."

"I am certain," he goes on to say, "that the result of such concerted action would be a body of social legislation of enormous value and a recovery by the Church of much of the moral authority which by her divisions she has lost."

This appeal, by far the most important and urgent legacy to Free Churchmen of Charles Silvester Horne, the "Sir Galahad" of nineteenth century Free Church life, is closed by an impressive echo of history:

"The story goes that in one of Cromwell's Parliaments, when a measure was introduced, the mover drew his New Testament from his pocket and quoted certain passages in support of the measure. Then, the historian says, the other members drew their Testaments from their pockets, verified the quotations, nodded to one another that the thing was so, and the measure passed without delay. I should be sorry to return to the process of argument from isolated texts. *But increasingly it ought to be the case that those measures which can make clear appeal to the spirit and teaching of the Son of Man should take their place on the statute-book.*" [1]

Such is the bold leadership bequeathed by Whitefield's most notable successor in the pulpit of Tottenham Court Chapel.[2] It looks towards an Appeal to Mankind by the Church, not in Word alone, nor in Individual Example alone, but in Concerted Social Action and in Corporate Social Life, which is ultimately the only perfect and adequate form of Evangelism.

---

[1] The italics are mine.

[2] The following relics of George Whitefield are in the possession of the Whitefield's Central Mission, Tottenham Court Road, and can be seen there:

1. The original deed granted to George Whitefield in 1756 by Earl Fitzroy for a piece of ground by the "Crab and Walnut Tree."
2. The original picture of George Whitefield preaching—his most widely-circulated portrait—by Hone.
3. Original Communion Table presented to Rev. C. S. Horne by widow of Rev. J. W. Richardson.
4. Original pulpit used by Whitefield, and from which Wesley preached the former's funeral sermon. Whitefield is reputed to have grown too stout to enter this pulpit at last, and humorously declared he would have to give up attacking representatives of the Established Church who had grown fat on pluralities.
5. The bust of George Whitefield, by the famous Enoch Wood, to which George Eliot refers in *Felix Holt.*
6. A secretaire of George Whitefield's and one of his shoe-buckles.

CHAPTER VIII

THE LAST PERIODS IN AMERICA

"Mutual Christian love will not permit you to forget a willing pilgrim, going now across the Atlantic for the thirteenth time."—GEORGE WHITEFIELD, in letter to Wesley, 1769.

WHITEFIELD paid in all seven visits to America, crossing the Atlantic to and fro thirteen times. Four of those visits remain to be outlined. The first of these was indeed a flying visit, for he landed in October, 1751, and within seven months was back in England. "Thanks be unto God all is well at Bethesda," was the report he was able to send to friends upon his arrival there. The prosperity of the Orphanage fired Whitefield with a new ambition to add thereto a college for preachers, and it was to present this petition in the right quarter before the time of the Trustees' Charter, which was near its end, could expire, that he hurried back to England. The scheme as we have already seen[1] was doomed to failure, and, as quaint John Berridge put it, Whitefield "was spared from becoming the father of a race of unconverted ministers." Doubtless he was the more relieved to have reason to return, seeing that his beloved mother had just "exchanged mortality for life," and there must have been domestic affairs calling for his attention. Whitefield's relations with his mother had always been of the most tenderly affectionate kind. His wandering life had made it impossible for him to enjoy her company very much, but he was always carefully solicitous for her welfare. On a recent birthday of his he had written to her thus:

"My dear and honoured Mother,

"To-morrow it will be thirty-five years since you brought unworthy me into the world. Alas! how little have I done for you,

[1] See p. 94.

and how much less for Him who formed me. This is my comfort: I hope you want for nothing. Thanks be to God for His goodness to you in your old age! I hope you comfort yourself in Him who, I trust, will be your portion for ever. After Christmas I hope to see you. My wife sends you her most dutiful respects. If you would have anything brought more than you have mentioned, pray write to, honoured mother, your ever dutiful, though unworthy son,

"GEORGE WHITEFIELD."

Previous to the Awakener's fifth visit to America a most interesting deputation arrived in England from the colonies, consisting of Gilbert Tennent, of the Log College, and Samuel Davies, the great Virginian preacher. They came to solicit subscriptions for a new college, founded by Governor Belcher at Princeton. This college was to supply ministers for the Presbyterian Churches of six colonies, New York, New Jersey, Pennsylvania, Maryland, Virginia and Carolina.[1] The Governor and his deputation were looking to George Whitefield for help in the prosecution of their design, and they did not look in vain. Every project of education, especially for the ministry, was dear to the heart of the Awakener, and he put the whole of his extensive connection in touch with the scheme, and his influence was simply invaluable to the founding of a cause that is to-day one of America's proudest institutions. An interesting side-light on the episode is provided by an extract from a diary kept by Samuel Davies.

"Wednesday, December 26, 1753.

"Mr. Whitefield having sent us an invitation to make his house our home during his stay here, we were perplexed what to do, lest we should blast the success of our mission among the Dissenters, who are generally disaffected to him. We at length concluded, with the advice of our friends and his, that a public intercourse with him would be imprudent in our present situation and we visited him privately this evening. The kind reception he gave us revived dear Mr. Tennent. He spoke in the most encouraging manner of the success of our mission, and in all his conversations, discovered so much zeal and candour, that I could not but admire the man as the wonder of the age. When we returned Mr. Tennent's heart was all on fire, and after we had gone to bed, he suggested that we should watch and pray; and we arose and prayed together till about three in the morning."

[1] Hodge's *Presbyterian Church in the United States*, quoted by Tyerman, Vol. II. p. 323.

Baptised with fire, cradled in prayer, the project could hardly fail of success.

On his fifth visit to the colonies (ninth voyage) Whitefield took twenty-two destitute children with him to house them in his Georgian home.[1]

On their journey they were held up at Lisbon for a month where, as we have already seen, Whitefield redeemed the time by an inquiry into "the full-blown Popery of the metropolis of Portugal." Four letters of his on his findings were published in England, and extensively quoted in the magazines and papers of the time. Even *The Monthly Review*, not at all friendly to Whitefield, was impressed and wrote, "Our celebrated itinerant preacher expresses a just and manly resentment of the miserable bigotry of the Portuguese and the priestly delusion with which they are led into even more ridiculous fopperies than ever disgraced the pagan theology."

Whitefield landed in South Carolina on May 21st, 1754, and proceeded at once with his young charges to Bethesda. Eight days later he was bound for New York, where he had a great reception and preached for a week. Thence, travelling in a chair, he proceeded to Newark, New Brunswick, Trent Town, *en route* for Philadelphia where he suffered a severe attack of "cholera morbus." There he preached in the New Building which he now calls "The Academy." On September 2nd he is back in New York, and talking of going on to Rhode Island but we lose all track of him here for about three weeks. He appears again in New Jersey at the opening of a new session of Governor Belcher's Princeton College. Here he was honoured with the degree of M.A., a "dubious honour," as Tyerman calls it, seeing that the college was in its infancy. This is undoubtedly why Whitefield never placed it beside his Oxford B.A. degree.[2]

New England could not fail to draw the Awakener on this revival tour, and in October 14th he is again flaming forth in Boston. "Thousands waited for, and thousands attended on the word preached." "At the Old North . . . at seven in the morning, we generally have three thousand hearers and many cannot come in." The numbers soon rise to four thousand and Whitefield is preaching in turn at four Meeting Houses, so

---

[1] Dr. Gillies.

[2] In view of his Pembroke degree no exception can be taken to M.A. after Whitefield's name, though it was never used by himself.

full that he has to be helped into the pulpits through the windows!

From Portsmouth, New Hampshire, he writes, "I am now come to the end of my northward line, and in a day or two purpose to turn back, and to preach all the way to Georgia. It is almost a sixteen hundred mile journey." Through Newbury, York, Kittery, Rowley, Byfield, Ipswich, Cape Ann and back to Boston he passes like a living flame, and then a month transpires with no news. The Awakener has set out on his great preaching trek, this time on horseback, for his preaching has again set him up in health. "The reader must try and imagine the great preacher pursuing his immense horseback ride, making the primeval forests ring with his songs of praise and preaching the Gospel of his Master twice and thrice every day."[1]

By Christmas he is in Maryland. From Bohemia in that State he writes to Lady Huntingdon on December 27th. "I am now forty years of age, and would gladly spend the day in retirement and deep humiliation before the Jesus, for whom I have done so little."

A great reception awaited Whitefield in Virginia, where Samuel Davies' first church, built upon the mere reading of Whitefield's sermons, had multiplied to seven, and where, in three years, three hundred communicants had been gathered and forty negro slaves baptised. On his visit to England, Davies had succeeded in getting the Toleration Act extended to Virginia, and the simultaneous appointment of a new and more sympathetic Governor (doubtless through the Whitefield-Huntingdon influence) had opened up the way for further progress.

"Scenes of wonder have opened all the way. A thousandth part cannot be told," wrote the Awakener to Charles Wesley of this visit.

On February 26th Whitefield, having been to Georgia and back to spend all too short a period at the Orphan House, was preaching at Charleston. Writing from there in March, just before embarking for England, he says: "Had I the wings of a dove how often would I have fled to Bethesda since my departure from it . . . the last few hours I was there were superior in satisfaction to any hours I ever enjoyed. But I

[1] Tyerman.

must go about my Heavenly Father's business. For this I am a poor but willing pilgrim and give up all that is near and dear to me on this side of eternity."

He sailed for England on his tenth ocean voyage on March 27th, and after a passage of six weeks, landed at Newhaven, little realising that the outbreak of the Seven Years' War would prevent his leaving for America again for some eight years. Not till 1763 was he able to pay his sixth visit to the colonies. He was at this time a very sick man indeed, and found the voyage a great relief. "I have enjoyed," he wrote from aboard ship, "that quietness which I have in vain sought after some years on shore. Not an oath has been heard even in the greatest hurry. All has been harmony and love. But my breath is short, and since my relapse in Scotland, I have little hope of much further public usefulness. A few exertions like the last struggles of a dying man, are all that can be expected from me." Soon after landing in Virginia he wrote a pastoral letter to his flock at Tottenham Court Road of which the following is an extract:

"Often, often have I thought of my dear London friends, when I guessed they were assembled together; and as often prayed, when I knew that they were retired to rest, that He, who keepeth Israel, would watch over them, and make their dreams devout. . . .
"Had I strength equal to my will I could fly from pole to pole. Though wearied and now almost worn out I am not weary of my blessed Master's service. O love Him! Love Him! . . . through His love I hope to see you again next year. Meanwhile, as long as I have breath, it shall be my heart's desire and prayer to God, that the labours of the dear servants of Jesus, who are called to preach amongst you, may be so blessed that I may not be missed a single moment."

The evangelist spent two months among his old friends at Philadelphia, but his health did not much improve. Full of plans for visiting Bethesda and continuing his itinerant ministry, nevertheless, through ill-health and also the menace of Indians on the warpath, he had to spend more than a year content, except for a minimum of preaching, namely twice a week, with writing only.

Then, with renewed strength, he spent four days at New Jersey College and two at Elizabeth Tower en route for New York, preaching with something of his old-time vigour. "My spirits grow better," he repeats. Of New Jersey College he wrote, "a blessed nursery, one of the purest, perhaps in the universe. The worthy president and three tutors are all bent upon making the students both saints and scholars."

In many of his letters at this time Whitefield uses the quaint phrase "new-creature ministers," and it serves to remind us that a notable feature of his work in both Britain and America was the large number of converted ministers he raised up to be a new strength to the Churches.

The colder atmosphere of the northern colonies assisted his steady recovery.

The correspondent of the *Boston Gazette*, writing from New York, was able to report, "The Rev. Mr. George Whitefield has spent seven weeks with us preaching twice a week with more general acceptance than ever. . . . For the benefit of Mr. Wheelock's Indian School, at Lebanon, in New England . . . he collected (notwithstanding the prejudices of many people against the Indians) the sum of £120. In his last sermon he took a very affectionate leave of the people of this city, who expressed great concern at his departure. May God restore this just and good man (in whom the gentleman, the Christian, and the accomplished orator shine forth with such lustre) to a perfect state of health and continue him long a blessing to the world and the Church of Christ!"

An overwhelming welcome awaited Whitefield in Boston because of his magnificent achievement in 1761 in raising in Britain such an enormous sum of money for the sufferers in the great Boston fire.

A great town's meeting was held, and a public vote of thanks was passed to him. Whitefield's letter of acknowledgement was characteristic:

"Gentlemen,
"This vote of thanks for so small an instance of my good-will to Boston, as it was entirely unexpected, quite surprises me. Often I have been much concerned that I could do no more upon such a distressing occasion. That the Redeemer may ever preserve the town from such-like melancholy events, and sanctify the present afflictive circumstances to the spiritual welfare of all its inhabitants, is the hearty prayer of
Gentlemen, your ready servant in our common Lord,
"GEORGE WHITEFIELD."

A further calamity to one of Boston's finest institutions gave George Whitefield at this time another opportunity of proving the value of his friendship to the city. In 1638 the Rev. John Harvard, a minister of Charlestown, near Boston, had died and bequeathed to the College at Newton, afterwards re-named Cambridge, one half of his estate and all his library. In honour of this benefactor, the college was henceforth named "Harvard." Other magnates and men of wealth followed suit, and left handsome bequests to this College, which has since exercised so profound an influence on American life. At one time every family in the colony gave to Harvard a peck of corn, or its value in twelvepence or unadulterated wampumpeag,[1] such was the veneration in which the citizens of Boston and its neighbourhood held the institution. The Library of the College was at this time entirely destroyed by fire. Whitefield immediately wrote home to England and secured fresh gifts of books, mostly of the Puritan school of thought, for a new library.

Preaching round about Boston, at Concord, Portsmouth, Newbury, he was able to report "there is a stir indeed. Oh for daily fresh gales!"

About a month later Whitefield turned his face southward for Bethesda, but the Bostonians sent a "hue and cry after him." They would not let the Awakener go! So great was their importunity and spiritual enthusiasm that he returned and ministered in the city for a further eight weeks, with lectures at six o'clock in the morning, concerning which Whitefield wrote, "I would fain die preaching."

The evangelist's apparent dilatoriness in turning southward was entirely due to his struggle against advancing disease. The colder, more bracing air of the north, however, in due time had its good effect upon him and in September, 1764, he reached Philadelphia again after most solemn and heartbreaking partings at Boston and New York.

No sooner had he arrived than he was impounded to preach the Commencement sermon of the College of Philadelphia, the provost of which was Dr. William Smith, educated at Aberdeen University, a most popular and talented principal.

"Dr. Smith," writes Whitefield, "read prayers for me; both the present and the late governor, with the head gentlemen

---

[1] Bancroft's *History of the United States*, quoted by Tyerman.

of the city, were present; and cordial thanks were sent to me from all the trustees, for speaking for the children, and countenancing the institution. This is all of God. To me nothing belongs but shame and confusion of face. O for a truly guileless heart." [1]

Writing to John Wesley at this time the Awakener says, "The gospel range [here] is of such a large extent, that I have, as it were, scarce begun to begin. Surely nothing but a very loud call of Providence could make me so much as think of returning to England as yet. . . . Here is room for a hundred itinerants. Lord Jesus! Send by whom Thou wilt send! . . . I am persuaded you are like-minded. I wish you and all your dear fellow-labourers great prosperity. . . . Methinks, for many years, *we* have heard a voice behind us saying, 'This is the way, walk ye in it.' I do not repent being a poor, despised cast-out, and now almost worn-out intinerant. I would do it again if I had my choice. . . . Even the last glimmerings of an expiring taper He blesses to guide some wandering souls to Himself. In New England, New York, and Pennsylvania, the word has run and been glorified."

Was this emphasis by Whitefield upon the need for itinerant preachers the challenge which aroused in Wesley's mind the vision of an American Methodism with Societies founded after the English pattern? Certainly the colonies had been well prepared, through Whitefield's labours, for such a venture. Moreover on his journey from Philadelphia, through Virginia and the North and South Carolinas, Whitefield met everywhere the "New Lights," as they were nicknamed, who were the analogue of the Methodists of Britain. These were plants of his own sowing, for everywhere throughout America the Awakener's strenuous and self-exhausting labours were bearing rich fruit. It was into this rich inheritance Wesley's preachers came.

At Bethesda once again Whitefield plunged into new plans for turning the Orphan House into a College, and within a week he was applying to the Governor of Georgia for a grant of two thousand acres for this purpose. Whitefield's memorial is too lengthy a document to insert,[2] but the Governor's courteous reply is a fine tribute to the evangelist.

[1] *Whitefield's Works*, Vol. III, p. 315.
[2] For account of opening ceremony, see p. 94.

"Gentlemen,

"I am so perfectly sensible of the very great advantage which will result to the Province in general, from the establishment of a seminary for learning here, that it gives me great pleasure to find so laudable an undertaking proposed by the Rev. Mr. White-field. The friendly and zealous disposition of that gentleman, to promote the prosperity of this Province, has been often experienced, and you may rest assured that I shall transmit your address home, with my best endeavours for the success of the great point in view.

"JAMES WRIGHT."

"December 20, 1764."

Not troubling this time to consult high dignitaries, ecclesiastical or political, in England, and being engaged also upon a more modest plan than before, Whitefield carried through his project with a bold hand, to a most successful conclusion.[1]

Writing home in February, 1765, Whitefield was able for once to record, "On Tuesday next, God willing, I move towards Charleston, leaving all arrears paid off, and some cash in hand, besides the last year's whole crop of rice, some lumber, the house repaired, painted, furnished with plenty of clothing and provision till the next crop comes in and perhaps some for sale." Unfortunately he was compelled to add, "the smallpox has gone through the house, with the loss of six negroes and four orphans. Before this, I think not above four children have been taken off these twenty-four years. . . . And now farewell, my beloved Bethesda, surely the most delightfully situated place in all the Southern parts of America."

After sundry preachings through Virginia and Maryland and around Charleston and Philadelphia, Whitefield left New York again for England, and after a quick passage of only twenty-eight days arrived in the homeland on July 7th.

An article that appeared about this time in the Lloyd's *Evening Post* is interesting enough to be noticed: After condemning "the incoherent, wild, and unconnected jargon" of Whitefield and his friends, the writer acknowledged "they had greater success than the Church of England clergymen."

He was profoundly grieved to see the "irreverent behaviour" at church services, such as "gaping and yawning, picking their noses, rubbing their faces, admiring and exposing to admiration their little finger with its ring on, and staring all round the

[1] See Tyerman. Vol. II. p. 479.

church even when rehearsing the most solemn prayers." For this he blamed the clergymen "their sloth and idleness!" "On the other hand," he wrote, "the Methodist preacher strains his voice to the utmost, that everyone may hear, and affects a tone of voice and manner of pronunciation most likely to impress and please his hearers." "In this really severe and fatiguing manner of utterance, he gives long discourses and exposes his person anywhere, in any corner, on any dunghill, and gets well pelted every now and then." [1]

Such was the character of newspaper comment on a new religious sect in the year 1765.

Only one more visit to America was to be permitted to the Awakener! On Monday, September 4th, 1769, he left his native land nevermore to return. His last day before embarking was appropriately enough a Sunday, and was spent in a characteristic way: "He preached on Sunday morning in the Methodist Tabernacle (Gravesend) and in the afternoon[2] in the Market Place. His last text, as he thought it would be, John xii. 32, to a Christian audience in this favoured land, was significant enough. "I, if I be lifted up, will draw all men unto Me"—there is the Awakener's world-outlook!

[1] See Tyerman. Vol II. p. 486.
[2] Not "in the evening" as the *St. James' Chronicle* for Sept. 7th has it.

CHAPTER IX

THE PASSING OF THE AWAKENER

"O to be kept from flagging on the latter stages of the road."—GEORGE WHITEFIELD.

CONSIDERABLE pathos attaches to the last utterances of Whitefield to his congregations at Moorfields and Tottenham Court Chapel. Though he could not be certain that he would never see them again he dwelt in these latter years so continually on the brink of collapse that doubtless he felt he must treat this thirteenth crossing of the world with deep seriousness The fact is stressed by some of his biographers [1] that his preaching had fallen off somewhat in these last years. Even Wesley, rather ungenerously, one feels, seeing that he must have known how fierce was Whitefield's struggle with sickness, refers slightingly to Whitefield's indebtedness for quaint turns of speech to Matthew Henry.[2] However that may be, the people still hung upon those eloquent lips and thronged to hear him preach. In the course of his last sermon in the Tottenham Court Chapel, Whitefield said:

"It is now high time for me to preach my own *funeral* sermon. I am going for the thirteenth time, to cross the Atlantic. When I came from America last, my health was so bad that I took leave of all friends on the Continent, from one end to the other, without the least design of returning to them again. But, to my great surprise, God has been pleased to restore to me some measure of strength; and though I intended to give up the Orphan House into other hands, God has so ordered it, that his Grace the late Archbishop of Canterbury refused me a charter, unless I would confine it to episcopacy. I could not, in honour, comply with this, as Dissenters, and other serious people of different denominations,

[1] See Tyerman, p. 566.
[2] In the preface to his *Explanatory Notes upon the Old Testament*. The reference is without a name but generally supposed to be to Whitefield.

217

had contributed towards its support. I would sooner cut off my head than betray my trust. I always meant the Orphan House to be kept upon a broad bottom, for people of all denominations. I hope, by the 25th of March next, all intended alterations and additions will be completed, and a blessed provision be made for many hundreds, and a comfortable support for poor orphans and poor students. This is my only design in going. I intend to travel all along the Continent. I am going in no further capacity. I am going, trusting God to bear my charges. . . . I might have been rich; but now, though this chapel is built, and though I have a comfortable room to live in, I assure you I built the room at my own expense. It cost nobody but myself anything, and I shall leave it with an easy mind. I have thought of these words with pleasure, 'I will bring thee again to this land.' I know not whether that will be my experience; but blessed be God! I have a better land in view. I do not look upon myself at home until I land in my Father's house. My greatest trial is to part with those who are as dear to me as my own soul."

In his final utterance at the Moorfields Tabernacle, Whitefield went further into financial matters. He said:

"As this place has been repaired, and I am wishful to leave everything clear before I go, a collection must be made for defraying the expense incurred. The world thinks I am very rich. A man, the other day, sent me word, that if I did not lay £30 in a certain place, I should be killed. You, yourselves, perhaps, think I get a great deal for preaching here; and therefore now I am going away, I will tell you my stated allowance for preaching at the Tabernacle. I have no more in this place than £100 a year; and yet, when I asked last night how the accounts stood, I was told there were £50 arrears. 'Well,' I said, 'ungrateful as it is to me, I will make a collection that all may be left free.' There are not six people in this Tabernacle from whom I have had the value of a guinea from last January to the present month of August; nor have I had a guinea from all the ordinances of this place towards bearing the expenses of my voyage." [1]

An interesting side-light this upon Whitefield's task of financing his churches and himself.

Whitefield set out on his last journey to America on September 4th, 1769, but was held up in the Downs for a month in similar fashion to the delay that occurred on his very first voyage.

[1] From Gurney's Volume of Whitefield's *Sermons*, printed 1770. Over this volume there was much unpleasantness. "Whitefield's discourses of late years were very unfit for the Press without undergoing considerable alterations."

THE PASSING OF THE AWAKENER

Writing to one of his preachers, Thomas Adam, of Rodborough, he said:

"On board the *Friendship* (Captain Bell), September 5th, 1769, six in the morning. My very dear Tommy, I will not write you whilst ashore, but drop you a few lines now I am come aboard. Just now we have taken up the anchor; and I trust my anchor is within the veil. I have not been better in spirits for some years; and I am persuaded this voyage will be for the Redeemer's glory, and the welfare of precious souls. Our parting solemnities have been exceeding awful. O England! England! God preserve thee from every threatening storm!

> "Less than the least of all,
> "GEORGE WHITEFIELD."

In a letter to John Wesley, Whitefield exclaimed:

"What hath God wrought *for* us, *in* us, and *by* us! I sailed out of these Downs almost thirty-three years ago. O, the height, the depth, the length, the breadth of Thy love, O God! Surely it passeth knowledge!"

By an appropriate coincidence at the very time the Awakener was leaving England to die in America, John Wesley's first two missionaries to the American colonies were crossing the ocean to take up their labours. Whitefield's work was drawing to its close, but already the sound of the swiftly following feet of many heralds of Methodism could be heard. He had prepared the way for Wesley's preachers to found a Church that is now the largest in the American Continent!

Driven by a tremendous storm into Deal, Whitefield was privileged to linger still, for a while, in his native land and preach other unexpected "final" sermons.[1]

To his friend Keen, Whitefield wrote:

> "Deal,
> "September 17, 1769.

"Mr. Bradbury put me under an arrest and is carrying me away to Ramsgate. I hope to arrest some poor runaway bankrupts for the Captain of our Salvation. For Christ's sake let all means be used to keep up the Tottenham Court and Tabernacle Societies."

Later: "I have just returned from Ramsgate. . . . I preached Friday and Saturday."

It took Whitefield and his companions, Cornelius Winter and Mr. Richard Smith, nine weeks to reach America. He

[1] *Memoirs of Cornelius Winter*, p, 88.

preached on board with all his old-time vigour, and finished the voyage in better health than he had enjoyed for many years.

At Charlestown, where they arrived on Thursday, November 30th, 1770, Whitefield preached to large congregations with great power. There his manager from Bethesda met him, and within a few days the little company set out in an open boat for Savannah.

"We had," writes Cornelius Winter,[1] "a pleasant passage through the Sounds, and frequently went on shore, and regaled ourselves in the woods. The simplicity of the negroes, who rowed us, was very diverting. We stopped at a plantation called Port Royal, where we were most kindly refreshed and entertained, and safely arrived at Savannah on December 14th. Mr. Whitefield was cheerful and easy, and seemed to have lost a weight of care."

Almost directly upon Whitefield's arrival at Bethesda there occurred the great red-letter day for the Orphan House— the opening of the extra Academy buildings[2]—two additional wings for apartments for students, a hundred and fifty feet each in length.

In a letter written on April 20th, 1770, Whitefield intimates his intention to resume his American itinerary as far, at least, as Philadelphia, and he bursts out:

"Was ever man blessed with such a set of skilful, peaceful, laborious helpers! O Bethesda! My Bethel! My Peniel! My happiness is inconceivable."

That was as it should be, for on the 24th of the month Whitefield left Bethesda for ever.

At Philadelphia he met Wesley's new missionaries to the Colonies, Boardman and Milmon, and did all in his power to help forward their mission.

An American Methodist historian[3] writes thus about Whitefield's ready co-operation in this matter.

"In the year 1770 Mr. W. passed through Philadelphia and, calling on our preachers . . . expressed to them his great satisfaction in finding them in this country where there was such a great call for faithful labourers. . . . His labours as an itinerant preacher have been greatly blessed to the people of America, and

---

[1] Memoirs.   [2] See page 94.   [3] *Georgia Gazette.*

thereby the way was opened for our teachers to travel and preach in different parts of the country."[1]

Whitefield preached in the city for nearly three weeks with as great effect as ever upon the people, and without apparent injury to his new-found health.

By June 23rd he was in New York, accompanied by one of the first and finest products of the New Jersey College, Rev. Samuel Kirkland, who afterwards became a celebrated evangelist to the Oneida tribes. His son, Dr. Kirkland, became President of Harvard College.

On July 29th, 1770, Whitefield, still "the Awakener," was able to report in a letter to Mr. Keen:

"During this month I have been above a five hundred mile circuit and enabled to preach every day. The congregations have been very large, attentive and affected, particularly at Albany, Schenectady, Great Barrington, Norfolk, Salisbury, Sharon, Smithfield, Powkeepsy, Fishkill, New Rumburt, New Windsor, and Peekskill. . . . O what a new scene of usefulness is opening in various parts of the new world! All fresh work where I have been! The Divine influence is as at the first. Invitations crowd upon me, both from ministers and people."

It is said that Whitefield's preaching was never more powerful or popular than at this time. It was as though God blessed him with an "Indian Summer" just before the end. Doubtless, however, the success attending these efforts increased seriously the strain upon his already sapped constitution.

Preaching at Sharon during this itinerary, Whitefield chose his favourite subject, "Ye must be born again." The enormous congregation that had gathered was simply overwhelmed with a flood of emotion but, extraordinarily enough, it was the concluding sentences of the sermon which sent an entirely peculiar and still richer wave of feeling over the assembly, so that an "impression for life" was made upon all who heard it.

"Awake, O north wind," cried that marvellous voice, "and come, thou South; blow upon this garden that the spices thereof may flow out. Let my beloved come into this garden, and eat his pleasant fruits."

[1] *History of the Methodists in America*, Jesse Lee.

221

Simple conclusion though it was, we are told that it was uttered with such melting pathos and beauty of cadence as to thrill the whole audience to an unforgetable degree.[1]

On another of these occasions, a well-known shipbuilder who heard him preach declared, in answer to the question "What do you think of Mr. Whitefield?"—"Think! I never heard such a man in my life! I tell you, sir, every Sunday, when I go to church I can build a ship from stem to stern under the sermon; but were it to save my soul, under Mr. Whitefield, I could not build a single plank."

The last two months of his life were spent in a grand itinerary of New England towns—a triumphal progress of impassioned evangelism. Commencing on August 4th at New Port, he visited Providence, Attleborough, Wrentham, Malden, and then had a spell of ten days in Boston! Thence he passed to Medford, Charlestown, and Cambridge, and back to Boston again! Roxbury Plain, Milton, Roxbury and Boston! Salem, North Head, Salem again, Cape Ann, Ipswich, Newbury Port, and Rowley—these made a tour that left him prostrated for several days with sickness! From September 17th to 19th he was again preaching in Boston and on the 20th at Newton. Then, although very ill, he managed to reach Portsmouth from Boston and preached for two days. Thence he went on to Rittery Old York and back to Portsmouth.

On the 29th of September he preached his last sermon in the open air at Exeter.[2] He was on his way back to Boston when the good people of Exeter prevailed upon him to preach.

"Sir," said a friend to him, "you are more fit to go to bed than to preach."

"True," replied Whitefield, and then, clasping his hands and looking up to heaven, he added: "Lord Jesus, I am weary in Thy work, but not of it. If I have not yet finished my course, let me go and speak for Thee once more in the fields, seal Thy truth, and come home and die!"

A vast multitude quickly assembled as he mounted a hogshead, and preached from the text, "Examine yourselves whether you be in the faith." One who was present and heard that last open-air sermon reports:

[1] Wakeley's *Anecdotes of Whitefield*.
[2] Since commemorated by a Memorial Stone.

MEDALLION STRUCK ON OCCASION OF
WHITEFIELD'S DEATH, 1770.

[*Face page* 222

"Mr. Whitefield arose, and stood erect, and his appearance alone was a powerful sermon. He remained several minutes unable to speak, and then said, 'I will wait for the gracious assistance of God; for He will, I am certain, assist me once more to speak in His Name.' He then delivered, perhaps, one of his best sermons. 'I go,' he cried, 'I go to rest prepared; my sun has arisen and by aid from heaven has given light to many. It is now about to set—no, it is about to rise to the zenith of immortal glory. I have outlived many on earth, but they cannot outlive me in heaven. O thought divine! I soon shall be in a world where time, age, pain and sorrow are unknown. My body fails, my spirit expands. How willingly would I live for ever to preach Christ. But I die to be with Him.'"

The Awakener on this last field-preaching spoke for two hours—spending himself to the last drop of his all too meagre strength. Though seemingly exhausted by his effort, White-field, after dining with Captain Gillman, started by boat for Newbury Port but, on arrival, he was too weak to leave the vessel. Eventually, with assistance, he reached the parsonage of the Old South Church, and towards evening he revived. Whilst he was at supper, crowds began to gather in front of the house. They even pushed their way into the hall of the house, hoping to hear that wonderful voice again.

"I am tired," said Whitefield, "and must go to bed." He took a lighted candle and sought his chamber, but the sight of the crowd filling the hall and street and patiently waiting was too much for him. Pausing on the staircase he began to speak, and then, insensibly, to preach. It was "the ruling passion strong in death," and his voice went on pleading, exhorting, flaming and waning and flaming again until the candle went out, *burnt down to the socket!*

At two o'clock in the morning a violent attack of his old enemy, asthma, took him. Unable to sleep further, he spent the time in prayer—asking God to bless the utterances he had recently made, to help him to bring more souls to Christ, to guide him in his future plans, to bless his great family at Bethesda, to be gracious to his London congregations at Moorfields and Tottenham Court Chapel.

At five o'clock he rose to open the window further, struggling for more air. Presently he turned to his friend, Richard Smith, and said, "I am dying." He ran to another window panting for breath. His friends did all they could to restore him, but nothing availed, and at six o'clock on Sunday morning, September 30th, 1770, he, who had awakened so vast a multitude of souls from the death of sin to the life that is life indeed, was himself awakened from this mortal dream to the Life that is without end.[1]

Those last sermons, however, which had cost the world so valuable a life, were they not worth even that price? Here is but one result known and measurable, but what others there were, who can tell till the great day of revealing? A young sailmaker of Portsmouth, named Benjamin Randall, had heard him and hated and reviled him for what he had heard. But about noon on the day of the Awakener's passing the crier went round Portsmouth calling, "Whitefield is dead! Whitefield is dead!" And a voice of thunder echoed in that youth's soul! "Whitefield is dead, Whitefield is in heaven, but *I* am on the road to hell." Shaken to his inmost depths, Randall gave himself up a willing prisoner to God. In the course of time he founded, in the United States, the Free-Will Baptist Church, a cause which consistently opposed slavery, and is to-day some one hundred thousand strong in membership. Thus did God own the Awakener's message and seal his power in the very hour and article of death.

On Tuesday, October 2nd, according to what is claimed to be his wish,[2] George Whitefield was buried beneath the pulpit of his friend, Jonathan Parsons, in the First Presbyterian Church of Newbury Port, better known as the Old South Church, which the evangelist had been instrumental in founding.[3] The scene was indescribable, six thousand members and ministers of all Churches crowding and surrounding the building. The hymns could not be sung for the crying and sobbing, and the outward demonstrations of grief seemed to eddy out from that little town by the Merrimac till they filled the whole world. The

---

[1] By a curious coincidence—Sept. 30th was exactly the date 30 years before, of Whitefield's first visit to Newbury Port.

[2] In 1927 the author, preaching in this church in honour of Whitefield, ventured to suggest that the American nation might present the body of Whitefield to Britain for interment in Westminster Abbey. It would be a gesture of friendship in the spirit of Whitefield's own love for both countries. The fact that Whitefield expressed a wish to be buried in Newbury Port, whilst undisputed, has been honoured for two centuries. Might not his bones now find permanent rest under conditions of greater honour to the man?

[3] See page 5, note.

THE CENOTAPH, IN MEMORY OF GEORGE WHITEFIELD,
which stands beside the pulpit in the Old South Presbyterian
Church, Newburyport, Mass., U.S.A.

[Face page 224

bells of Newbury Port were tolled, the ships in the harbour fired their guns in salute of the departed leader and hung their flags at half-mast, but, as the news spread over two nations, vast audiences began to gather everywhere to express their loss and to feel once more, often with overwhelming power, the force of the Gospel the Awakener had preached with such love. In Georgia the stores ran out of every stitch of anything black, so widespread was the population's mourning, and Governor and Council led the procession to the Memorial Sermon.

In London, not only did multitudes surge about the Tabernacle and the Chapel to hear John Wesley's eloquent tributes to the great pioneer—tributes of love and grief and triumph—but Churches and Chapels and Societies all over the metropolis and the country seemed to vie with each other in the magnitude and solemnity of their Commemoration Services. It was as though the Mighty Spirit of the Awakener, released by death, swept once more over the cities and towns and villages, where his wonderful voice had been so often heard, in one last grand Visitation of pleading love and Gospel appeal, sealing thousands finally in the Faith.

The tribute, that Whittier so eloquently and truly bears[1] to Whitefield, living and preaching, was just as true of Whitefield dead:

"So the flood of emotion deep and strong
Troubled the land as it went along,
And left a result of holier lives,
Tenderer mothers, worthier wives.
The husband and father whose children fled
And sad wife wept when his drunken tread
Frightened peace from his roof tree's shade,
And a rock of offence his hearthstone made,
In a strength that was not his own, began
To rise from the brute's to the plane of man.
Old friends embraced, long held apart
By evil counsel and pride of heart;
And penitence saw through misty tears
In the bow of hope on its clouds of fears,
The promise of Heaven's eternal years,—
The peace of God for the world's annoy,—
Beauty for ashes, and oil of joy!"

"And he being dead *yet* speaketh!"

[1] *The Preacher.*

225

PART IV

The Awakener's Challenge

"To awaken a drowsy world, to rouse them out of their
formality, as well as profaneness, and put them upon seeking
a present and great salvation."—George Whitefield.

CHAPTER I

THE MAN—PIONEER OF MODERN EVANGELISM—PHILANTHROPY AND EDUCATION

"Oh! for a mind divested of all sects and names and parties. I care not if the name of George Whitefield be banished out of the world so that Jesus be exalted in it."—GEORGE WHITEFIELD.

IN trying to focus the challenge of this eighteenth century story upon our own life and times we must begin with the man himself. We have seen his humble beginnings and glimpsed something of the amazing range, profundity and value of his ultimate influence on the world; yet how meagre is his fame among men!

It is difficult for humanity ever to do justice to two heroes simultaneously, and without detracting in the least from the worth of John Wesley, there is little doubt that Whitefield has been seriously underrated. It is difficult to escape the conclusion that the fierce and contemptuous criticism that Whitefield's daring policy inevitably drew upon him, the sheer amount of "mud" flung at him, combined with the irritation with which the "natural man" tends to react towards the evangelist, accounts for the very adverse verdicts passed by some well-known writers upon George Whitefield. For people cut off from the life of the multitude and sheltered in cultured literary or aristocratic circles, it is fatally easy to slip into the fallacy of dismissing every man who captures the crowd as a shallow-pated demagogue and mountebank. Wesley tended to escape this ready-made condemnation because he entered later upon the practice of unusual methods and an older man (he was eleven years senior to Whitefield) can always challenge the world

229

more successfully than a youth can do. Moreover, Wesley was undoubtedly, as a Fellow of Lincoln, the more reputable scholar, and also he was a constructive ecclesiastic. Was there nothing of sheer impatience with demagogy and subconscious bias against the Gospel-preacher in Dr. Johnson's references to Whitefield? Says Boswell:

"We talked of Whitefield. He said he was at the same college with him and knew him *before he began to be better than other people* (smiling); that he believed he sincerely meant well, but had a mixture of politics[1] and ostentation, whereas Wesley thought of religion only." Robertson said: "Whitefield had great natural eloquence which, if cultivated, would have done great things." Johnson: "Why, Sir, I take it he was at the height of what his abilities could do, and was sensible of it. He had the ordinary advantages of education; but he chose to pursue the oratory that is for the mob." Boswell: "He had great effect upon the passions." Johnson: " Why Sir, I don't think so. He could not represent a succession of pathetic images.[2] He vociferated and made an impression. There again was a mind like a hammer."

Two other verdicts of Johnson's are quoted elsewhere by Boswell.

"Whitefield never drew as much attention as a mountebank does; he did not draw attention by doing better than others, but by doing what was strange. Were Astley to preach a sermon standing upon his head on a horse's back, he would collect a multitude to hear him, but no wise man would say he made a better sermon for that."

"I never treated Whitefield's ministry with contempt; I believe he did good. He had devoted himself to the lower classes of mankind, and among them he was of use. But when familiarity and noise claim the praise due to knowledge, art and elegance, we must beat down such pretensions."

"His (Whitefield's) popularity, Sir, is chiefly owing to the peculiarity of his manner. He would be followed by crowds were he to wear a night-cap in the pulpit, or were he to preach from a tree."

It is time this was dismissed as so much ill-natured "coffee-house" gossip by a rather snobbish, cross-grained, clever old *littérateur* whose interest was in "knowledge, art and elegance" rather than in the moral and spiritual salvation of the "lower

[1] Where is this evident in Whitefield's story? Does not the Doctor mean ' demagogy ', isn't he fearing the politics of the rabble?
[2] As to the truth of this statement *cf.* sermon quoted on p. 210.

classes." There is much to be said for Macaulay's judgment of Johnson, "The characteristic peculiarity of his intellect was the union of great powers with low prejudices." This judgment is confirmed both by Johnson's cheap dismissal of other celebrities[1] and more especially by his attitude to certain Methodist students expelled from the University of Oxford in 1768.

"Sir," said Johnson to Boswell, "the expulsion was extremely just and proper. What have they to do at a University who are not willing to be taught but will presume to teach? Where is religion to be learned but at a University? Sir, they were examined and found to be mighty ignorant fellows." Boswell: "But was it not hard to expel them, for I am told they were good beings?" Johnson: "I believe they might be good beings, but they were not fit to be in the University of Oxford. A cow is a very good animal in the field, but we turn her out of a garden."

One of the charges brought against these men was for extempore praying, and in his defence of them, Whitefield made a caustic comment which is sufficient answer to the "great Bear" Johnson himself: "It is also to be hoped that as some have been expelled for extempore praying we shall hear of some being expelled for extempore swearing. The voice of spiritual melody would be as much to the honour of the University as the more frequent noise of box and dice at the unlawful games of hazard and back-gammon."

Gledstone's remarks on such contemporary opinions about Whitefield are sound. He writes: "It was principally states-men—Pitt and Fox among the number, never Burke—who went to hear him. Hogarth disgraced his genius by some indecent caricatures of him; Pope by abusing him in the Dunciad. Not one of the celebrated Literary Club, Garrick excepted, was ever seen in the soul-trap. Oglethorpe was a kind of link between the Club and the Tabernacle. A friend of Whitefield's; he was also a friend of Goldsmith. . . . But the easy ways of many of these sons of genius, their wine sipping, their gaiety and their sins, sufficiently explain how it was that in all Whitefield's career not one of them crossed his path."

[1] *Cf.* conversation about Burke.

One fears that the Johnsonian strictures have had an undue share in the depreciation of Whitefield. Thus, for example, the picture of the great evangelist outlined by Mr. Arnold Lunn, in his recent book *John Wesley*, is marred by not a little misjudgment at least in its tone and implications, if not in its definite statements. Dr. Lavington's grossly exaggerated description of Whitefield's boyish confessions of sin as "a perfect jakes of uncleanness" is quoted with insufficient protest.[1]

The evangelist's artless pleasure in the patronage of the aristocracy (*cf.* Dr. Johnson's complaint of his preoccupation with the "lower classes") to whom, mark, Whitefield never stinted the truth, is described by Mr. Lunn as "vanity." Finally, Sir James Stephens' reflections upon Whitefield's lack of scholarship and culture (an inference from silence not from howlers), which entirely ignore the terrific concentration of Whitefield upon one task and one alone, is adduced with apparent endorsement. I leave my readers to judge, with the evidence here before them, whether this man, whose emotional passion and clear insight into the heart of the Christian faith combined to form one of the great watersheds of human history, can be justly viewed as a "common servitor" turned religious and social upstart. Whitefield was no fool, but a great natural genius who most generously and severely disciplined and denied himself in an overwhelming passion for human good, a passion born of a most profound spiritual change.

Numerous are the stories of Whitefield's prowess as a preacher that one might mention did space allow in defiance of Dr. Johnson's opinion. We have already described the complete carrying away on one occasion of the sedate Lord Chesterfield.[2] Once, when Whitefield was preaching in New York, before some seamen, he suddenly assumed a nautical tone and manner that were simply irresistible. "Well, my boys," he cried, "we have a clear sky, and are making fine headway over a smooth sea, before a light breeze, and we shall soon lose sight of land. But what means this sudden lowering of the heavens, and that dark cloud rising from beneath the western horizon? Hark! Don't you hear distant thunder? Don't you see those flashes

[1] Compare remarks on page 14.
[2] See Wakeley's *Anecdotes of George Whitefield*. See also page 201.

of lightning? There is a storm gathering! Every man to his duty! How the waves arise and dash against the ship! The air is dark! The tempest rages! Our masts are gone! The ship is on her beam ends! Then what next?" This appeal instantly brought the sailors to their feet with a shout, "Take to the long boat!"

Said David Garrick once; "I would give a hundred guineas if I could only say 'Oh!' like Mr. Whitefield," whilst Horace Walpole, no easy critic to please, ascribed to Whitefield "the fascinations of a Garrick."

The judgment of that admirably balanced mind and careful historian, John Richard Green, though sober enough, is nearer the mark: "Whitefield, a servitor of Pembroke, was, above all, the preacher of the Revival. . . . Whitefield's preaching was such as England had never heard before, theatrical, extravagant, often commonplace, but hushing all criticism by its intense reality, its earnestness of belief, its deep, tremulous sympathy with the sin and sorrow of mankind. It was no common enthusiast who could wring gold out of the close-fisted Franklin, and admiration from the fastidious Walpole or look down from the top of a green knoll at Kingswood on twenty thousand colliers, grimy from the Bristol coalpits, and see, as he preached, the tears 'making white channels down their blackened cheeks. . . .' In power as a preacher he (John Wesley) stood next to Whitefield."[1]

It is due to Whitefield's reputation that emphasis should be laid on the fact that he pioneered all the characteristic features of the ultimate form of Methodism. Thus he was the first of the sacred trio to enjoy the great experience of soul liberation. Charles Wesley followed, and John, as we have seen, ultimately arrived. Whitefield was the first to essay open-air and field preaching, and the first to get into touch with and realise the potentialities of the Religious Societies of the period which undoubtedly contributed to the Methodist model. He was the first to see the necessity for and to appoint lay preachers and the first to perceive the possibilities of religious journalism. Finally, and perhaps most important of all, he saw very vividly the spiritual need of the wider world of his time, and pioneered the Methodist gospel in Scotland, Ireland, and the American

[1] *Short History of the English People*, Vol. II. p. 694. Everyman edition.

colonies before Wesley had fairly got under way. Let it be granted that in all these matters Whitefield was somewhat shallower, as well as swifter, than Wesley, and that Wesley eventually proved himself a supreme master in constructive leadership; nevertheless the *breach-maker* and *frontier-breaker* is surely deserving of peculiar honour and but for him, it may be fairly claimed, Wesley might never have secured his opportunity, or at least such an opportunity as he actually enjoyed.

Whitefield we may say gave *mobility* to the Revival, Wesley contributed *stability* to its results. Let both be honoured as indeed each honoured the other! A minister was once questioning Wesley's hopes of salvation and asked Whitefield, "Do you think we shall see John Wesley in Heaven?" "No, sir!" thundered Whitefield in swift reply, "he will be so near the throne and we at such a distance that we shall hardly get a sight of him." That "we" is delicious!

The stupendous achievements in preaching of these two men owed much to the extreme simplicity and noble discipline of their way of life. Both men were extremely orderly. They were men of system and self-discipline. Cornelius Winter, who lived with Whitefield during the last five years of his life, tells us that before leaving the sitting-room for the night, every piece of furniture, every chair, must be put in its right place, not a book or paper left about, even his gloves must be in their appointed place. Whitefield was remarkable for his moderation in eating and drinking. If he had a favourite viand it was cow-heel. "How surprised would the world be," he said once, "if they were to peep in on Dr. Squintum and see a cow-heel only on the table."[1]

All through life, like Wesley, he was an early-riser. His day began at four o'clock all the year round, and he would retire just as punctually at ten in the evening. If any company were present he would cut proceedings short very courteously with "Come, gentlemen! It is time for all good folks to be at home." He was punctuality incarnate, being as careful of other people's time as of his own. The test of popularity is one of the fiercest a man can endure, and from the age of twenty-one to his life's end Whitefield stood that test well. For Whitefield to be announced to preach in any part of England was the instant signal for

[1] Dr. Gillies' *Life of Whitefield*.

hundreds of working men to down tools and leave workshops and gather round him in eager, tumultuous expectancy, to be accompanied, presently, by the wealthy in their carriages or on horseback, until all classes were well represented in the crowd hanging upon his words. Hence, no phase of Whitefield's character is more attractive than his ready and genuine humility. He had a positive dread of being spoiled by popularity. To one who ventured to warn him once of certain criticisms made against him, he replied, "I thank you heartily. May God reward you for watching over my soul; and as to what my enemies say against me, I know worse things of myself than they can say concerning me." These, Dr. Johnson, are not the traits of a mountebank orator!

Nothing is more impressive in Whitefield than his consuming zeal for the saving of men. He was as ready to spend himself for the individual and for the few as for the vast congregation. His individual work must have been simply colossal, costing him, as it did so often, whole days of patient endurance, and leaving him scarcely any time even for food. As lesser ministers know, there is no work that can be so mentally and nervously exhausting as this. His Calvinism did not suffice to hinder his deep and passionate humanitarianism. He would, if he could, place the offer of salvation at the feet of all human beings on the face of the earth, whatever their ultimate fate might be. Even Sir James Stephens, whose adverse reference to Whitefield on the score of his ignorance has been noticed, was obliged to admit, "If ever philanthropy burned in the human heart with a pure and intense flame, embracing the whole family of man in the spirit of universal charity, it was in the heart of George Whitefield. He loved the world that hated him, he had no preferences but in favour of the ignorant, the miserable, and the poor."

Whitefield was indeed the pioneer of modern philanthropy. In an age of cruelty, when the sympathetic social imagination of mankind was incredibly dulled and blurred, he went the length and breadth of two great nations teaching them to see the woes and perils of distant sufferers, and enabling them to taste the joy of the generous heart. After his insistent and continuous association of the Gospel with practical charity, the work of a Robert Raikes for the waifs and strays of our cities, of the Shaftesbury Society, and the Ragged Schools, of Dr. Barnardo and George Muller, was rendered far easier, if not altogether inevitable.

Whitefield had strict views concerning money, yet whilst he never made a purchase without paying cash down, he was generosity personified. One delightful story is told of this trait in him receiving unwonted reward. Whitefield was travelling on horseback with an acquaintance through rather lonely country. On their journey they passed a cottage at which obviously there was trouble. Upon inquiry they found a poor widow in straits for money and food. Whitefield immediately parted with a five-pound note, all the money in his possession. They resumed their journey, and the friend lectured Whitefield upon his extravagant charity. But Whitefield maintained that such a crisis was a call of Providence, and that God would not see him in want. Presently, on the moor they were held up by a highwayman, and this time it was Whitefield's turn to crow, for he pointed out that he had nothing to lose, whilst his friend's pockets were emptied. The highwayman, however, before he left, compelled Whitefield to exchange his good broadcloth coat for the footpad's ragged jacket, at which the friend laughed heartily. They went on their journey, when suddenly the noise of galloping hoofs sounded behind them, and they saw the thief returning at top speed. By now, however, they were nearer habitations, and by spurring their horses they escaped. Later on, Whitefield discovered in the ragged coat he was wearing a bundle of notes amounting to one hundred pounds, evidently the proceeds of several crimes. The exchange of coats had been disastrous for the highwayman, but Whitefield's friend was compelled to admit that it showed a very handsome profit for the evangelist upon an investment of five pounds!

But not only was Whitefield pioneer philanthropist, he was pioneer educator as well. However true it may be that in giving himself to his supreme task George Whitefield sacrificed his own hopes of profounder scholarship or his chances of displaying what he already possessed of that commodity, nevertheless, he remained always deeply sensitive to the perils of ignorance, and was eager to promote education in every conceivable way. Kingswood School at Bristol, Dr. Doddridge's Academy at Northampton, Harvard College at Boston (to-day a great University), and Dartmouth College, together with Mr. Wheelock's College for Indians, were some of the educational establishments indebted either in their foundation, or in their furtherance, to his influence, whilst two other great American universities actually emerged from foundations for which he was directly responsible.

We have seen the part he played in the encouragement of the Log College, founded by the Tennents at Neshaminy. This was afterwards removed to Princeton, New Jersey, through the patronage of Governor Belcher, and gradually passed into the modern Princeton University. Somewhat similar was the progress of the New Building, as it was first called, which was erected in 1740 by Benjamin Franklin and others for White-field at Philadelphia. Whitefield was allowed to add to the scheme a Charity School for "the instruction of poor children gratis, in the knowledge of the Christian religion and in useful literature." This school developed first into an academy, then into the College of Philadelphia, and finally into the magnificent University of Pennsylvania. In commemoration of this origin, there was erected at Whitefield's bi-centenary in 1914, in the dormitory triangle of the University, a most noble statue of the great preacher. The sculptor was Dr. R. Tait MacKenzie, who was also responsible for the statue to Benjamin Franklin, which adorns the University grounds. At the erection of this monument—the finest artistic tribute to Whitefield anywhere in the world—the following statement was made of the evangelist's services to the University:

"The inspirer and original Trustee of the Charity School of 1740, the forerunner of the University of Pennsylvania, he solicited the first donations to the Library of the University of Pennsylvania, guided the new school of learning by his godly counsel, heartened it by his masterful preaching, and inspired it with his noble life." Among the eloquent inscriptions on the panels of the pedestal on which the statue rests appears the following most fitting tribute: "Zealous advocate and patron of higher education in the American colonies." Upon another panel is the affectionate tribute of his friend, the quaint scientist-statesman of Philadelphia, Benjamin Franklin, "I knew him intimately upwards of thirty years.

His Integrity, Disinterestedness and Indefatigable Zeal in prosecuting every Good Work I have never seen equalled, and shall never see excelled." That warm-hearted testimony is from a man of such keen intellectual interests that he would hardly have made an intimate friend of one who did not possess kindred abilities. The fact is that Whitefield never lost the taste for learning which drew him to Oxford, and which was undoubtedly nourished there, and perhaps because his own mode of life made the pursuit of learning difficult he was the more earnest in seeking to ensure an educated ministry for the new Churches that sprang up in the wake of the Revival.

When we turn to consider the social impact of the Awakener's work a great vista of far-reaching consequence opens up before our gaze.

CHAPTER II

WHITEFIELD'S IMPACT UPON SOCIETY

It would be hopelessly impossible to trace out and to measure the personal consequences of such a ministry as Whitefield's. It is estimated that he addressed at least ten million souls in the course of his thirty-four years of ministry from his open-air pulpit alone. We can only think with wondering awe of what it must have meant for men and women by the thousand to begin to live new lives by the grace of God! The Awakener set hundreds of thousands of people thinking for themselves, under the guidance of the New Testament, on matters of the soul and of the right conduct of life. Moreover, so many of his converts became in their turn kindlers and transformers of other lives. Such men as Robert Robinson,[1] the Baptist minister of Cambridge, author of "Come Thou Fount of every blessing"; Thomas Rankin, of Dunbar; John Fawcett, of Yorkshire, author of "Blest be the tie that binds"; John Edwards, of Dublin; Thomas Adams, of Minchinhampton; Cornelius Winter, who in turn captured the great William Jay, of Bath; Samuel Davies, of Virginia; Samuel Cooper, of Boston; Gilbert Tennent, of Philadelphia; these were but a few of a great company of mighty preachers drawing and working upon their own crowded audiences in Britain and in America. There were at least twenty ministers, at one time, in the Boston area alone who claimed George Whitefield as their spiritual quickener. All this must have meant widespread leavening of society with more conscientious and altruistic citizenship. So close to the Divine and Universal centre did Whitefield draw his converts that his own catholicity of spirit—a catholicity all the more notable for being that

[1] This man became an invaluable controversialist in the struggle for Nonconformist Liberty and religious tolerance.

a Calvinist—powerfully affected them. As one writer has remarked concerning the religious controversy in which Whitefield and Wesley were involved, "The removal from the scene of Whitefield's great personality meant the withdrawal of an influence that was consistently cast on the side of harmony and peace."[1] Whitefield's preaching was always above and beyond denominationalism. When he was preaching once from the balcony of the Court House in Philadelphia, he cried suddenly, "Father Abraham, whom have you in heaven? Any Episcopalians? No! Any Presbyterians? No! Have you any Independents or Seceders? No! Have you any Methodists? No, No, No! Whom have you there? We don't know those names here! All who are here are Christians —believers in Christ—men who have overcome by the Blood of the Lamb and the Word of His testimony." "O! is this the case?" continued Whitefield, "then God help me, God help us all, to forget party names, and to become Christians in deed and in truth."

This catholic spirit in Whitefield was amazingly illustrated in his church relationships. He was an ordained Anglican priest, yet lived a Methodist, and was the co-founder of Methodism, he was a willing preacher among Dissenting and Nonconformist bodies, chaplain to the Countess of Huntingdon, and thus responsible with her for the founding of many causes that were, to say the least, "irregular." Moreover, across the Atlantic, "he helped," to use Gledstone's words, "more than any man to bring into existence in America a hundred and fifty Congregational Churches within twenty years."

Added to this were his peculiar contributions to Calvinistic Methodism in Wales, to Presbyterianism in Scotland and also in America, where he actually founded Presbyterian Churches and lies buried in a Presbyterian Church.

Thus, as a direct result of his labours, Whitefield's work is woven into the history and progress of every Protestant Church in both lands, and to nearly all of them he brought great numbers of new converts. We are not surprised, therefore, to find emerging steadily from so world-wide an outlook and so universal a spirit, the noble efforts at World-Evangelism represented by the various Missionary Societies. Through

[1] C. Silvester Horne, *Popular History of the Free Churches.*

Newton, Thornton, Scott and Venn, all trophies of the Revival, the Church Missionary Society was founded; through the quickening of the Baptist Churches, William Carey, the father of modern Missions emerged to create the Baptist Missionary Society. Through the reaction of Carey's heroic achievements and the active interest of Matthew Wilks, one of Whitefield's successors at the Tabernacle and Tottenham Court Chapel, the London Missionary Society came into being, with its nobly simple purpose, "to send neither Episcopacy, Presbyterianism, nor Independency to the heathen, but simply the Gospel of Christ." Within twenty-six years of Whitefield's death the good ship, *Duff*, purchased and equipped by the new Society, left the Thames with twenty-nine missionaries on board. As a result of the combined labours of the group that formed the London Missionary Society there came into existence two great auxiliary forces of Home and Foreign Mission effort, the Religious Tract Society and the British and Foreign Bible Society. Finally, there was the inevitable arrival of the Wesleyan Missionary Society, which resulted from the selfless labours of Dr. Thomas Coke, a Church of England clergyman dismissed for his "enthusiasm," who became one of Wesley's preachers. The first year's income of the Wesleyan Missionary Society was no less than twenty thousand pounds!

Still more fascinating lines of associated influence lead us to three of the greatest figures in subsequent history. No name stands higher among the English-speaking peoples in the annals of social reform than that of Ashley Cooper, Earl of Shaftesbury. His epic struggle on behalf of the workers of England, and especially of the shamefully exploited child-workers, sprang directly from his new life in Christ. The Earl's actual spiritual father was John Wesley, but we have already noted Wesley's debt to the Awakener. "I am an Evangelical of the Evangelicals," declared Lord Shaftesbury, adding, "Christianity as applied is absolutely and essentially practical." In a recent "Life of Shaftesbury"[1] occurs the following passage:

"To Shaftesbury, as to all ardent Evangelicals, faith is illumination, dynamic; it is desire and restless energy for human betterment, a yearning to see the will of God 'done on earth as in

[1] By Rev. J. Wesley Bready, M.A., B.D.

Heaven.' Thus Shaftesbury was Evangelical . . . because it represented an ardent endeavour to appreciate the Spirit of Jesus, and to apply that Spirit to all the complicated problems of human relationship."

Shaftesbury himself declared of the Evangelicals late in life reviewing his century's developments, "I am satisfied that most of the great philanthropic movements of the century have sprung from them."

His own personal sacrifices were a fine proof of his utter religious sincerity—mortgaging his estate up to the hilt, despoiling his picture-gallery of masterpiece after masterpiece, living in obscure simplicity, in order to pay for the passion of social reclamation and reform that belief in Christ had brought to him.

Outside Westminster Abbey, on the day of Ashley Cooper's funeral, one of the many thousands of working-men who stood bareheaded in the rain, cried out, "Our Earl's gone! God A'mighty know'd how he loved us, and we loved him. We shan't look upon his like again." The voice of millions spoke in that verdict, but the love so wondrously kindled and kindling is not really gauged until it is seen to be that Love of Christ for all mankind which George Whitefield revealed anew to his generation.

But if George Whitefield, through Wesley and the People's Earl, blessed England in this vital way, he was instrumental in reaching a still wider area through another great emancipator, William Wilberforce. It must always be a matter of profound regret that Whitefield, *like so many other eminent Christian men of his century*, was unenlightened in conscience regarding the sin of slavery as, alas, still so many are in regard to the sin of war. The best that can be said for his personal liability for slave-holding is that he was the trustee of a great philanthropic effort for which he had to give a good account to God and man, and negro labour appealed to him as an economic necessity in the conditions and climate of Georgia, and, further, that he had invariably in view the physical and spiritual well-being of all in his employ. Moreover, he was fierce and courageous in his defence of fair and good treatment of slaves wherever he went, and dared the wrath and active hostility of slave-owners again and again in his protests against cruelty—but he was blind to the iniquity of the institution. All the more gratifying is it, therefore, to find that through his distinctive work of leading souls to individual salvation he set in train forces that ended ultimately in the abolition of slavery. It seems that in 1769, just before Whitefield left England for the last time, there was in his audience, at Tottenham Court Chapel, a boy *Wilberforce* of ten years of age, in the care of one[1] of the many aristocratic hearers that waited upon the great evangelist's ministry. As this lad of tender heart and years listened to the fiery eloquence of that Voice of God his soul was stamped for life with an indelible religious impression. In after years the impression was weakened for a while, and the youth plunged into a life of reckless gaiety and thoughtless self-indulgence. But the influence of religion set siege to his heart again in the form of a book written by good Philip Doddridge, *The Rise and Progress of Religion*. The book was lying on the table of a hotel in Italy, and the gay young spark from England turned its pages idly, only to be gripped suddenly by the combined forces of the printed page and the indelible memory. William Wilberforce threw self-pleasure to the winds in a new consecration of his life to the service of humanity. The liberator of the slaves had arrived!

The story of Whitefield's quickening effect upon freedom, however, does not end here—it only begins. Another great figure looms on the scene—the lanky form of the young railsplitter of Kentucky, Abraham Lincoln. It is no mere coincidence that the soil of Boston and New England is holy ground for all the sons of Freedom. It is drenched with the passion of liberty from thousands of dedicated souls. The Pilgrim Father tradition begins the great story, the struggle for Independence carries it on, and into that historic contest there enters the significant contribution of Whitefield, the Awakener. The old Pilgrim spirit was decaying and crumbling away when Whitefield burst like a flame of fire upon New England. This part of America became the scene, over and over again, of mighty triumphs of spiritual liberation due to his preaching. Souls were born again by thousands[2] over all that area, and when

[1] Probably his aunt.
[2] In New England alone an estimate for but one period of the Revival was 30,000 souls. *History of First Presbyterian Church, Newburyport*, by Hovey.

at last the great crisis between the colonies and the home country came—actually on the occasion of Whitefields' last visit to Boston—the great Evangelist gave his verdict without hesitation, stern patriot though he was, on behalf of Liberty.[1] For once Whitefield's political sagacity here excelled that of John Wesley, who, in spite of the fact that Nonconformist opinion in Britain was generally on the side of the colonists, made an attack on the latter which, as Silvester Horne says in his *History of the Free Churches*, "was unworthy of his shrewd intelligence and generous heart." Well! well! even Homer nods!

This double strain of influence—first the spiritually liberating grace of the Great Awakening spreading over the States and represented in Kentucky by the itinerant preacher, Pastor Elkin, and by Peter Cartwright, the revivalist, who so powerfully affected the Lincoln family, then later the spirit of the men of Concord and Lexington—caught the rising young Kentuckian advocate and swept him into sane and healthy religion and into that devotion to a free humanity that made him at last the Abolitionist President.

No outline, however, of the social impact of Whitefield's personality and work could be complete that does not reckon with the peculiar effects of Methodism itself upon the life of Britain at one of the most critical periods in European history. One of the weightiest, as well as one of the most recent verdicts on this feature, is that offered by the great French historian Halévy in *A History of the English People in* 1815.[2] He says:

"During the eighteenth century England had been the scene of a great religious movement unparalleled on the Continent—the last Protestant Movement which has given birth to permanent institutions. This was the Methodist or Evangelical Revival."

"Why was it that of all the countries of Europe, England has been most free from revolutions, violent crises, and sudden change? We have sought in vain to find the explanation by an analysis of her political institutions and economic organisations . . . the élite of the working-class, the hard-working and capable bourgeois had

[1] There was another line of connection, too. A man whom Whitefield greatly influenced in Scotland was the Rev. Alexander Craighead. He, in turn, inspired the Presbyterian patriots who framed the Mecklenburg Declaration. This became the Model of the Declaration of Independence made only a year later at Philadelphia.

[2] One of his three volumes of *A History of the English People in the Nineteenth Century*.

been imbued by the Evangelical Movement with a spirit from which the established order had nothing to fear."

Thus, in Halévy's judgment, England was saved from the chaos and horrors of an impending bloody revolution which had already caught Europe in its toils, mainly by the steadying effect of the Evangelical Revival. It was religion which gave to the forces of social change in England, not only a dynamic, but a dynamic so controlled by Christian temper that desperate policies were in the main eschewed, and social sufferers given a capacity for patient endurance which allowed time and opportunity for considered reform. To quote Halévy again:

"If the materialistic interpretation of history is to be trusted, if economic facts explain the course taken by the human race in its progress, the England of the nineteenth century was surely above other countries destined to revolution, both political and religious. But it was not to be so. In no other country of Europe have social changes been accomplished with such marked and gradual continuity. The source of such continuity and comparative stability is, as we have seen, not to be found in the economic organisation of the country. We have seen, also, that it cannot be found in the political institutions of England, which were essentially unstable and wanting in order. To find it we must pass on to another category of social phenomena—to beliefs, emotions, and opinions, as well as to the institutions and sects in which these beliefs, emotions and opinions take a form suitable to scientific inquiry."

It is a pity that in their invaluable work on social conditions in the eighteenth century, *The Town Labourer*, James and Barbara Hammond should have emphasised the restraining elements in Evangelicalism, and have missed so badly the dynamic elements in it. They dismiss the potent force of the Revival as almost purely conservative in its political effects. But as J. Ernest Rattenbury has pointed out in his telling criticism of their position[1] they are able to do this only by identifying the Evangelical Movement too exclusively with the findings of the Wesleyan Conference, and by ignoring many features that tell in the other direction. Mr. Rattenbury writes:

"Their treatment of the reaction of the Wesleyan Movement on the social and political development in England at first sight seems

[1] *Wesley's Legacy to the World.*

convincing, and no doubt it contains considerable elements of truth. But it is unsatisfactory because it does not sufficiently realise that the Evangelical Revival was a watershed from which many streams other than the Wesleyan denomination issued, and that the activities of that denomination in the early nineteenth century can by no means be identified with the resolutions of that purely clerical and unrepresentative body, the Wesleyan Conference."

What the Hammonds fail particularly to take into account is the inherent dynamic quality of the impulse to liberty contained in the essentially Christian and Pauline Gospel of Whitefield and Wesley. This impulse could be trusted to work out, *as in history it has always worked out*, to its social and political applications, and whilst this tremendous fact, constantly ignored by the sceptic, is no excuse for the social blindness and political ineptitude and class-prejudice which have constantly hindered its out-working, nevertheless, so powerful is the impulse that in *some* disciples the Gospel simply must focus itself on social life. To adapt a clever sentence of Abraham Lincoln's, one might say that social myopia may afflict "some Christians all the time, and all Christians some of the time, but *never* all Christians all the time." Even this sentence does not do justice to the social passion which breaks forth from the Evangelical faith. We should have to query "some Christians all the time," for if a man really has the Christian root of the matter in him, his progression to some altruistic social philosophy is inevitable. A capital case in point can be cited from this period in John Wood, the manufacturer friend of Richard Oastler, about whom Oastler tells the following story:

"My friend was in bed, but he was not asleep; he was leaning upon a table beside his bed. On that table were placed two candles, between them was the open Bible. On my advancing towards the side of the bed, he turned to me, reached out his hand, and, in the most impressive and affectionate manner, pressing my hand to his, he said, 'I have had no sleep to-night. I have been reading this book, and in every page I have read my own condemnation. I cannot allow you to leave me without a pledge that you will use all your influence in endeavouring to remove from our factory system the cruelties which are regularly practised in our mills.'"

Oastler continues:

"I promised my friend that I would do what I could. I felt that we were, each of us, in the presence of the Highest. I knew that that vow was recorded in Heaven. I have kept it; the grace of God having upholden me, I have been faithful."[1]

It is perfectly true that the Evangelical doctrine did at first engross its believers with that spiritual and eternal salvation which lies beyond all external conditions of life, and which takes into account reasonably the immortal destiny of personalities, and that in that "light of eternity" social and political interests seemed to be proportionately very secondary things. This was due, however, not merely to an inadequate presentation of the Gospel which obscured the immediate social goal of Christianity and reduced it to innumerable individual ends, but also to the starved and ill-educated social sense of the period which characterised the people in general. This impoverished social sense in the people at large, Methodism, with its institutions, *was already in process of changing most profoundly*. Here again is something the Hammonds have missed. We must not forget that one of the simplest and yet strongest influences of the Revival was the gathering of large numbers of earnest-minded working people into communities which were in some degree self-governing. Whilst Whitefield strove to avoid creating such societies, and Wesley deliberately and successfully made it his special care, yet everywhere in the wake of Whitefield's work they leapt into being. The training in self-expression and in the filling of offices and the control of public affairs which these Societies provided for a great host of working men and women was invaluable as a preparation for industrial combination and for the future work of Trade Unionism.

The Dissenting Chapel and the Methodist Society were the pioneer forms of the later self-governing Labour organisations, and they became the nurseries of popular aspirations after place and power in civic and national government. Neither Church nor State at this time were providing anything of this kind, or

---

[1] Alfred's *History of the Factory System*, Vol. I. p. 94, quoted by W. Bready and J. E. Rattenbury.

indeed of any other kind, to meet the spiritual and intellectual
needs of the people. No effort was being made in the direction
of religious or educational improvement excepting by those
Charity Schools and Religious Societies for which Whitefield
preached his earliest sermons, and which impressed him as
so valuable.

By Methodism a newly-oppressed, bewildered and miserable
proletariat, degraded and drink-sodden, received a new infusion
of sheer Life from spiritual sources. Into its manhood
and womanhood there was breathed a new moral heroism
capable of the championship of unpopular causes and
martyrdom for them. And all this was achieved on so
widespread a scale, and was characterised by so profound a
faith in God that a universal revolution steadily but slowly
occurred hand in hand with a constant mood of sublime
patience. Thus the strong current of liberty was controlled
and guided.

Out of such nurseries of public service there arose inevitably
a body of leaders in social life, of high moral character and of
dependable, tried, efficiency—leaders of infinite value to the
workers in their future struggles. As Halévy says: "To this
movement British Liberalism of the opening nineteenth
century owed its distinctive character." "The majority of
the leaders," Halévy continues, "of the great Trade Union
Movement that would arise in England within a few years of
1815, will belong to Nonconformist sects. They will often
be Local Preachers. Their spiritual ancestors were the *founders
of Methodism*. In the vast work of social organisation which
is one of the dominant characteristics of nineteenth century
England, it would be difficult to overestimate the part played
by the Wesleyan Revival." [1]

The latest product of this vein of Methodist influence
is the present Government of Great Britain,[2] led as it is
by a galaxy of ex-local-preachers of various denominations,
who are every whit as capable statesmen as any poli-
ticians drawn from the aristocratic or plutocratic classes of
society.

[1] Halévy, Vol. I. p. 372.
[2] 1929, Second Labour Government in British history.

One cannot do better, in closing these observations in reply to the position stated by Mr. and Mrs. Hammond, and which it is to be feared has very generally influenced Socialist judgment in this country about the Evangelical Revival, than by quoting a very true and penetrating statement made by Mr. Rattenbury in his most valuable book. [1]

"A religious society, in the nature of the case, includes men of every grade of piety and education. It is not merely an army, but a school, often with a large infant department. Its corporate life expresses its average, not its exceptional attainments. The objection to the Church that it does not comfortably follow its highest ideals is quite true as a matter of fact, but, if it is to be a school for saints, it must have its elementary classes, and they necessarily retard the rate of progress. It has often been said that many Christian reforms have been advocated by the unorthodox, by people outside the Churches, and illustrations no doubt could be given, but it will be found that, when the antecedents and early training of such men are examined, they have usually been deeply Christian. The Church is always leading men into a Christianity higher than that of the average Church life, and she often damps the enthusiasm of the men she trains; and indeed such men loosen themselves from her, and represent her teaching as individuals apart from her more truly than she herself does corporately. But it cannot be otherwise; if the Church is to be really universal in her comprehensiveness, she must include in her embrace undeveloped and imperfectly developed people. Social reformers often come up against the average corporate life of the Church and get no effective backing from her for their schemes of amelioration. For this reason we are more likely to trace the results of the Evangelical Revival in the social service of individual Methodists than in the resolutions of their Conferences."

That is not the last word, as we shall see, as to the capacity of Corporate Church life for social redemption, but it is so true as to deserve the careful consideration of all who would discredit Christianity as a force making for the ideal Social Order.

One final word upon the far-reaching effects of Whitefield's work. It contributed its share of impetus to the enfranchisement of the people. The sign-manual of a man's freedom is the degree in which he is included in the task of government —the government of his own life and that of his fellows. Until

[1] *Wesley's Legacy to the World*, p. 239.

his share in that task is equal with that of his fellow-citizens he is so much of a slave, and in that degree he cannot be deemed a responsible being. There can be no true responsibility without adequate freedom, and the lack of freedom is therefore the parent of all injustice. The quickened but controlled stream of liberty pouring forth on innumerable lives from the Awakener's work was bound, sooner or later, to find its outlet in this direction.

The little Methodist Societies, as we have seen, were a powerful social force, educating innumerable groups of the poorest and most socially insignificant in public affairs, and in the application of religion to real life. Thus Cornish Methodists became keenly interested in the American War of Independence, and Lancashire Methodists took a definite and enlightened interest in political reform.[1] Methodists like . Michael Sadler and Richard Oastler, Fielden, Bull, Bretherton, and Joseph Raynor Stephens flung themselves passionately into the struggle for Poor Law and Factory Reform, and were invaluable to Lord Shaftesbury. Through their continued efforts the Ten Hours' Act was passed, and a number of other Acts revising the cruel conditions of Labour—especially among children.

"The historian of the movement which produced the Factory Acts must not forget the many tributaries which swelled the main stream. But the source of the river was the piety and Christian sentiment of the evangelicals."[2]

Such interests, however, were bound to focus at last into electoral reform and the power of the people in Parliament. It was particularly through the moral-force group of Chartists[3] that the spirit of liberty released by the Revival, found its leverage on the future of the franchise. This included such men as William Lovett (1800–1877) the Cornish Methodist of New-quay, a co-writer with Joseph Hume and Richard Cobden; Samuel Bamford, author of *Passages in the Life of a Radical*, Thomas Cooper, tribune of the people and famous Chartist, Methodist by training and a local preacher, author of *Purgatory of Suicides*, and model for Charles Kingsley's *Alton Locke!*

[1] A. E. Dobbs, *Educational and Social Movements*, quoted by Rattenbury.
[2] Halévy.
[3] *Christian Responsibility for the Great Order*, Rev. S. E. Keeble.

So we might go on adding to the list. It is true that, as the Hammonds have emphasised, Methodism officially erred on the side of caution in regard to movements that seemed to it to be fraught with revolution, but to quote Rev. Samuel E. Keeble: "many noble Christians braved that peril sooner than be silent under wrong." From these men it is only a step to the first Christian Socialists, Kingsley, Maurice, Ludlow, Tom Hughes, etc., and it is interesting to find Kingsley writing to Thomas Cooper about his ancestors who had fought in Cromwell's army and left all for the sake of God and liberty and sailed with the Pilgrim Fathers. So the old strain of Free Religion, Evangelical and Political, vindicated itself once more in personalities and deeds that changed history.

CHAPTER III

THE EVANGELICAL REVIVAL IN THE LIGHT OF TO-DAY.

THEOLOGICAL AND ETHICAL

WE have asked whether the Evangelical Revival can be repeated. The answer we suggested at the beginning of our study was an affirmative one, yet it was very far from our intention to suggest that if repeated it could or should be identical in all respects with the eighteenth century achievement. History does not repeat itself, yet there is a spiral movement of human progress in history which, as it were, takes humanity over the same ground again and again, but often at a much loftier height. A revival of religion in our time, if it is to be central either to modern religion or modern society, cannot possibly be in either the precise terms of Whitefield's and Wesley's Gospel or within the limitations of their social outlook. The first Evangelical Revival has changed the world and the mind of Protestantism too profoundly for that to suffice.

There are at least three great factors of change which distinguish the religious and social world of our time from that of George Whitefield. They are:

1. The emergence of new attitudes to Scripture and to Human History yielding a purer Christian Theology and Ethic.
2. The arrival of the Science of Psychology and a resultant new approach to the experience of Conversion.
3. The existence of a highly Socialised World necessitating a Collectivist approach to moral and religious problems.

Each of these factors is a distinct and wonderful gain if rightly used.

1. *The Emergence of New Attitudes to Scripture and to Human History Yielding a Purer Christian Theology and Ethic.*

The bondage of the great Evangelists to the letter of Scripture is evident throughout their story. Wesley's magical use of haphazard Scripture reference was on more than one occasion attended by ludicrous results.[1] Whitefield's defence of slavery[2] was only possible by the use of a theory of Scriptural authority which placed the patriarchs on a level with the apostles. There is a new knowledge of the Scriptures abroad in the Church of to-day that delivers modern evangelism from these serious pitfalls. Moreover, this new knowledge is abroad amongst the people at large. Whereas Whitefield was appealing to a public for whom, however ignorant they were of the Bible, the letter of Scripture still possessed *direct* Divine authority, the modern preacher is faced with an audience that is becoming increasingly conversant with the apparatus of Biblical criticism, and with the chief findings of scientific Biblical research.[3] This means that the appeal of the modern preacher must go behind the text of Scripture to the inherent reasonableness, within a definite and coherent philosophy of religious thought, of the sentiment involved in any particular text or passage. This makes preaching intrinsically a harder task and inevitably more rational and argumentative, and, unless one is careful, less emotional. The two main factors, outside the actual research of Biblical scholars, which have forced this change of view regarding Scripture, have been, on the one hand, the discovery associated with Copernicus and Galileo, of the movement of the earth round the sun and the earth's comparative roundness,[4] and on the other hand, the discovery of evolution as the Divine method of the creation of man.

These contributions from Science, everywhere accepted to-day by secular scholarship, and therefore the constant mental assumptions of the younger portion of the modern public, are absolute challenges, not to the truth and value of the Bible as a progressive revelation of God and Morality, but to the old

[1] See page 66.
[2] " As to the lawfulness of keeping slaves I have no doubt, since I hear of some that were brought with Abraham's money." *G. Whitefield.*
[3] Cf. *The Bible in the Light of To-day,* by An Enquiring Layman. (Obtainable on all public bookstalls).
[4] See the author's volume *The Greater Christ* for fuller treatment of this.

conception of Scripture as infallible in its scientific information and its account of human origins. The spiritual and moral gains, however, of this liberation from the letter of Scripture are sublime. For the supreme mischief of the older attitude, illustrated all too sadly in Whitefield's attitude to slavery and Wilberforce's attitude to English poverty, was that the Highest Ethic of Scripture, together with the Highest Vision of God, were reduced to such a mixed average of the differing levels of Scripture that Christians were able to behave like St. Paul at one time and like Abraham or David—*in their weaker moments*—at another. No single factor has so tragically delayed the ripening within Christendom of as clear a conscience concerning War as was at length achieved concerning Slavery, as this tendency to pull back the Ethic of Jesus to the standards of the Old Testament. That this tendency is inherent in the view that the Bible from cover to cover is infallible and inerrant in its teaching, information and example, is illustrated by the confused morality of eighteenth century Evangelicalism.[1] That John Newton could write, "How sweet the name of Jesus sounds," whilst navigating his own ship full of slaves, shows that something was badly wrong somewhere. But the mischief has a darker aspect still in the way in which it has clouded the glory of God in the face of Jesus Christ. The attempt to draw a composite Divine Being from the inconsistent presentations of God from Genesis to Revelation has enabled Christians to stress the more tender and more cruel elements in such a composition, according to the convenience of the occasion. There was a God of Battles always available whenever the country was plunged by political ineptitude into strife, and a God of Mercy whenever a sinner was seen to be penitent enough, or when one's own peccadillos were in question.

We know how many an evangelical preacher, like Grimshaw of Haworth stressed the fiercer elements of the composite Biblical picture of God. To Whitefield's credit, we can say that it appears much less in his public utterances than his doctrine would have warranted, whilst to Wesley's greater credit, there is a concentration on the Love element that brings him very near to Universalism, with its hope of the ultimate salvation of every soul.

[1] See page 88.

But the emancipation of modern Christianity from this flat and mechanical theory of inspiration takes it sharply back to the supremacy of Jesus and of the higher elements in His teaching and example. The intrinsically lower moral levels, even in the records of Christ's own teaching, as well as in that of Old Testament books and characters, are to be judged by the higher levels. The effect of this obviously sane method is to clear the vision of God of all vindictive shadows. "The dark line" in the face of God disappears and Divine Love shines unclouded.

Within the scope of this book one cannot elaborate adequately the new theology and clearer ethic that emerges from this release of the pure gold of Scripture from the dross that has clung to it all too long. Yet the clarification of our Gospel is such an urgent necessity if modern Christianity is to find the greatest revival of its history, that some attempt at it must be made. Let us understand, then, very clearly that the sharp and effective spearhead of the eighteenth century Revival was quite clearly the Love of God, not His terror. Fear elements there were in the Gospel of Whitefield and Wesley, and fear effects there were in their preaching, but when full allowance is made for these it was not Fear that brought peace and new life to all sorts and conditions of men, but a Love upon which they could rest. There is no better expression of this Gospel of the Revival than Wesley's own statement in his *Earnest Appeal to Men of Reason and Religion* (1741):

"The Love of God and of all mankind, we believe to be the medicine of life, the never-failing remedy for all the evils of a disordered world, for all the miseries and vices of men. Wherever this is, there is virtue and happiness going hand-in-hand. There is humbleness of mind, gentleness, long-suffering, the whole image of God, and at the same time a peace that passeth all understanding, and joy unspeakable and full of glory. . . . This religion we long to see established in the world, a religion of love, and joy and peace, having its seat in the human soul, but ever showing itself by its fruits, continually springing forth, not only in all innocence (for love worketh no ill to his neighbour) but likewise in every kind of beneficence, spreading virtue and happiness all around it."

Wesley then goes on to speak of:

"the straight way to the religion of love, even by faith. By this faith we are saved from all uneasiness of mind, from the anguish of a wounded spirit, from discontent, from fear and sorrow of heart, and from that inexpressible listlessness and weariness, both of the world and of ourselves, which we had so helplessly laboured under for many years, especially when we were out of the world and sunk in calm reflection. In this we find that love of God and of all mankind which we had elsewhere sought in vain. This, we know and feel, and therefore cannot but declare saves everyone that partakes it from sin and misery, from every unhappy and every unholy temper."

There is a very modern atmosphere about that clear and eloquent statement of Wesley's Love Gospel. We are fortunately able to place beside this statement of Wesley's an equally delightful letter of Whitefield's to John Wesley in 1747, which arrives practically at the same conclusion:

"Dear and Reverend Sir,
    "Not long ago I received your kind letter, dated in February last. . . . My heart is ready for an outward, as well as an inward union. Nothing shall be wanting on my part to bring it about, but I cannot see how it can be affected till we all think and speak the same things. I rejoice to hear that you and your brother are more moderate with respect to *sinless perfection*. As for *universal redemption*, if we omit on each side talking for or against *reprobation*, which we may do fairly, and agree, as we already do, in giving a universal offer to all poor sinners that will come and taste the water of life, I think we may manage very well."

The pity is that even with Whitefield's and Wesley's stress upon Love the more sinister elements in Scripture tended to flow back upon this clear vision and blur it.

The inability of these great spirits to detach the Gospel of Love from the punitive elements of Scripture explains the theological confusion which caused them so barren a feud over Calvinism and Arminianism. Whitefield, too occupied with immediate human necessity to delve very deeply into theological profundities, was caught in Calvin's obsession with the element of Necessity in Life, and in the Gospel, and held abstractly that a number of human souls were doomed to reprobation. Wesley, leaning towards the brighter side both of Life and the Gospel and emphatic in his belief in free-will, looked for a mightier—if not a universal—triumph of Divine Love.

In the light of modern theological findings we see now how much both were in fault, through their bondage to a Scriptural theory. Mr. Arnold Lunn waxes indignant over Calvinism in his recent *John Wesley*, but there is a strong movement in modern theology, through the influence of Rudolph Otto, and, more particularly, Karl Barth, towards a Neo-Calvinism. Yet the temper of modern theology is extraordinarily Arminian, and even Neo-Calvinists look for an entry of God into the human situation that may bring universal salvation.[1] In other words, a higher synthesis of the old apparently irreconcilable attitudes is in process of being worked out. The present author would scarcely dare to claim that he can make a contribution to this task, and yet the way forward seems to him to be possible only along some such line of thought as the following:

The vindictive punitive elements in Scriptural teaching, insofar as they arise on pre-Christian levels in the pages of the Old Testament, can be dismissed as incidental to moral evolution and need receive from us no more attention than that.[2] But as they arise from the actual teaching of Jesus, as presented in the Gospels, they call for closer consideration. Without wearying my readers at the end of this book with numerous quotations from the Gospels, let me be content with an outline treatment of the matter whilst referring them to the fuller explanation contained in the joint work of Dr. Cyril Emmet and Miss Lily Dougall, *The Lord of Thought*. One of the most serious effects, as already noted, of the mechanical flat-level value idea of Scripture has been the obscuring of delicate lights and shades and subtle genius in the statements attributed to Our Lord. Everything has been taken too much at its face-value. For example, it would seem to be the most obvious of facts that the Christ of the little children of Matthew xviii, xix, the Christ who dealt so tenderly with the woman taken in adultery, the Christ who strongly rebuked his disciples when they wanted to call down fire from Heaven on certain villages

---

[1] *Vide The Word of God and the Word of Man.* Karl Barth, pp. 281 and 282.

[2] For effective treatment of them see such a book as Fosdick's *Modern Use of the Bible*.

that rejected Him, either could not have uttered His terrible doom on Tyre and Sidon at all, or could not have done so with *quite the orthodox meaning current to the period.* Was Christ to be of that evil spirit He rebuked in His disciples? What right have we to assume that the language of judgment on the lips of Jesus of Nazareth, *who never refers to God excepting in terms of exquisite tenderness and utmost protectiveness of humanity*, is, of the same value and meaning merely that it possesses in say, the Book of Enoch or on the lips even of an Amos or John the Baptist? Can Jesus be so original in His Vision of God (and his originality consists particularly in His concentration upon the Love of God), and yet be so banal in His ideas of punishment and judgment? Surely to do justice to His supreme genius we must ask what was His connotation of Love? Certain theologians are never tired of telling us that it was Holy Love. Yes, but that means a Holiness ever suffused with Love as well as a Love ever suffused with Holiness. What it really means, of course, is a *Love that honours the Whole!* A Love therefore that *never* fails! A Love that flows equally and eternally to ALL His children. The Holiness of God is the Strict Equity of His Love. No other meaning can be given to it. To try to reach the meaning of Holiness in terms of loyalty on God's part to moral values is simply to arrive at last at the query: Why loyalty to these values? The only answer is: For the sake of each personality involved, that is—for Love's sake in all its fullness. It is because God must serve the Harmonious Good of ALL that there comes into play the two tremendous twin policies of Judgment and Atonement. Judgment, however, is by Consequence and not by Punishment. By a searching examination of passages of judgment in the teaching of Jesus it is possible to detect that quite a number of them are vindictive utterances attributed to Jesus, but evidently due to the backwash of inferior current thought upon the minds of the evangelists or of copyists. As a case in point, the well-known doom: "They shall be cast into outer darkness, and there shall be weeping and wailing and gnashing of teeth," is repeated by St. Matthew five times over, and each time with an atmosphere of vindictiveness. St. Luke, on the other hand, has it but once and in a much less sinister context—a context of consequence, not of punishment.[1] The remaining passages of judgment in the teaching of our Lord are not of a *vindictive* but of a *consequential* character and capable of an interpretation that does no violence to the Personal Tenderness of God in Christ.

Referring to apparently vindictive passages in the Parables, Dougall and Emmet write as follows:

". . . It does not follow that what is done as a direct personal action of the potentate in the parable is to be thought of as done in exactly the same way by God Himself. In view of the fact that anger and punishment are not attributed to God in the ordinary teaching of Christ, we are justified in refusing such an interpretation of the parables unless it is forced upon us.

"On the other hand, Christ did wish to emphasize beyond the possibility of mistake the unrelenting law of consequence and retribution; it was necessary that it should be presented vividly and dramatically, and it may well be that one of the reasons for His choice of the parabolic method was that it enabled Him to teach the working of consequence in a vivid way without attributing it to the personal action of the Father."[2]

To see this clearly we must mark the distinction between "consequence" and "punishment." The idea of "punishment," as an activity of God, must be discarded—for what is punishment? It is the infliction, by a personal agent, of penalty *over and above* natural consequences. To quote an excellent illustration: A father sees his son playing football clumsily—the lad does so at some risk, receiving many a kick and blow. But in this case the father, as a penalty, steps up to the boy and breaks his ankle! That is punishment: it adds a penalty, loss, injury to an already mischievous situation. Let us imagine, however, that this youth breaks his ankle naturally in the course of the game, taking the risks of the numberless chances of hurt that must occur with constantly colliding bodies. That would not be punishment but consequence; and a father might look on and see it happen, and be not one whit changed in his perfect love and tenderness towards his son, being willing for his boy to take such risk and to accept such calamity bravely should it come.

To change the illustration: A mother who wishes to see her baby walk must be ready to see it fall over in the process,

---

[1] Cf. *The Lord of Thought*, pp. 238-9.
[2] ibid. p. 237.

and permit it to run some risk of injury and pain. Such injury would be judgment but not punishment. If, however, the mother, seeing her child fall over, were to go to it and push it over again on its attempting to rise, with a "Serve you right, there!"—that would be punishment. Alas! it is what too often happens in our human relations! But we cannot reconcile such action with the God revealed in Jesus Christ.

Now it is everything for the prospect of a Univeral Gospel —a real "Good News to all People"—thus to clear the Vision of God of the grim and awful shadow of cruelty that has lain on it so long. For Man becomes inevitably what his God is —worship is emulation and imitation. As Dougall and Emmet so truly point out:

"Man is, after all, instinctively godly. He can never whole-heartedly seek to be what he does not believe that God is. It is only lack of knowledge of human nature that has allowed any religious teacher to assume that men could be taught to forgive where God did not forgive, or to refrain from cursing in his heart those accursed of God, or to fail, whenever he had the power, to lift his hand to smite those whom God intended to smite. . . . War can never cease until men cease to think of God as a man of war and a legal judge, i.e., as a Being who, sooner or later, will vindicate right by using *force majeure*."[1]

There is nothing vindictive and merely punitive in God as Jesus reveals Him. The Universe is built by Love for Love. Its laws are infinitely beneficent and harmonious, but not to be defied without loss and injury and retribution to the defier. This vast mechanism of Law is an expression of Love, and its maintenance in perfection of operation is an act of Love. A universe made for Holy Love cannot be something else at the same time. It must be essentially irrefragable—it is never the Law that is broken, but the lawless. And that is an act of Love. It would certainly not be an act of Love to permit the unloving and unlovely to break such a Universe successfully. Thus we believe that working through all the objective process of the Universe there is a Personal Love "working all things together for good"—a process of At-one-ment complementing the process of Judgment. This process of Atonement has

[1] *The Lord of Thought*, pp. 149 and 150

been wonderfully epitomised by the American philosopher Royce thus: "The human community, depending as it does upon its loyal human lovers, and wounded to the heart by its traitors . . . utters its own doctrine of atonement as this postulate—the central postulate of its highest spirituality. No baseness or cruelty so deep or so tragic shall enter our human world, *but that loyal love shall be able in due time to oppose to just that deed of treason its fitting deed of atonement.*" [1] For souls do break and bruise themselves upon the Universe most pitifully and terribly. "He that hateth Me wrongeth his own soul." People sin brutally, ignorantly, and suffer terribly. Yet over all such the "loyal love" Inviolable, Unchanging and Unchangeable is for ever brooding and toiling, incessantly working as a Living Power upon the living minds and hearts and wills of men to save them from their sins and from their miseries. There is no terror in God but there is and there must be in life that is Godless. "Perfect love casteth out fear"; but equally when Perfect Love is cast out, fear must enter in. But though cast out, the Perfect Love does not abandon its foolish child.

So the way is clear for the master-truth of the character of God, that Gospel which Jesus preached and which He was. "And Jesus came into Galilee preaching the Gospel of God," what God is like and what man therefore must and may become! The Divine sovereignty, therefore, if it is to be vindicated— and, with Calvin, we believe it must be—can only be so in terms of Love, a Love such as Arminius taught: eternal, free and Universal. Love must win at last, but He must win freely, and therefore His method puts man in risk from his own folly and wilfulness. Nevertheless there is always an ever-open way of escape.

Now with this clarified theology this truer knowledge of God, comes into view the true and full ethic of God in Christ.

Jesus always based His ethic on the character of the Father. "Be this," He said, "do that," "that ye may be sons of your Father in Heaven." Because of this ideal that He sets before men, Christ speaks of New Birth. George Whitefield, it is said, had but one theme in all his preaching—the New Birth. "Why, Mr. Whitefield," inquired a friend one day, "why do

---

[1] The *italics* are mine.

you so often preach on 'Ye must be born again'?" "Because," replied the Awakener solemnly, looking his questioner full in the face, "because *you* must be born again!"

This experience of new birth, however, that Jesus demanded, sadly needs to be definitely related to the rest of His teaching. It has been isolated from the organic unity of Christ's thought and used all too much as Whitefield and Wesley used it, with only a magical content. The matter stands closely related, surely to Christ's teaching of the Divine Fatherhood. All experienced parents know that there is a deep sense in which the child must be twice-born to them to become really their child. The first birth is physical, though full of deep unrealised potentiality. It is also quite compulsory, from which its inadequacy arises. As the child ceases, however, to be a mere creature and becomes more responsible and self-conditioning, an absolute necessity arises for the child to endorse spiritually, that is, personally, from the deepest inmost reality of its being, its relationship to its parents. Where that spiritual response to a love ante-dating the child's very birth does not arise, sonship or daughter-ship is not consummated, nor is parenthood. A. S. M. Hutchinson, in *This Freedom*, says of Dora, the elder daughter of Rosalie, "Dora was never really born to her mother." We can see clearly what the author means. Dora had never endorsed with her real inner being her relationship to her mother. There was no *spiritual* life between them. That "spiritual birth" is the only way for child and parent into the Kingdom of Home. Is not this what Jesus meant? "Except ye become as a little child (to your Father in Heaven), ye shall not enter into the Kingdom of Heaven." When the relationship is accepted, trusted, answered by full personal surrender, then the floodgates of the Divine Fatherhood can open wide and Life descend in its fullness upon the soul, yielding rebirth and newness of life and "the powers of the world to come." That is salvation—Oneness with God.

But in that surrender to the Divine Father one is making choice of unclouded and inviolable love as the new principle of one's being and life. It is a new principle, indeed, for in the passage from *creature* to *child* one passes over from Nature to Super-Nature—from the working principle of one form and level of life to the working principle of another and a higher form and level of life. This is the fact that our Evangelical fathers did not get sufficiently clear. Whitefield and Wesley preached the New Birth in the main as a mystical experience. It was something that happened to the soul in its acceptance of a formula of belief which, more or less, as the case might be, made real to the believing soul the might and mercy of the Love of God. It was a supernatural change of heart or nature. All of which was good so far as it went, but not quite good enough. They were not sufficiently clear as to the *poles of change and the precise differences between the old and new natures—especially the specific Christian difference.* All too often they were satisfied if the change brought about was little more than that from the breach to the observance of any one or all of the Ten Commandments. They must have made many an Englishman into a good Jew rather than into a real Christian! It was from this failure to grasp the oneness of the Lord's Gospel in Teaching Life and Sacrifice that there sprang the serious inhibition of the social passion inherent in the Divine Love. It is quite true that Wesley, and consequently Methodism at its best, were peculiarly open-eyed as to the ethical results of conversion, but unhappily those results had rather to be inferred from the Divine Love somewhat laboriously, and in some references dubiously—the process of surrender to the Person of God was not integrally one with surrender to His Programme and Policy—His Principle of Life.

Before we turn to see what this *Christian difference* really is, and so mark clearly the poles of Christian conversion, let us see how an approach along psychological lines leads us to the same issue.

CHAPTER IV

THE EVANGELICAL REVIVAL IN THE LIGHT OF TO-DAY

II. PSYCHOLOGICAL

2. *We of the modern world have to reckon also with a new science of Psychology which requires a new approach to the experience of conversion.*

The work of Professor William James, as illustrated in his *Varieties of Religious Experience*, is widely known, but a great deal of water has flowed under the bridge since that great book was written. Probably from no quarter in the modern world is there arising so subtle a corrosive of religious faith or so powerful an enemy of Christian evangelism as from the New Psychology in certain of its schools and interpretations. Yet this is only half the truth, for in forcing religion to vindicate itself in psychological terms the New Psychology is inducing in modern religion a fierce realism that will be of incalculable blessing at last. Religion is going to be *aerated* thoroughly in our age, forced to face stark reality, and to stand the test of the "light of common day." What would modern psychology say of George Whitefield and John Wesley? Mr. Sidney S. Dimond, M.A., has given us a very full and valuable treatment of John Wesley and of the Revival in general in his *Psychology of the Methodist Revival*. Undoubtedly the manse at Epworth played a big part in shaping the future evangelist. For one thing it had a ghost, a fact which may help to account for the often pitiful strain of superstition in John Wesley. Further, as a tiny child he was almost miraculously saved from death by fire when the vicarage was burned down. This fact would, with family comments on it, build up his sense of destiny. But more particularly we have, what Mr. Dimond seems to have missed, the extreme probability of a mother fixation, and a resulting complex on the evangelist's part. Susannah

264

Wesley was a most remarkable woman and a wonderful mother. She was the twenty-fifth child of her father, and had nineteen children of her own. Of the ten that survived infancy she tells us in a letter that she managed to give to each one of them a definite time regularly for private religious instruction and guidance. When, later on, people marvelled at her remarkable influence over her children, she wrote, "There is no mystery in the matter. I just took Molly alone into my own room every Monday night, Hetty every Tuesday night, Nancy every Wednesday, Jacky every Thursday, and so on, that was all!" That was all! "Jacky every Thursday!"

No wonder John Wesley could write later, "I cannot remember ever having kept back a doubt from my mother; she was the one heart to whom I went in absolute confidence from my babyhood until the day of her death." Undoubtedly the Methodist discipline—its Method-ism, lies rooted in the sharp discipline and stern repression of normal joys that his mother inflicted on John's boyhood. Mr. Dimond, indeed, notices this, remarking on page 79 of his most valuable work "the discipline of his mother's *régime* was responsible in his infancy for a repression of the instinct of play and of the expansive emotion of joy. The mirth and buoyancy of childhood were cut out of his life." Consequently, when Wesley obtained his freedom upon going to Charterhouse School he could write in his *Journal* "outward restraints being removed, I was much more negligent than before, even of outward duties, and almost continually guilty of outward sins, which I knew to be such, though they were not scandalous in the eyes of the world." The repressions of childhood had a further effect in leading John to seek the company of the younger boys of the school, whom he used to harangue as their leader. When taxed with this by his master, he calmly admitted his reason, "Better to rule in Hell than serve in Heaven." The shadow of his mother was upon him, and hence his ultimate obedience to God came to be couched in terms of reconciliation to his mother, terms, that is, of interest in a very strict mode of life leading to ascetic practices. Wesley's mother took the most acute interest in John's work all through his career, and later in life we find her installed by her son in a house next to his headquarters in London where she died in

1742. Doubtless that mother-fixation very strongly affected John Wesley's leaning to Arminianism, by producing a strong reaction in the direction of freedom. It would be interesting, too, to trace the relation of it to Wesley's unhappy attempts at love making and marriage. This is the kind of root influence the New Psychology would delight to trace, and probably succeed in finding.

With George Whitefield the dominating unconscious motive was undoubtedly a strong reaction to an inferiority feeling. One needs but to consider his circumstances, the child of an innkeeper, then pot-boy and later a menial servant at Oxford, to see how he would be driven in upon himself and obliged to find his own compensations. One of the commonest reactions to such inferiority conditions is the development of a sense of destiny. The obstacles being too great to overcome naturally, the native egoism of the soul posits a supernatural aid to their conquest. "Nothing can keep me back! I am chosen of God." Did we know the facts of their early life, doubtless we should find that many of the world's great men have come that way. As the grass grows by cutting so man becomes great often by being "sat on." See Whitefield in later life! With what audacity the lad of twenty-one hurls his dogma, born of an experience of Divine visitation, at the heads of the London public and clergy alike! Literally, he takes their breath away. With what poise and command, moreover, he sways the mighty audiences that wait upon his speech in Britain and America! On such occasions it is his sense of destiny that fills him with power. Yet see how increasingly he speaks disparagingly of himself. He is a "worm," a "vile creature," "utterly unworthy." This is not cant, it is deep, agonising self-shame plunging him sometimes very near to despair. Thus, inwardly he oscillates between two extremes: profound misgiving and profound exaltation. He is constantly swinging between the depths of penitence and the heights of faith, emotionally unstable and emotionally ablaze. This it is that gives him the courage of a lion in his public work and makes him timorous as a mouse in personal danger. From this inner chaos, molten in its heat, flashed forth those thunderbolts of feeling that electrified and overwhelmed his audiences!

Now we understand better those boyish confessions of sin

that he noted so elaborately in his *Journal* and which gave such offence to Dr. Lavington. The tendency to grovel explains their publication with secret pride that Deity should have stooped to rescue such. Fact enough behind these confessions doubtless—sins born of the foul atmospheres of his early upbringing and city life! These youthful follies would reinforce powerfully that sense of inferiority, and lead him to seek still stronger compensations which would come more readily from religion than from any other source. This is the explanation modern psychology would give of George Whitefield, and superficially it looks a rather sorry one. Yet the facts we cannot deny, and an element of truth in such an explanation we must admit. But as an explanation it overlooks the simple fact that such a mental history can be used of God for His own ends, and, indeed, can be consciously consecrated by the possessor with such noble result as is evidenced in the case of Whitefield. Without the least doubt, for example, it was the sheer desperation of his case, his tragic sense of unworthiness, which enabled him so early, compared with the Wesleys, to appreciate the meaning and the exquisite value of the " free grace " of God. We notice, too, that it was not until the Wesleys had tasted sharp failure in Georgia that they, too, arrived at the great change. After all, what does such a psychological analysis do more than reveal how simply possible and wise it is for a man to come to God, as the hymn puts it, "Just as I am." How else can he come? God Himself cannot detach us from our personal history, nor can He use what is not there. He must take a man as He finds him—but what He makes of what He finds, ah! that is another matter! The psychological doctrine "accept thyself"[1] has a profound value, especially for the soul that has discovered itself and suffered shock in the process. To take one's particular psychological stress and look it squarely in the face, and then dedicate it to the good of men and the service of God is to find one's homely quartz shot through and through with golden value. Nothing is really more beautiful, when one thinks of it, than a soul gallantly struggling against its own profound self-discouragements, often finding such to be mysterious and all but unbearable, as Whitefield found them, and yet for the sake of others transforming them into a gracious

[1] See Dr. Hadfield's *Psychology and Morals.*

humility of spirit towards men and a holy boldness on God's behalf. After all, it is not the roots of our emotional constitution that matter so much as the flower we grow upon them, the goal to which we direct them, the end for which we consecrate them to Life, to God! As Professor James has put it in that inimitable discussion of the matter that opens his famous Gifford Lectures,[1] "By their fruits ye shall know them, not by their roots," and again, "If the *fruits for life* of the state of conversion are good, we ought to idealize and venerate it, even though it be a piece of natural psychology; if not, we ought to make short work with it, no matter what supernatural being may have infused it." Or as Mr. Fearon Halliday has so well expressed it, "victory is the spiritualization, and not the denial of the instinctive. It is a positive, not a negative thing—the replacing of the wrong love by the right one."[2] And indeed, it is a unique kind of power at which a man arrives who so utterly comes to the end of himself that he is entirely concentrated on and given over to God, and who knows what it is to find "power perfected in weakness," to quote Paul's great paradox. Such was Whitefield's experience over and over again.

It is encouraging and helpful to more prosaic spirits like ourselves to see the natural history of an evangelist, and to see how marvellously the "Power, other than ourselves, making for righteousness," can use such humble material. "We have this treasure," says one of the greatest of evangelists, "in earthen vessels that the glory may be of God."

Let us turn now from the psychology of the evangelists to that of the evangelised. Here, again, modern psychology has a great deal fresh to say. Perhaps the first thing to say is that in the overwhelming majority of cases the psychological effect of the revival was absolutely healthy and morally invaluable. That being said, we may admit that we are not so surprised and startled at the less normal psychic phenomena that attended these preachings as our fathers were, nor do we give them an immediate supernatural origin either from above or from below. We can trace their origin more accurately in the bitterly starved instincts of the poor amongst whom they mostly occurred.

[1] *The Varieties of Religious Experience*, pp. 20 and 237.
[2] *Psychology and Religious Experience.*

It has already been noted that there were fewer of these incidents of convulsions, outcryings, fallings, faintings, etc., among Whitefield's audiences than among John Wesley's, though in the latter case they characterise mostly only the preaching of the years 1739–1743. The reason for this, too, we have found in the different styles of the two men. Whitefield was himself so fiery and even lachrymose at times, so expressive of the whole gamut of emotion, that he relieved by proxy the pent-up feelings of his hearers. Wesley, on the other hand, gave his audiences no such relief because his emotional expression was so restrained and his appeal so logical. What is particularly notable, however, regarding Wesley is that it is evident that, with certain audiences, he could induce these phenomena when he liked, and that they waxed and waned according to his encouragement of them or not. In his careful examination of these incidents, Mr. Dimond[1] analysed no less than two hundred and thirty-four cases of pathological symptoms, and his verdicts are very interesting. Many of them he found to be due to sheer imitation, which is a far greater force in social behaviour than is usually realised. The percentage of women was 64·5. Mr. Dimond also marked a curious geographical distribution of these cases. Of the eighty-five cases mentioned in Wesley's *Journals* of people who "dropped as dead," fifty-six occurred at Bristol, nineteen in London, seven in Newcastle and three in Cornwall. The Celtic fringe, with its traditional excitability, seems to have behaved in a comparatively normal manner under Whitefield's and Wesley's preaching, whereas Bristol and Newcastle are the centres of marked psychological disturbance. What is the answer to the riddle? It is a sad one. "Bristol and Kingswood at that time contained a population the most primitive, brutal and ignorant in England. From what we know," writes Davenport, "of the primitive nature of man, unmoulded by experience and civilised environment, where more certainly would the peculiar phenomena be likely to appear in the England of the eighteenth century than in the neighbourhood of Bristol and Kingswood."[2]

This verdict is confirmed by the fact, noted by Dimond,

---

[1] *The Psychology of the Methodist Revival.*
[2] *Primitive Traits in Religious Revivals*, quoted by Dimond.

that after an interval of four years, the phenomena appeared again at Gateshead Fell and Chowden, and Wesley described these places as "the very Kingswood of the North."

"Twenty or thirty children ran round us," he writes, " as soon as we came, staring at us in amaze. They could not properly be said to be either clothed or naked. One of the largest (a girl about fifteen) had a piece of a ragged dirty blanket some way hung about her, and a kind of cap on her head of the same cloth and colour. My heart was exceedingly enlarged towards them, and they looked as if they would swallow me up."

It was particularly among these demoralised human types of eighteenth century England that the more sensational psychic phenomena appeared. Perhaps the "primitiveness" was a bigger contributing factor than were poverty or privation, for in the simpler, healthier life of the New England States the same kind of thing repeatedly occurred in times of revival. "Experience and environment had never developed the inhibitions of civilisation," is Davenport's explanation.

Mr. Dimond attributes the occurrence of these disturbances mainly to suggestion on the part of John Wesley.[1] Wesley had been reading of similar occurrences in the revival under Jonathan Edwards and was at first inclined to agree with the American preacher's favourable opinion of them.

"Wesley appealed to the ethical fruits of conversion as a proof of the Divine origin of the bodily disturbances."

It was not until he had expressed regret that "the grace of God" did not sink so deep at Newcastle as it did at Bristol and Kingswood, that bodily effects followed his preaching. Then after six or seven had dropped as dead, he writes, "There seemed in the evening to be a deeper work in many souls than I had observed before."[2] On closer examination, however, Wesley revised his opinion, and began to feel that the origin of these things was rather Satanic than Divine. "I can make no doubt but that it was Satan tearing them as they were coming to Christ."[3] "From this point," remarks Dimond, "extreme physical disturbances are a diminishing quantity, and rarely appear in any part of the country after the year 1743."

[1] *Psychology of the Methodist Revival*, p. 130.
[2] Dimond, ibid.
[3] Wesley's *Journal*, Vol. III, pp. 69-70.

Lecky's unhappy verdict upon this strain in Methodism needs only to be quoted in these days to be set aside:

"A more appalling system of religious terrorism, one more fitted to unhinge a tottering intellect and to deepen and embitter a sensitive nature, has seldom existed."

That is a very one-sided picture.

These extraordinary convulsions of the emotions, for which social conditions were more responsible than Methodism, were a small price to pay, after all, for the cleansing and exalting effects of spiritual revival with the manifold consequences we have seen. In connexion with the more recent Welsh Revival, it was shown that cases of insanity reported to the Glamorgan County Asylum numbered one per cent. above the normal, but during the same period the number of cases of insanity due to alcoholism *decreased* from seventy-one to forty-two, from sixteen per cent. in 1904 to twelve per cent. in 1905. The verdict of Dr. Fursac, the French investigator, is therefore, as Dimond points out, perfectly justified. "It is better that one man become mad by religion than a hundred by alcohol."

With regard, of course, to the great mass of normal conversion resulting from the revival, modern psychology would insist upon a rigorous analysis of each case in terms of natural, mental and emotional history. It would find operating in every case mother and father fixations, sex-instinct complexes, herd-instinct complexes and so on. It is just this reduction of the most glowing experiences of the human soul to mere natural, very natural, history, by the New Psychology, that has so damping an effect on the faith of many to-day. It must therefore be dealt with further.

Religion to-day, in general, and therefore Christianity included, has to face a double form of the charge of Unreality. One of these is popular, and comes from the masses of the people; the other is academic and comes from the new psychological thought and discoveries of the time. In between these two profoundly serious entities there are playwrights and authors and journalists busy popularising both forms of the indictment, and helping to fuse them together into the most formidable attack religion has ever had to face. The form which the popular accusation takes is in the now well-known phrase, "Religion is Dope." The academic form may be summed up in the statement, "Religion is Phantasy."

It is said that in Russia the Soviet Government have placed above the altar in the Church of the Kremlin, Moscow, the announcement, "Religion is the opiate of the People." Whether that be true or no, the phrase represents a charge against religion which is widespread throughout the democracies of the modern world. Nor can we lightly rebut the charge. No institution on earth should be so humble and self-examining as the Church of Christ, and in face of a situation like this, for her own soul's sake as well as for humanity's, she will do well to examine the case patiently. With the story of Whitefield and the Evangelical Revival behind us, we cannot fail to see the measure of justification for this verdict in the history of religion in our own land. The terrible hardships visited on the masses of workers in the Industrial Revolution originated from a class of employers and owners, many of whom were ostentatiously religious. Moreover, religion and morals were actually used by many, such as Paley, Wilberforce and Hannah More, to make the pitiable slavery of the poor palatable to them.

"*One of Hannah More's Cheap Repository Tracts* [1] told the story of a Lancashire colliery girl, who was taken down the pit when nine years old to act as drawer with her brother, who was two years younger. 'She cheerfully followed her father down into the coal-pit, burying herself in the bowels of the earth, and there, at a tender age, without excusing herself on account of her sex, she joined in the same work with the miners, a race of men rough indeed but highly useful to the community.' The father was killed by an accident down the pit in sight of his children. The girl continued to work in the pit for fourteen years at wages of 2s. a day, sometimes earning 3s. 6d. in twenty-four hours by taking a 'double turn', and supporting her mother and two brothers for some years. Then her health broke down, 'and her head was also troubled by some of those strange and unpleasant imaginations which are known by persons conversant with the diseases of the poor to be no unusual consequence of bad food and great bodily fatigue joined with excessive grief.' She applied for employment as a servant, but there was a prejudice against her because she had been a collier, and her application failed. Fortunately, by that comforting dispensation whereby afflictions are turned into blessings, her bearing and patience attracted notice. Enquiries were made at the colliery, and she received such a glowing character that she was taken into

[1] Quoted by J. and B. Hammond in *The Town Labourer*.

employment. 'This story,' the tract concludes, 'may teach the poor that they can seldom be in any condition of life so low as to prevent their rising to some degree of independence if they choose to exert themselves, and that there can be no situation whatever so mean as to forbid the practice of many noble virtues.'"

Though that is not couched in specifically Christian language, yet it indicates the atmosphere whereby religion and morals were used to reconcile the poor to their lot, with a sickening blindness to glaring iniquities, by otherwise quite good people.

There is no need to multiply illustrations. It is one of the blots on the fame of Wilberforce that his *Practical View of the System of Christianity* was couched in the same sub-consciously hypocritical vein. We recall how Charles Dickens pilloried "dope" religion in his Chadband and Pecksniff, and perhaps most cleverly of all from the point of view of the "doped" in Mrs. Jellyby of *Bleak House*—the good poor little woman who was all the time so keen on the dear natives of Borrioboolaga whilst *her own children were busy falling down the area-steps*. One has often queried whether Dickens meant Mrs. Jellyby for a picture of Mother Church, so busy just then on foreign missionary enterprise and still so blind to the sufferings of her more immediate children round her doorstep!

It is far from the present writer's intention to dispute that a real religious faith is a sublime help under all conditions of human life, but when such faith is used to blind one to what *others* are suffering, and suffering needlessly and unjustly, then it becomes an opiate of the most poisonous kind. That is what has bitten into the soul of the workers. Religion has been misused again and again to make people so content within their lot that they have grown insensible to the injustice resting like a death pall upon their fellows and upon little children. Whilst, therefore, we cannot agree entirely with the Hammonds in their all but wholesale rejection of Evangelical forces as being all of this character, one cannot but agree to the large and dis-tressing measure of truth in the terrible limitation set to the influence of religion by this subconscious use of it to bolster up class privilege and position.

But it may be claimed matters are different now. Since those bad old days we have had Methodism and the growth of

Central Missions and a new approach to the poor—Shaftesbury Societies, the Salvation Army, Church Army, and Charity Organisation Society, &c., &c.

Certainly a social conscience of a kind has developed in the Churches, but the workers still do not respond. Why? Because the fundamental injustice still operating in wealth distribution robs charity of all the graciousness of true love, and clothes it with the insult of the bribe. "There is no gratitude in the poor these days," one hears. How can people be grateful who have come, for good or ill, in error or in truth, to the conclusion that what is given them is but *the meanest instalment of their own*, withheld from them by fraud of system if not by fraudulent intent. *That is an all but universal conviction of the modern poor.* Consequently, all the elaborate and expensive machinery of social service provided by the modern Church misses its mark, and will continue to do so until in some way the Church can convince the mass of the people that she is spiritually and morally on their side. It is not more blankets and coal, more institutes and billiard-rooms, that will move the modern masses, but a Church which, like Christ, is the champion of the common people *in principle and in programme*.

But it is just at this juncture, so difficult a one for the modern Church, that a scientific movement from the schools of learning emerges to clinch the popular judgment about religion and to provide a philosophy for the people's attitude. The New Psychology, in its main stream of teaching, tends to dismiss religion as phantasy.[1] And here, again, we cannot afford to adopt a lofty tone of disdain as some are attempting to do. There is so much truth mixed up with this teaching—salutary truth for would-be religious people. Starting from the well-known fact of animal instincts as lying at the foundation of the human organism, the New Psychology stresses the conflict that is set up, as humanity progresses in its community life, between the tendency of every instinct to express itself fully in competition with other instincts, and especially in competition with the requirements of happy and harmonious social life. As a case in point, the instinct of hunger tends in us all to express itself with primitive rudeness and ravenousness,

[1] See Freud's *The Future of an Illusion*.

but it is powerfully inhibited in most of us by the customs of society. Much of the energy of the instinct in its primitive condition has been drawn off into the etiquette and the art of table manners and food preparation and service. The energy of the human being is drawn from these powerful animal instinctive emotions—an emotion being the suffusion of the organism with the energy of the instinct preparatory to action. Obviously the full energy of these emotions are not used up by social life. Where does it go to? It is drawn off to become the raw material of intellectual, artistic, philosophical, scientific and religious activities. All the life of man other than physical is explicable as the sublimation of the "libido" or energy of his instincts, the most powerful of which are those that are associated with Sex, Herd, and Self interests. Now with the inadequate and haphazard character of our social organisation it is inevitable that many and often serious conflicts should arise, bringing stress and strain upon the organism, and it is under the pressure of such conflicts that men and women turn to sublimating agencies such as art, literature, sport and also religion. Thus, your modern knowing young student or even man-in-the-street feels able to explain all the intense interest of religious people in religion in terms of psychological stresses and complexes which their religion is meant to relieve. Religion is thus viewed as subtly selfish in its motive, and without any more adequate object. It is a trick of the human mind to bring itself relief. Your pompous deacon is over-compensating an inferiority feeling worked into him in childhood or youth; others are filling out the starved emotional impulses of sex-desire in spiritual experiences of passion, innocent enough, but essentially self-serving. In all such religion the human organism never escapes itself, is always serving itself.

See, for example, how the new psychology would explain Mrs. Jellyby. She is a mother who cannot control her own offspring. They disappoint her self-appreciation of her proud rôle of motherhood. Very well; she must restore her hurt pride somehow. She will mother the natives of Boorioboolaga which happens to be conveniently far enough away for her "mothering" in this case to escape criticism. Her mind is eased, but *her children still fall down the stairs.*

It is just here that the popular but profound novelist fulfils his task of interpretation by helping us to pass over from the "Dope" accusation of the people to the "Phantasy" criticism of the schools. He helps us to understand how morality and religion is being "found out" along these lines to-day. John Galsworthy, more obscurely in the *Forsyte Saga*, but very plainly in his great novel on brotherhood, *Fraternity*, presents us with the following interesting thesis. The only people with a social conscience in Great Britain are the well-to-do middle class. The workers haven't a social conscience; all they have is a social need. They know what they want and that they want it; they don't need a conscience about it. The aristocracy haven't a conscience about it either; they have heredity. They set out to do "what is done," and never by any chance to do what isn't done. In between these two classes comes the "middle-class," which, by its very position, gains a sense of balance, and is uneasy about the extremes that are upon either hand. It is between the nut-crackers. The middle-classes have a sense of balance and also leisure and culture to use it. Hence they develop a conscience about social inequality. Such a thing, however, is very disturbing to people whose supreme aim in life is "comfort." Desiring comfort they must ease this social fear—hence their interest in philanthropy and reform.

But, here is the acid test, philanthropy and reform must never fundamentally affect the balance of power in Society. The poor must take what is given them and be grateful, and "the poor ye have always with you" is the favourite text of the middle-class. The social morality and religion of philanthropy of the British Middle Classes is thus seen to be largely phantasy—a subtle means of making *oneself* more comfortable. Galsworthy gives a capital instance of the kind of thing he means in *Fraternity* itself. Thyme, the gently-nurtured daughter of Hilary, has a lover, Dr. Martin, a rather terrible person for facts. He takes Thyme round the poorer parts of London. He has them marked in colours on the map, blue, red, black. Thyme trips beside him, full of happy plans of amelioration and betterment—a youthful idealist warming her hands at the fires of her own goodwill. When the tour is ended they are in the park resting. Suddenly Thyme flings

herself face downwards on the sward sobbing her heart out.
The reason is made apparent in her reply to her lover's inquiry:
"Oh! I don't really care for these people. It is the ugliness
of it all that offends my sense of beauty. I'm thinking of
myself all the time."

So Thyme finds herself out, and thus middle-class Morality,
Social Politics and Social Religion are pilloried as elaborate
devices of self-relief and self-pleasing, socially useful to an
extent, but sheer phantasy-solutions of social fears. One of
the proofs that this analysis is all too true is the rather cold-
blooded secret determination, that vitiates so much social
reform, that no real difference shall ever come to pass in the
relative positions of the various classes. All change must be
very moderate, and there is an inordinate fear of going
too far.

Here, then, we find a disquieting conaensus of judgment
from three vital quarters of society, from the masses, the scholars,
and the men of letters upon religion in general and Christianity
in particular, as being shot through and through with unreality,
and as being only a make-believe escape of man to God. Man
does not escape himself. What are we to say to it?

We must admit its large and disquieting element of truth.
But fortunately we can say much more. In the first place, we
might pause to be thankful that there is a power—namely,
Religion, that can take these fierce instincts as they rage in
disappointment within us, and give them some degree of coherent
expression and preoccupation. That, to begin with. Life
will always need Religion for that purpose at least. Psychology,
after all, can only lay bare the processes and tendencies at
work; with no unification and harmonisation of these tendencies
we get a dissatisfied life and often an exhausting conflict; with
repressed tendencies we get a neurosis. Unification enables
the processes to enter the service of the conscious mind and
there is no power so effective for this as Religion.

"He draws all things to an order fair." Religion helps us
to take ourselves as we are and then unifies us and remakes
us.[1] Secondly, we can see that to discredit the objective validity
of religion is to risk serious injury to this process of sublimation.
If, found out to be fundamentally selfish, Religion is shown

[1] See last chapter of Prof. J. McKenzie's valuable book, *Souls in the Making*.

to be a mere trick, the power will go out of the trick as the spell of the conjurer vanishes when he is found out. A religion known not to be real will not sublimate—yet sublimation says psychology is essential for social life!

The chief reply, however, leaps to the challenge from that vein of religion in history, where self-sacrifice has been supreme. It is in the sign of the cross, the only sign in which it ever conquers, that Christianity conquers here. Much religion there has been, and is, that was, and is, "dope," but there is another type of religion vastly different. Was religion dope for Jesus of Nazareth, hanging from the Cross with the prayer of forgiveness falling from anguished lips? Was it dope for St. Paul placing his head on the block of execution? Was it dope for St. Francis embracing my lady Poverty? Or for George Whitefield vomiting blood in his passion for souls? For John Wesley riding and preaching hard and late in perpetual sacrifice of himself? For their followers mobbed, imprisoned, persecuted, ridiculed, yet without malice or reviling! Or for William and Catherine Booth penetrating haunts of vice with no protection save a great love for men? This kind of thing cannot be resolved into a mere sublimation of the herd-instinct. It must be examined in its own light and right. *God is to be found with vivid reality in Morality and Religion wherever man has truly escaped himself!* "Whosoever seeketh to lose his life shall find it." "He that dwelleth in love, dwelleth in God." The Great Other does not appear till self is surpassed. But then He appears!

The same reply attaches to the charges of Phantasy-religion. The acid test of reality is the victory over that secret inner core of selfishness. That this has been successfully achieved over and over again is indisputable. Again, it is not the *root* of the impulse to religion that matters, but the *fruit* of it, the goal of beauty and power in which it fulfills itself. Let a man "accept himself" and "just as he is" give himself to God, and he will see the "selfishness" taken up and used by that other for the ends of altruistic Love.

Meanwhile the New Psychology, in its "explanation" of religion, is making all the more reasonable the fundamental conversion of the human soul demanded by Christianity. It is showing us plainly that the Divine reality of religion cannot emerge until the self is over-passed, and the centre of attention and devotion shifted from self to the Other!

There is then a kind of natural conversion that the New Psychology admits. It is willing to concede, indeed must do so, that Religion does "turn" human minds from being stormy battlefields of instinctive conflict into more or less harmonised and unified abodes of peace. Instincts are sublimated, complexes are aired and resolved by the power of Religion. *There is a natural conversion.* This natural conversion, moreover, is common to all really powerful religions, whether primitive or developed. This, too, we must concede. Professor Underwood has written fascinatingly and with great illumination in his *Conversion, Christian and Non-Christian*, about this. His account of the degree and value of "conversion" in other World Religions helps to sharpen the challenge to Christian Conversion. Is all conversion merely *natural?* Does it never step outside nature? Does it never carry the soul beyond itself and into a new life? Does it never become new birth, but remain merely a refinement of the old being?

That is the challenge the modern evangelist must answer.

So we see how the modern psychological approach to the evangelist's problem brings us to the issue with which our last chapter closed. What are the poles of true Christian conversion? Men may be changed by religion but inadequately. They may be changed from dirty sinners to cleaner ones. They may be changed in certain areas of feeling or activity, but not over the *whole* of their being or life. Is it possible that much Christian conversion in the past has been of this inadequate character, "natural" conversion masquerading as "supernatural," a change that did not change sufficiently, was not radical and thorough-going enough?

Alas, it is quite certain. Much conversion has been undoubtedly phantasy-conversion—conversion motived entirely though secretly, by the self-instinct—a fear-reaction and therefore a selfish one. The self-hood of the person involved has not been transcended or fulfilled in a true self-giving—it has simply escaped to a subtler form of selfishness. It is this that explains what is called area-conversion—those types of change that pertain curiously to only one phase of the soul's interest or life—there are intellectual area-conversions, mere theological conversions often, involving only a change of thought, doctrinaire and aloof from life—emotional area-conversions, flooded with feeling yet curiously and determinedly impractical and confused in thought—there are volitional area-conversions, where there is a change of life, often limited to one feature, but where there is no attempt to revise opinions or ideals and little appreciation of truth or love-values.

It is this fact of purely *natural-conversion* that explains the curious hitch that occurs all too often between an apparent acceptance of the Lordship of Christ and the ethical fruitage of acceptance. It explains an Elmer Gantry[1] and many another unworthy preacher and minister of the Gospel. Especially does it explain those most tragic failures that break upon the rock of the sex-instinct.

Here, of course, "self" is most deeply intrenched in man— here it fights for predominance with peculiar fury. Failure here is failure everywhere—victory here is all but victory everywhere. This is why the sex-ethic will yet prove the supreme battle-ground between the Church and the world. Already the world-ethic of marriage is shaping itself with apparently no interest in chastity or belief in continence as either desirable or possible.[2]

"He that is begotten of God doeth no sin," says the Apostle,[3] and in that statement there is an undoubted truth. Let a soul really escape itself and reach God and all motive for sin disappears, the *nature* is changed. But there may be a big difference between *a* change in the soul and *the* change. The right and full escape of the soul to God is not the easy ready-made thing that a cheap evangelism sometimes tends to suggest. Its initiation and its technique may be sublimely simple, but its achievement involves a profound travail, even as of birth, in the soul.

Our Evangelical forefathers used to declare that "the state of nature was not the state of grace." It is a useful distinction, though we should make it in a different way from them. They were thinking of the distinction between a mystical righteousness of God and the claims of ordinary human honesty

---

[1] By Sinclair Lewis.
[2] *Cf.* Bertrand Russell's *Marriage and Morals.*
[3] 1 John iii. 7 and v. 18. (The Greek "is begotten" implies continuity "has been made and remains a child of God.")

and goodness. It was the issue between faith and good works. But for us, thinking in the light of evolution as God's method of creation, we can see a deep and illuminating distinction in it. What is the state of "Nature?" We see it vividly in the animal world. It is a way of life dominated by the self-instinct. So marked is this that obviously it is the explanation of the great mechanism of the natural world culminating in the curious "menagerie" the earth carries. Nature manufactures "selves" and a "self" is made by self-concentration.

The "individual efficient in his own interests" as Benjamin Kidd[1] expresses it, is Nature's goal, and her very successful achievement. This is animal-nature, and it has its own ethic or customary way of behaviour—an ethic that never passes beyond reciprocity of action. "You scratch my back and I'll scratch yours" is a useful phrase in which to sum up the ethic of nature—that is of animal behaviour. "A little piece of sugar—and a little trick." "But you bite me! and you look out!" The story of Androcles and the lion illustrates it perfectly. On their second meeting in the Roman arena, the lion, remembering how Androcles helped it in the desert, resolutely refuses to eat him. But Androcles and the lion should meet a third time. Then the "natural ethic" would be tested indeed. "So!" the lion would argue, "he helped me when the thorn was in my paw, and I did *not* eat him in the arena. We are quits! Now I may have my dinner!" The animal ethic of reciprocity—sometimes called "justice" by human animals, this is the highest "state of nature." It can be very refined, very intellectual. It is still the general ethic of mankind. *But in it there is no redemption*. That is the glaring awful fact. To be good only as others are good, to regulate your behaviour by the other animal—this is to make evil set the pace for good—it keeps society gravitating towards the level of its most selfish and evil members. There can be no human salvation on that method as Jesus warned us. "Except your righteousness exceed the righteousness of the Scribes and Pharisees ye cannot enter the Kingdom of Heaven." "If ye love them that love you what do ye more than others?" Do not even the *heathen* the same? The state of nature is not the state of grace. Grace, the most beautiful word in human

[1] *The Science of Power.*

speech, means the very opposite of this animal ethic. It is the going out of love to the unlovely and unloving, it is the stoop of wealth to poverty, of holiness to the sinful, of the wronged to the wrong-doer, it is all that we mean by forgiveness, by that "mercy" which "becometh a monarch better than his crown." It only comes into being as the last conquest is won over the "self" and as the "self," gathered in a true self-possession, devotes itself to a higher interest than its own. This new attitude of the "self" is essentially "redemptive." It sets inflexibly a standard of Inviolable Love up to which other lives must come, by which it will stand unto death and from which it will never descend. It thus becomes a new rallying level for Society. It is, to quote Kidd once more, "the Individual efficient in the interests of Others"—a new creature.

Here then the "poles of Christian conversion" come into view. For this radical opposition between "self-preservation" and "self-devotion" as the dominant instinct in life is the issue that Christ thrusts peculiarly upon men. He does so by His Cross as well as by His teaching. "Whosoever seeketh to save his life shall lose it, but whosoever will lose his life for my sake shall find it." But such a change shifts the biological level of the soul from the animal world to a higher kingdom—it shakes the animal-human organism to its foundation—it involves a self-revolution that in its inception is often attended by emotional agony, but certainly in its out-working means a perpetual spiritual warfare.

Conversion so interpreted is more than a sublimation of natural instinct undertaken for pure self-relief and carrying the soul no further. It is an over-passing of inbred, natural selfishness in a launch-away of the soul to God, as real, as concrete, as *biological* probably in its ultimate achievement, as the launch-away of a butterfly from its chrysalis.[1]

But finally, such conversion carries the Individual out into the splendour and spaciousness of the Divine Sociality.

Christ's ultimatum of New Birth to human nature is seen by the foregoing to be grounded in a profound necessity. Man must rise from the animal to the Divinely human, and the Divinely human is perfectly social.

[1] Middleton Murry's new word "meta-biological" might be useful to express this achievement. See his book, *God*.

In His statements about Conversion Jesus is quite plain about this. "Except a man be born again *he shall not see the Kingdom of God*." "Except ye turn and become as this little child *ye shall not enter the kingdom of heaven*." Conversion is a means. The goal is a Society of Souls living together in the Spirit of God. Conversion is not for individual salvation merely—it is not in order to store up bright specimens of humanity in a kind of everlasting celestial museum. It is for the enrichment of the Kingdom of God.

That Society is Eternal. The Kingdom of God for Jesus was quite immediately Real. It possessed the Unseen. It was the Only Real World there is! This world of ours is not yet real—it is only becoming so. It is in process. But beating down through and around all the life of lesser growing worlds like ours is the One True World of God and His Family, into which all children can only enter as they achieve *the nature* of that Kingdom. "Thy Kingdom *come*," Jesus taught us to pray. "Thy will be done *as it is done in heaven*." Heaven is just the Divine Social Order which is ever seeking to colonise this planet. The Church is, or ought to be, the nucleus of that colonisation—the society of dedicated and associated personalities through whose opened souls and surrendered lives God's Unseen Kingdom may become the visible City of God on Earth. But the Church must therefore, in its internal organisation, foreshadow that ultimate City of God—as the nucleus of that New Order she must organise her life on the Divine Principle of Self-Devotion, not on the Natural Worldly principle of Self-Centredness. She must become in our day what she was in Christ's day—the People of *the Way*—Method-ist indeed!

Her Industry and Commerce, as one case in point, must not be like that of the world. "*Not* so shall it be among you."[1] A System of Private Profit culminating at intervals in universal War is *not for her*.[2] For her the Corporate Life is utterly sacred, and the only true goal of Individual being. She is God's Pioneer of Organic Racial Salvation—the Body of Christ doing His Deeds, expressing His Ideas, for the saving of all the world.

[1] Matt. xx, 26.
[2] It is an interesting fact that Toyohiko Kagawa, the great apostle of Japan, is keenly alive to this requirement of the gospel, and is organising his converts into great Christian Co-operatives. See also his book, *Love the Law of Life*.

Now all this was implicit in the Revival gospel of the eighteenth century. So powerful was this inherent sociality of the Truth about God that nothing could prevail, as we have seen, to prevent its finding some degree of expression. But before the evangelism of our day there rises this dazzling prospect. *If the Evangelical Revival of the eighteenth century has been fraught with such socially transforming power whilst so blind to the social meaning of the Gospel, what might not a New Revival accomplish with an explicit consciousness of the Social Goal of Christianity and a truer psychological technique?*

the successful unification, in a free way, of the human race the old slow, tortuous plan of one by one conversion, the old easy-going "wait for everybody" method is bankrupt. *There is no time to spare!* The old crass individualism in any walk of human life is dead or dying, and there is no vainer hope than for its resuscitation except by way of the new anarchy and barbarism that may come from the destruction of civilization.

Sir William Harcourt is credited with the statement: "We are all Socialists nowadays." If that was true so long ago how much truer it is to-day. Look at the political parties vieing with each other in social legislation, each becoming increasingly committed to the task of treating the nation as a whole, and indeed humanity as a whole. It is safe to say that only the party which succeeds in doing that will make any real impression on the world of to-day. For good or ill, mankind is taking its attention away from men, and finding itself compelled to attach it to Man. It is dreaming a Unity of the Race the first attempts at which possibly will be upon a national scale. By the foregoing reference to the inadequacy of the "one by one" method the writer does not mean that the moral suasion of the individual should be abandoned, but that there must be added to it the conception of massed education, massed emotional change and massed redirection of life on a scale hitherto undreamt of. The miracle of the radio points the way to the possibility of mankind sharing great mental illuminations very rapidly, suffering bombardment of facts to the shattering of prejudice on a wholesale scale, receiving emotional impetus to a degree that may make for dramatic and unanimous changes in the popular way of life.

A new docility will undoubtedly settle down upon a humanity maintained in prolonged peace especially in a disarmed world. This need not be a sheep-like docility, it may be, instead, the disciplined co-operation of a humanity rendered more homogeneous in character and purpose by a great common worship of one Ideal. We do not complain of the docility of the body's limbs, indeed, we should be a bit surprised to find insurrection. They find their true freedom and health only in the closest co-operation, and their supreme joy in united action.

This new humanity is already shaping towards vast co-operative efforts of massed action in the moral realm in such movements as that of Prohibition of the Liquor Traffic in America,[1] and, of course, in the kind of effort represented by the League of Nations.

Now the sheer pressure of population may give to individuals a trend in this direction by reinforcing the herd instinct, but it cannot of itself direct the movement to a successful and happy issue. The danger is that unless this growing crowd-consciousness is dominated by right ideals, baptised into a true and adequate purpose, it will be swept away on tidal floods of lower feeling by storms of panic and passion, and humanity may cast away the golden opportunity of this age of consummation. It is necessary, therefore, for this goal, the Unity of the Race, to become a religion, to be seen as sublimely possible because Divinely purposed. It must draw to itself the authority of that Other who haunts the silent corridors of every mind of man. This is where the Church's function lies. In such a world as this for the Church to remain individualistic in her outlook and methods is for her to become obsolete.

Modern society will soon be faced with the need of deciding whether it can afford any longer to tolerate individual enter-prise IN SIN, FRAUD OR FOLLY out of superstitious regard for a liberty of the individual which is rendered barren by the crowded state of society. The Freedom of the Whole will take on such an urgency that the licence of the part will have to yield to it. There will be new scope, therefore, in this modern world for a collective will to righteousness, to purity, to temper-ance, to kindness, to freedom, providing such collective will can be successfully organised. Politics will therefore become more and more for the socially-minded the medium of such an active collectivist ethic, the expression of a religion that sees a passionately social God as the centre of a divinely-human kingdom, as the Father of a divinely-human family.

In the light of this development, so surely and even rapidly coming, the hesitancy of the Churches to frame their own political policy and to organise their own united ethic and to apply it by their unique modern weapon, the vote, will be

---

[1] In the author's judgment, considering the inherent difficulties of this kind of approach to moral and social problems and the added difficulties incidental to conditions in America, the success of Prohibition is phenomenal, cf. "Prohibition at its Worst," by Prof. Irving Fisher of Yale University.

seen by posterity to be crass blindness and folly. The modern Church might rise in majesty to be the moral leader of the whole of mankind into harmonious social life if she would herself but "see life steadily and see it whole," and apply her resources practically to this task of shaping and planning vast collective decisions for right living.[1] For this is the goal to which Christianity looks; it is nothing if it is not the Religion of Human Unity. The Cross, which is its symbol, binds all together. Even as in that Cross, East runs into West and West into East, North into South and South into North, and height and depth and breadth are all conjoined in one, held together by a "Passion" stronger than sin or death, so humanity is one Man in the eyes of that God who is revealed in Jesus Christ.

It is this vision of a united world made one in the Inviolable Love that lives from God to man, and therefore can live from men to men, that is the lode-star of our age, the supreme fascination for the modern soul. It is this that must be the proclaimed goal of the new evangelism. Our faith teaches us that no men can be really free till Man is free, no men be really rich till Man is wealthy, no men be really happy till Man is set in happy conditions. Is there not a clear policy for the Church in this truth, in this unity of love which must be man's because it is God's? Must she not insist that Industry and Commerce be made a Fellowship and the Nation be made a Family and the World be made a Friendship? Must she not be the sworn foe of all conditions or forces that oppose those consummations? But most searching question of all, *must not her own united life pioneer these achievements?* It is not enough for her to exercise any longer the Gospel of the Word only, or even of individual conviction and witness, her evangelism must now be expressed in her own organised life as throughout the world at Peace with All, in Love with All, in Service of All. This is the true catholicism of the true Church, not all thinking alike but all loving alike (which may indeed bring the thinking), not all worshipping alike but all worshipping, with the same reverence, the same Ideal Love, and, in certain definite relations at least, all acting alike, discovering a common ethic and living it out with a grand unan-

[1] Cf. C. Silvester Horne's "legacy" to the Free Churches, p. 205

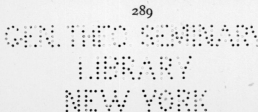

imity. That is the evangelism this wistful, clear-eyed, modern world requires, and would welcome with tears of joy. This is the Evangelism to which Christ Himself looked for final victory, for did He not pray for His followers that "they may be one . . . that the *world* may know, that the *world* may believe!" This must be the new Evangelical Revival.

．　　　．　　　．　　　．　　　．

Here then is our final conclusion. It is still possible for the Christian evangelist to face the modern man with the demand for a radical change of human nature, a new birth, the power to achieve which is nowhere so surely derived as from Jesus Christ. But the Christian community making that demand must demonstrate the new nature. A verbal gospel, however necessary and however effectively it changes the ideas and lives of people, is still an unfulfilled gospel, by the test of Christ, until it produces a social order, on whatever scale, in which the self is fully devoted to others and comes thereby to its own perfection. The Christian Church must be that social order, the nucleus of the Kingdom of God as it is coming on earth. Her own organisation, therefore, is her best and only true evangelism.

A unity in herself (of spirit and ethic not of sterile uniformity), observing in all her members over all the earth an inviolable peace towards all men, demonstrating perfectly the only conceivable principle of a stable social order, namely the self-devotion of all individuals to the community by the grace of Divine Love, such a Church could preach indeed. She would be the irresistible Architect of the Temple of Humanity, and would need no longer the rebuke and challenge of that great lover of men—George Whitefield the Awakener.

INDEX

INDEX

A

B

C

INDEX

D

E

F

G

INDEX

INDEX

INDEX

O

P

Q

R

INDEX

INDEX

INDEX